Million Dollar
Home-Based
Businesses

Million Dollar Home-Based Businesses

Successful
Entrepreneurs
Who Have Built
Substantial
Enterprises
From Their
Homes

Sunny Baker and Kim Baker

ADAMS MEDIA CORPORATION
Holbrook, Massachusetts

Published by
Adams Media Corporation
260 Center Street, Holbrook, MA 02343

ISBN: 1-55850-246-7

Printed in the United States of America

C D E F G H I J

This publication is designed to provide accurate and authoritative information with
regard to the subject matter covered. It is sold with the understanding that the publisher is not engaged in rendering legal, accounting, or other professional advice. If
legal advice or other expert assistance is required, the services of a competent professional person should be sought.
— From a *Declaration of Principles* jointly adopted by a Committee of the
American Bar Association and a Committee of Publishers and Associations

Cover Design: Marshall Henrichs

This book is available at quantity discounts for bulk purchases.
For information, call 1-800-872-5627
(in Massachusetts 617-767-8100).

Visit our home page at http://www.adamsmedia.com

This book is dedicated to the diverse, exceptional,
inspired, and energetic people
who through dedication, tenacity,
and entrepreneurial spirit,
have built auspicious businesses
from their bedrooms,
garages, lofts, and backyards.

Table of Contents

Introduction

Homemade Millionaires: Who Are They? 13
Criteria Used for Selecting Million Dollar Home-Based Businesses 14
What Are the Common Threads Among Homemade Millionaires? 17
Do You Have What It Takes to Become a Homemade Millionaire? 20

Chapter 1

Homemade Superstars 21
The Computer Millionaires 22
Other Homemade Success Stories 29
Did You Know That These Giants Started from Home? 30

Chapter 2

Where Do the Ideas Come From? 34
✦ These Entrepreneurs Get Their Ducks in a Row for Big Bucks 35
✦ A Blazing Success with Strings of Bacon and Fried Eggs 39
✦ King of the Fixer Uppers Makes a Royal Living 43
✦ Entrepreneur Gets Down to the Dirt 46
✦ Movie Buff Tracks the Nude Scenes for Posterity and Prosperity 49
✦ Imprinted Towels Soak Up Orders 52
✦ It's Not the Goodyear Blimp, But It Takes Great Photos 56
✦ In-Store Samples Promote Partners to Prosperity 59
✦ Who Needs an Office when You Live in a Dorm 63

Chapter 3

Should You Do It for Love or Money? 66
Choose a Business or Service that No One Else Wants to Do 67
✦ A Corporate Magic Carpet Ride 68
✦ A New Angle for L.A. Law 71
✦ The "Business Book Guy" 76
✦ Leapin' Lizards! Former Rock and Roller Sings a Better Song for
   Kids 79

✦ Only Out to Change the World 82
✦ Dreams, Rag Dolls, and Love Are Transformed into Rewards
  Beyond Imagination 85
✦ "Unemployable" Homemaker Paints Her Own Path to Success 90
✦ Packaging Anything to Go Anywhere 93

Chapter 4

Home-Based Businesses Are Healthy, Politically Correct, and
  Ecologically Sound 97
✦ Fabulous Person Makes Politically Correct Faux Furs 98
✦ Products that Are Good for People Are Good for Business 102
✦ Dollars and Flowers Blowing in the Wind 105
✦ Plant Entrepreneur Grows Plenty of the Green Stuff 110
✦ Turning Fat into Dollars 114
✦ "Your Research Findings Have Brought Us Much Hope" 118
✦ The First Wealth Is Health 122
✦ Ballooning School Profits Soar Over Rockies 124

Chapter 5

Do You Really Need Home-Office Technology to Make a Million? . . . 128
Avoid Boondoggle Technologies 129
Some Home-Based Businesses Depend on Technology 130
✦ From Underground Comics to Aboveboard Businessman 131
✦ Video Script Writer Opens His Own Show at Home 134
✦ Former Oboist Writes His Way to Success 137
✦ Teaching Math a Better Way Adds Up to Profit and Independence . . 140
✦ In Search of a "Real" Job, a Genuine Opportunity Is Discovered . . . 144

Chapter 6

Should You Stay Home-Based or Expand to an Outside Facility? 150
✦ Arizona Entrepreneur Makes Money Under the Sun 152
✦ Two Former Execs Get Off the Ladder to Take Control of Their
  Destiny 156
✦ Former Flight Attendants Build a Million Dollar Cookie Monster . . 160
✦ Entrepreneur Saves Company By Chasing Truck! 165
✦ How Can You Start a Garage-based Business if You Don't Have a
  Garage? 168
✦ Her Stuffed Animals Are Not Toys 171
✦ Houses for Equestrians Is Not Horse Play 174
✦ The Ultimate Iced Tea Makes a Very Cool Business 178
✦ Saving Lives Leads to Savings in the Bank 184

Chapter 7

Get Credible Information and Advice Before You Start 188
Check Out the Trade Magazines First 188
Read Business Books and Listen to How-to and Motivational Tapes . . 190

Join Clubs, Be Active in the Community, and Network as Much as
  Possible 191
Don't Be Afraid to Get Professional Help When You Need It 192
✦ They're the Carpet Store at Your Door 193
✦ A Second Mortgage Fosters a Magazine for Parents 196
✦ Next Time Someone Mentions Amway, Maybe You Should Listen . . 200
✦ Selling Humanistic Programs to Corporations with Dollars and Sense . 204
✦ Direct Mail Is a Twice-Traveled Route to Success 211
✦ Professional Dancer Falls into Successful Public Relations Act 214

Chapter 8

The Truths About Home-Based Entrepreneurs 218
Ther Are a Disproportionately Large Number of Home-Based
  Businesses Started by Women 218
It Looks Like 1985 through 1989 Were Watershed Years for Homemade
  Millionaires 219
Homemade Millionaires Are Ageless! 220
✦ Don't Underestimate the Power of a Gas Can or the Impact of this
  Entrepreneur 222
✦ This Lady Knows How Much Your Business Is Really Worth 229
✦ The Weekend Entrepreneur 232
✦ The Exceptional Entertainment Company Delights Corporations . . . 235
✦ Partners in Venture Become Partners in Life 238
✦ A True Believer in the American Dream 242
✦ An Up-and-Coming Millionaire: Sixteen-Year-Old Started on Road to
  Success at Age Eight! 245

Afterword

Avoid the Losers and the Dabblers at All Cost 249

Index

Index 251

Acknowledgments

Foremost appreciation goes to all the people profiled in this book for the time they took from their busy schedules to talk with us about their businesses and their lives. Some were kind enough to send us samples of their wares (we never asked for them), including cookie bouquets, printed towels, weight-loss formulas, vitamins, books, music cassettes, skin care products, and more. When you actually see (or taste) the products, it's clear why the people profiled in these pages have been successful. They all prove that American (and sometimes Canadian) ingenuity coupled with a quality product and a large measure of hard work still comprise a valid formula for success. The integrity, quality, and passion of these people is difficult to duplicate in prose, but if we partially succeed in relating their ideals, we will have served our purpose in writing this book—to provide role models for others to transform their dreams into viable enterprises. If more Americans follow this lead, on their own initiative as a people and without government intervention, they could guide the nation to economic stability from the comfort of their homes.

Homemade Millionaires: Who Are They?

In a Newsweek *report on the more than 2 million*
millionaires in the United States, more than 90 percent
claimed to have earned their wealth by starting their own
firms. Many of these ventures were started from
home-based offices in bedrooms and garages.

"I made over $1 million in less than 60 days!" "Earn $80,000 per month in your spare time!" "From zero to $4 million, a Rolls Royce, 560SL, and my own private lake in less than a year!" Claims like these are too often the ploys of unscrupulous advertisers. Usually for a fee, companies (some of them legitimate) will set you up with the equipment and train you to earn a respectable living with a knife sharpening business or make millions with a balloon delivery franchise. Too quickly the promise and premise of running your own successful home-based business melts into a pile of useless training guides and boxes of moldering equipment, disposed of years later for pennies on the dollar at a garage sale.

Are the claims of these advertisers always deceptions used to swindle money from ignorant wanna-be entrepreneurs? Can anyone really make a million working at home? Can a business that starts at home really be taken seriously? Well, perhaps not if you get involved in the rackets of charlatans, but in our own experience we know it is possible to prosper in home-based enterprises of all kinds. The quick-money, any-one-can-do-it claims of the junk tabloids have turned many would-be entrepreneurs into unemployed skeptics. People need legitimate role models and realistic expectations of home-based businesses to inspire them, not the fraudulent representations of swindlers. We see too many people simply giving up on their futures. Because of financial pressures, unemployment, and economic malaise, people everywhere are blaming others for their situations or just not trying any more. Though recessions are hard on everyone, it isn't time to throw in the towel. Just the opposite—it's time to try harder. The people profiled in this book prove that there are still limitless opportunities out there—you just need to grab them and make them happen on your own. No one else can do it for you. There are no quick fixes or simple solutions, but there are many legitimate and potentially lucrative options to consider.

Million Dollar Home-Based Businesses provides a diverse range of role models and success scenarios, some of them ordinary, others exceptional, that demonstrate that there are almost no restrictions on the type of enterprise or size of business that can be started from home. Many of the businesses were started during the turmoil of tough economic conditions, both personal and global. Most of the people we talked to started out broke or unemployed. Some are severely "handicapped" by others' definitions—they just failed to see themselves that way and prospered in spite of limitations that others would pose as insurmountable.

There are about one hundred real people profiled in this book. The in-depth profiles tell how they got started, describe the keys to their success, and reveal the characteristics that make them tick as entrepreneurs. After reading the book, which includes general guidelines for building your own business, you'll be convinced that anyone with the drive to succeed can reach financial independence on the strength of personal initiative alone. While it's true that some of the people described in these pages are extraordinary—gifted with talents or training that few of us possess—the majority of the entrepreneurs in this book have only one special attribute—the desire to get ahead on their own power in their own business.

Criteria Used for Selecting Million Dollar Home-Based Businesses

When we started our search for home-based success stories, there were five basic requirements established to qualify a person for coverage in the book. The five criteria are simple. They have nothing to do with college degrees, high IQs, or opening a business in a city where the streets are paved with gold. The requirements were used simply to separate the successful home entrepreneurs from those who inherited wealth, happened to open a McDonald's franchise before 1965, or started conventional businesses in an office or factory.

Criterion 1

The business must gross at least $200,000 per year with a rapid growth profile or have made more than $1 million total in the past four years. The majority of people in the book more than meet these financial criteria. However, as we spoke to people and networked with entrepreneurs around the country looking for home-based success stories, we discovered some entrepreneurs who didn't quite meet the gross income requirements, but were so interesting, successful, and growing so rapidly, that we included their stories here anyway. We call them the "up and coming" millionaires—because they will certainly be there in a year or two.

Criterion 2

The business *must* have started at home. The business principals had to live where they worked, instead of simply using a house as an office building or store front. Some of the businesses profiled became so successful that they had no choice but to leave home for larger quarters in an office or commercial plant; others who needed more space have expanded their homes to maintain the advantages of home-based operations.

There are certainly many self-made millionaires who did not start their operations from home, including retailers, consultants, manufacturers, and restaurateurs. Why restrict the book to only home-based success stories? There are two motivations for including only entrepreneurs who started their businesses at home. First, when people find themselves without jobs and they need to start from scratch, a home-based enterprise has significant advantages in lower start up costs and reduced overhead. As a result, hordes of people in these unpredictable economic times are looking into home-based businesses. There are also a growing number of magazines supporting home-based endeavors and special organizations for home-based businesspeople.

Since so many people are looking into home-based businesses, it makes sense to provide role models for them to follow. Second, new technologies make it more feasible to operate a business at home. Why spend the extra money for an office if you don't have to? Fax machines, portable copiers, desktop computers, and office-quality telephone services are all technologies that can be used as easily in a home as in a traditional office setting. It's no longer necessary to visit the office to communicate. To the outside world, thanks to modern communications technologies, there is no reason why a home-based business cannot provide the same level of service as an office-based business.

Third, we decided to concentrate on home-based entrepreneurs to dispel the myth that home-based businesses aren't true enterprises. Home-based businesses are often given a bad rap in banks and singled out by the IRS as hobbies. Bankers arbitrarily refuse to loan money to these businesses, just because they are home-based. We hope this book will convince financial institutions, and the IRS, that home-based enterprises have the same potentials (and the necessity for fair taxation and deductions) as office-based and store-front businesses.

Criterion 3

The business must have been founded with less than $100,000 in start-up capital. Most of the personalities profiled in this book used much less than this to start their businesses. The point of this arbitrary capitalization limitation was to make sure that the people profiled in the book started out without special privileges or assets to support them. For example, this criterion rules out "entrepreneurs" who got started using the family jewels as collateral for a business that made millions dealing in Picassos or meddling in the stock market.

Criterion 4

Purchased businesses were not considered unless the purchase of another business was used to expand an existing home-based enterprise. We did include a few successful entrepreneurs who bought franchises that could be operated from the home. While there are plenty of people who become successful with companies set up by someone else, *Million Dollar Home-Based Businesses* is mostly about people who thought up their own concepts for businesses and successfully executed them.

Criterion 5

To be considered for a profile in this book the business had to have started with only family members or five or fewer employees. The idea here is to show that people can do things with little help from others on the outside and still make significant incomes.

While these selection criteria may appear restrictive at first, the number of companies we found that meet the specifications is astounding. When assembling this book, we had to leave out many interesting and successful enterprises that fully met the criteria. Sometimes the choice was arbitrary—because we had already described a similar business. To include all the home-based millionaires would require a multi-volume set. We chose to include a wide range of personalities, enterprises, approaches, and attitudes that represent the diversity of successful home-based entrepreneurs. In this way, almost anyone can find a role model to relate to based on age, education, and/or enterprise criteria.

What Are the Common Threads Among Home-Made Millionaires?

The people and businesses presented in the book are diverse. They come from disparate cultural, socioeconomic, and educational backgrounds. In fact, it surprised us at first that formal education is not a predictable component in the profile of our homemade millionaires. Some of these moneyed people have never finished high school. Others are college drop outs. Still others have advanced graduate degrees from prestigious universities. While many of the people profiled in this book run a business directly related to their education, sometimes education seems to propel them in another direction. For example, one entrepreneur we interviewed found that his master's degree in clinical psychology placed him in a field he disliked intensely. So, using the skills gained from his childhood fascination with electronics, he began a business designing computerized control systems—a long way from the psychologist's couch. Some of the people educated themselves instead of going back to school to gain the required skills formally. This leads us to the conclusion that other factors are more important in gaining home-based millions than a formal education.

Though the educational achievements of our profiled millionaires are unpredictable, as you read the accounts you will notice distinct qualities that these people share in attitude and approach. We have interviewed hundreds of home-based entrepreneurs to write this book and based on these interactions have concluded that there are three significant factors contributing to all the success stories. Since these qualities seem to represent a common thread among all participants, we thought that we should highlight them in the next section in order that readers considering a home-based business are clear on the prerequisites to prosperity. As you read on, keep in mind that these qualities were almost universally mentioned when the home-based entrepreneurs were asked about the key factors in their success. The same traits were brought up by people in all parts of the country regardless of the gender, age, personal profiles, or business of the entrepreneur.

Perseverance

Perseverance is the number one trait you'll see revealed again and again in this book. To be successful in a home-based business you must be capable of prolonged effort, even in the face of adversity.

Many of the people profiled cite their ability to hang onto their dreams through thick and thin as being the single most important trait responsible for their success. A few of the homemade millionaires have started previous businesses that ended in the bankruptcy courts, only to pick up the pieces and try over and over until they made a business work. Others have taken years to get things off the ground but eventually succeeded. For many of these individuals, the tenacity to cling to their businesses in the face of mounting losses and problems saw them through the crises.

As one person put it, "Whenever I feel like I just can't keep the company going because of problems, overwork, or slow sales, I think about the way Monday at the office used to be before I moved out of corporate America and set up my company at home. Even during the worst time in the history of my home-based company, when product problems were producing more returns than sales, just thinking about the grind I gave up at the office makes my company and its problems take on a new and positive light."

Dedication is a related success factor in the homemade business stories we've documented. While the owners of competing companies, especially large, established ones enjoy a weekend at the beach, the dedicated home-based entrepreneur may work all weekend to satisfy a customer. It is their willingness to put in the extra three hours a day or an extra day a week that ultimately helped these people succeed where others would have failed. Homemade millionaires simply don't give up or give in.

Fierce Need for Independence
After perseverance and drive, you'll notice that most of the homemade millionaires share a fierce determination to remain independent. Many of these people went through a bad experience with an uncaring boss or unstable company that motivated them to work for themselves. Many homemade millionaires run enterprises that allow them to make money doing what they would be doing for fun anyway. For the most part, the people in this book love their work and this romance fuels the drive required to keep them going. While we heard many variations of this theme, almost all of the home entrepreneurs dislike or are not very good at working for someone else. They are not corporate players and some are proud of this fact. Many of these people were regarded by companies and corporations as "problem" employees who liked to make their own decisions and who refused to go along with the party line for the sake of inter-company politics. Instead, these people made their views known when they felt

a decision was incorrect, even if it placed them in an unpopular position. For many of these people, their ideas and foresight materially contributed to the success of their previous employers, but for their efforts, they received little or no recognition or financial reward. As one homemade millionaire put it, "I made my company a lot of money by recognizing opportunities for growth that they missed. But, on my performance reviews I would get told that I wasn't a good employee in the company's eyes because I made too many political waves."

For some of the people profiled in this book, running a successful home-based business was a way to "get back" at their old employers by proving that they could make it on their own. Although some experts recommend against it, many homemade millionaires actually set up flourishing businesses that compete head to head with their old companies. These entrepreneurs take candid pride in beating their old bosses at their own games.

A Willingness to Take Risk

Every homemade millionaire was willing to take a risk of some sort when starting his or her new venture. While the degree and kind of risk varied considerably among individuals and companies, no one (at least not in this book) fell into a successful business without putting something on the line: financial risk, personal failure, or loss of a "secure" job to start the business. Many of the people in the book started their businesses against the advice of friends, family, and even their employers. They were left to achieve success entirely on their own. Some of the entrepreneurs even risked their marriages, going ahead with ventures without the approval of their mates.

They Share Traits, but Not Business Practices

While it appears that the three characteristics of persistence, a need for independence, and a willingness to take risks are almost universal traits among the homemade millionaires, the similarities among the success factors seem to stop there. The ways entrepreneurs conduct their lives and build businesses are as diverse as the products they sell. There were many differences in the way people selected a business, got it started, and built it to success. Where one homemade millionaire turned a hobby into a major business over a period of years with almost no start-up capital, another mortgaged the house and took every risk possible to build a business overnight. Especially surprising was the variety of start-up capital sources. Some funding came from traditional sources like small business loans or loans from friends or family. Other people put savings away methodically and had specific financial security goals that had to be met before they allowed themselves to even start their own businesses. But most of the capital came from odd or impulsive sources, including insurance settlements for car accidents, money sequestered away for a boat or vacation, or even a reimbursement check for a business trip overseas. Some of the ventures, like Donna Friedman's The Exceptional Entertainment Company, Inc., opened with no start-up capital whatsoever. Another unexpected anomaly was the difference in the attitudes about planning. Some claim planning is a waste of time—others swear by it. Some cite the development of a solid business plan as the single most important aspect of their success. Others work on a fly-by-night basis, running more on instinct than anything else—and they prefer it that way. The homemade millionaires described in this volume also have different working hours, sometimes controversial attitudes about reinvesting in the company, and completely diverse approaches to marketing their products. There is no one single formula that works for everyone—though it does seem you must have the three prerequisite traits of perseverance, independence, and ability to take risk to get started.

Do You Have What It Takes to Become a Homemade Millionaire?

As you read this book you'll see how everyday people made themselves successful with little more than an idea, some occasional luck, and a strong will to succeed. Can you picture yourself in their shoes? Do you want to become successful in a business that you actually *like* working in? Is freedom from domination by others an important goal in your life? Are you willing to take the risk? If you answered yes to these questions, then you may have what it takes to become a homemade millionaire. After reading the book, you'll know it is possible.

CHAPTER 1

Homemade Superstars

Our exploration of homemade success stories begins with some of the most successful entrepreneurs of this century. You are probably already familiar with most of their names, or at least their products, but you may not know that some of these people and their companies got a start at home. What's even more intriguing is that with only a few exceptions, most of these stories read like the sagas of the lesser-known entrepreneurs profiled in this book—a start from home with little or no money, little support from others around them, and a not-necessarily-unique idea. Many of these people used something ordinary as seed for what would eventually become a major corporation.

Amanda W. Smith of Mrs. Smith's pies is a classic case. In 1919, Amanda took the ordinary recipes handed down through her family and with a dose of her own invention and care she produced a unique product—her pies. With the help of her son, Robert, she sold her pies to local customers from a rumble seat converted into a pie rack in the back of the car. Her baking skills set in motion the events that would one day produce the massive food conglomerate that still bears her name. She kept baking at home until 1925, when she retired. At that point the company was on its way to being the megacorporation known as Mrs. Smith's Delicious Homemade Pies, Inc.

As the story of Mrs. Smith's reveals, home-based start-ups are not a recent development. In fact, most of American industry owes its beginnings to cottage industries started in homes and farms. But as the country grew and companies became larger, home-based enterprises seemed to be the exception. It wasn't until the recent recessions, coupled with the development of technologies that allowed people to work and communicate from home, that the home-based business phenomenon started getting serious attention again as a viable alternative to nine-to-five corporate life.

Now, home-based enterprises are so common that they are finally being recognized as the legitimate companies they are. Even the once-skeptical *FORTUNE* 500 corporations now regularly do business with home-based vendors because they see that people who work from home can provide the same or better quality products as office-based workers. Customers enjoy the superior service and competitive pricing that these home-based companies typically provide.

Before we introduce some of the homemade millionaires we found around the country, here are some of the better-known homemade entrepreneurs from both the recent and more distant past who started flourishing empires from their homes.

The Computer Millionaires

You've probably heard the story of the patent office clerk who quit his job around the turn of the century because he felt that everything important had already been invented. As one of the most shortsighted fellows of all time, he would have been amazed today to see the machines that pervade our lives. If he had been told that a tiny silicon chip would be the single most important invention of the twentieth century, he would have laughed in disbelief. Yet today microcomputers on a chip are embedded in almost everything, including our toasters (yes, really!). Microcomputer technology has done and will do more to change the way we live than the electric light bulb and the telephone changed the world in the nineteenth century.

Naturally, computer technology has made a lot of people rich and many of the pioneering computer architects started out of their homes designing equipment that would eventually make them both rich and famous. One of the hotbeds of home-based entrepreneurial activity has been California's Silicon Valley. Beginning in the 1950s, this area adjacent to San Jose and about forty miles south of San Francisco, spawned many of America's premier entrepreneurial success stories. Most of the Valley's fortunes are tied to computers and electronics. During the early 1980s, people in the Valley joked that every two-car garage secretly housed a start-up company that would make the owners millionaires. Most home-based enterprises in this book began in a spare bedroom, but for some reason most computer companies in the Silicon Valley seem to get started in the garage.

We only have room to profile a handful of the computer entrepreneurs. Listing the few profiles of the people and their well-known companies is to somehow shortchange the large number of homemade millionaires the Valley has produced. For every one of the well-known people like Steve Jobs and Steve Wozniak who founded Apple Computer, there are probably hundreds more people who started or continue to run highly successful, but low-profile companies from home or small offices. Many of these entrepreneurs are publicity shy and make their money on royalties from a handful of brilliant patents. Others write software programs and sell their wares to major companies that market them as their own. One of these "invisible" people—one *very* interesting Jerry Seagraves who still lives in the Bay Area, is among the detailed profiles provided later in the book.

The Homemade Hardware Millionaires

The saga of the development of the first microcomputers is full of colorful names, oddball machines, and overnight successes. Some of the personalities are worth a book unto themselves such as the eccentric Adam Osborne of Osborne Computer and Osborne/McGraw-Hill Books, Jack Tramiel, and Nolan Bushnell, to name but a few. We profile five others in this section who were among the most successful of the hardware innovators and they all started their companies from home—mostly in the garage.

Profile: David Packard and William R. Hewlett

Company Name: Hewlett-Packard

Business Profile: The company builds a wide variety of test equipment, sophisticated calculators, computers, and computer peripherals. They manufacture medical instruments as well.

The Office: The company was started in David Packard's garage in 1939.

Starting out with $538 and income from their wives' jobs to support them, David Packard and William Hewlett set out to build an electronic test instrument called an audio oscillator. (An audio oscillator creates an audible tone. The frequency [pitch] of the tone produced can be varied by adjusting a knob.) The first sale of eight audio oscillators was made to Walt Disney's company. Disney wanted them for use on the sound track of *Fantasia*. From there, HP went on to dominate the electronic testing and scientific instrument industry. Growth at HP got a second wind beginning in 1972 when the company's immensely popular line of scientific and engineering calculators quickly replaced clumsy and imprecise slide rules, and then again when Hewlett-Packard made forays into computer peripherals markets starting in the 1980s. Today the company is a vast enterprise employing more than one hundred thousand people, but it all started in one garage.

You'll see references to the HP name spread throughout the profiles of the computer start-up companies in this section, because their encouragement to innovate spawned many of the second generation start-up successes in the Silicon Valley. The company allows its engineers to develop their ideas and if the company isn't interested, go off and start a business, as long as HP is given nonexclusive rights to market the product. And, many of the spin-off companies are naturally started at home, perhaps the most famous being Apple Computer, profiled next.

★　　★　　★

Profile: Steve Wozniak and Steve Jobs

Company Name: Apple Computer, Inc.

Business Profile: The company builds easy-to-use personal computers, starting in the early days with the Apple II (still manufactured today). Apple introduced its Macintosh computer in 1984 and the Newton and other personal information managers (PIMs) in 1993. It is one of the major players in the personal computer industry. Steve Wozniak left the company some years ago to pursue personal interests. Steve Jobs left the company after eventually being forced out by a new CEO, John Sculley, who was brought in from Pepsi-Co. Mr. Jobs started another computer company, NeXT Computer, with money he realized from his Apple stock. NeXT is still struggling to win a significant market share from the Macintosh.

The Office: The company was started in the garage of Steve Job's parents' home in the 1970s.

Replete with mythical history, a whimsical cast of characters, and a six-color apple logo, Apple Computer makes the second most popular computer architecture available in today's marketplace—the Macintosh. The Apple 1 was originally built in a garage using parts obtained from Hewlett-Packard and Atari, using the talents of high school buddies Steve Jobs and Steve Wozniak. Jobs sold his Volkswagen and Wozniak sold his two Hewlett-Packard calculators to start the venture. Fifty Apple 1 computers were sold to friends and a couple of computer stores in the area. The initial success and a rough business plan allowed them to convince the investment firm of Hambrecht & Quist to help put the funding together to start Apple Computer. Jobs convinced "the Woz" to give up his job at Hewlett-Packard and get the company moving. With bow-tied Jobs guiding the company with his innate entrepreneurial spirit and the computer whiz kid Wozniak designing the computers, Apple was quickly on its way to selling the Apple II. This computer, while not the first commercial microcomputer to reach the market, quickly became a favorite of small businesses, educators, and novice computer programmers. Eventually eclipsed by first the IBM PC and later Apple's own Macintosh, the Apple II dominated a large niche in the history of computing and made the founders multimillionaires of almost legendary proportions.

Profile: James Toreson
Company Name: Xebec Corporation
Business Profile: Computer disk drives and disk drive controllers.
The Office: The company was started in the family room.

Perhaps less celebrated than the founders of HP and Apple because his company's products are an internal component of computers that purchasers rarely see, James Toreson is another Silicon Valley mogul who started his huge corporation from home. His company's first product was a hard disk controller. His company was then called Microcomputer Systems Corp. A controller board is a "go-between" computer circuit board that reads and writes data to a computer's internal hard disk at the direction of the central processor.

Visiting big companies such as HP, IBM, and Memorex (remember Memorex?), Toreson's MSC sold drive controllers but kept the rights and ownership of the technology. Sales were brisk because most of his customers did not want to take the time to design their own controller systems. MSC quickly became the country's largest independent supplier of controllers. The name was changed to Xebec when MSC bought a competitor. (A Xebec is reportedly a three-masted ship used by pirates in the Mediterranean.) Today the company, complete with its own corporate jet, still makes controller systems, now assembled by robots in a factory located near Carson City, Nevada. Xebec actively supports new entrepreneurs who have high-technology ideas. We hope these spin-offs get a proper start in someone's garage!

The Homemade Software Millionaires

Software design is a less capital-intensive endeavor than developing hardware and less space-consuming because the work takes place on a computer rather than a workbench full of prototypes with parts and ganglia filling the room. A software company can be started just about anywhere you can put a computer keyboard, although that didn't stop Software Publishing Company from starting in the garage anyway. The personalities of the software millionaires are as diverse as the hardware people. The chief nerd among them is Bill Gates, who started Microsoft in 1974. Still chairman of Microsoft, Mr. Gates is a multibillionaire touted to be the richest man in the United States—and he's only thirty-seven. There are also tragic figures including George Tate, founder of Ashton-Tate who contrived the name Ashton before his to make the company name sound better, who died while still in his early thirties. Here are profiles of some software gurus who started at home and made millions.

Profile: Fred Gibbons

Company Name: Software Publishing Corporation

Business Profile: Software Publishing markets a variety of graphics and productivity software programs. The company is best known today for its Harvard Graphics products.

The Original
      Office: The first Software Publishing product was written in Janelle Bedke's garage.

When Hewlett-Packard rejected employee Fred Gibbon's idea for software, he and two co-workers formed their own company to write the database package, *pfs: file*, as part of a package of programs that would later include several other pfs-series software packages. The task of writing *pfs: file* went to colleague Janelle Bedke, who left

Hewlett-Packard and set up shop at home in her garage in proper computer start-up style. To bankroll her work, Fred and partner John Page contributed part of their HP paychecks and Gibbons kicked in his life savings of $50,000. They also worked evenings and weekends to help code the product and produce the instruction manual. Once the program was complete, the product was announced to computer dealers all over the country. Orders rolled in so fast that Gibbons and co-founder Page were forced to leave HP to keep up with the demand. Finally, to build the company, they approached venture capitalist Jack Melchor who assembled financing from a list of people that reads like a Who's Who of Silicon Valley. The funding propelled Software Publishing out of the garage and into a position as a major player in the microcomputer software market.

Profile: Sandra Kurtzig

Company Name: ASK Computer Systems, Inc.

Business Profile: ASK develops software for specialized business applications such as the control of manufacturing systems.

The Office: The company was started from a spare bedroom in Sandra's Silicon Valley apartment.

Sandra Kurtzig is one of the few female CEOs of a major corporation in the United States. Regardless of equal opportunity laws, few companies promote females through the glass ceiling and into the star chair in the president's office, so Sandra put herself into that chair by starting her own company. She also wrote a best-selling autobiography titled (what else?) *CEO.*

While working at General Electric, Sandra decided that she wanted the freedom to have a family that her job as a sales representative didn't provide. Quitting her job, she took her $2,000 in savings and started a contract computer programming company, ASK Computers, from her spare bedroom. Initially intended as a part-time venture, she quickly had so many clients that her dreams of quality time with the family evaporated. As she puts it in A. David Silver's book *Entrepreneurial Megabucks,* "My part-time job was taking up to twenty hours a day. I had the other four to start my family."

Why was there so much demand for ASK's services? Because of a perpetual problem within the computer industry that Sandra solved. New hardware requires new software, but in many instances the software can't even be started until the hardware is complete. In addition, many companies require custom software to be developed that meets special needs, and that's where Sandra's company excels—in developing custom software solutions for medium to large-sized companies. In fact, ASK's first hit product was a manufacturing inventory control program written for Hewlett-Packard's 3000 series minicomputer, developed when HP gave Sandra and her team time to test and program their software on one of its 3000 series machines at night. Reportedly so determined were they to complete the product on time that the team slept in sleeping bags at HP during the product's final phases in order to complete it! With that kind of drive it's no wonder that this enterprise is now a 400 million dollar corporation. Sandra is a CEO to be reckoned with.

Profile: Philippe Kahn

Company Name: Borland International

Business Profile: Borland is one of the biggest software players in the nineties, having gobbled up one-time competitor Ashton-Tate.

The Original
Office: The company was started from Philippe Kahn's home in Scotts Valley, California.

As one of the more eclectic personalities in an industry filled with such people, Philippe Kahn got his start by writing a Pascal compiler, a programming language used to develop other programs. To launch the product, he convinced one of the computer magazines to run an ad for his product on credit. Good thing, too, because Philippe didn't have any money to pay for it had they demanded prepayment. Fortunately, Philippe's Turbo Pascal sold incredibly fast, being the first Pascal compiler priced low enough that high school and college students could afford to purchase it. (We even bought a copy back then.) Packaged with a miserably incomplete and incompetent user manual, it was a unique program because Philippe allowed purchasers to distribute copies to friends for free as long as no one charged money for copies. After selling a mountain of Turbo Pascal compilers, Borland International began developing and acquiring other software products and the company grew from a mail-order house to the mainstream company it is today. Known for packing more power into a product for less than half the competitor's price, Borland ranks as one of the five largest software concerns and sells a complete line of microcomputer software, including the popular spreadsheet program, QuattroPro, and other leading products. And yes, they still sell Pascal.

Other Homemade Success Stories

Of course, not all homemade mega-millionaires were involved in the computer industry. For example, most successful cartoonists work from home. Homemade millionaires in this category include Charles Shultz of *Peanuts* fame, Gary Larsen and *The Far Side*, Berke Breathed who created the now defunct *Bloom County*, and a host of others. Humorist Dave Barry works from home and as he wrote in a pre-1992 election column, "Today's career question is, Should you work at home? Working at home is an idea that's appealing to more and more people, such as George Bush. One day he got sick and tired of constant foreign travel and said, 'Barbara, I'm going to put a desk and a phone in the oval office and just stay home and veto legislation.' Other famous people who work at home are Queen Elizabeth II and the American farmer."

And almost every best-selling author, including Amy Tan, Danielle Steele, James Michener, and many, many more create their manuscripts in home offices. In these careers you are expected to work at home, but, for other enterprises, success at home seems less ordinary. Here are a couple of examples.

Is Lamb Chop a Homemade Millionaire?

Remember Shari Lewis and her homemade puppets Lamb Chop, Charlie Horse, and Hush Puppy? Shari had a popular kids show in the early 1960s that has been revived for PBS in the 1990s by perpetually perky Shari. There must be quite a bit of interest in Shari's simple puppet characters because a recent production run of seven hundred thousand Baby Lamb Chops sold out in just three and a half weeks over Easter season. Shari and Lamb Chop work out of Shari's Spanish-style house in Beverly Hills, which is the center of Shari Lewis Productions. Her twenty-nine-year-old daughter works as a creative consultant to the show. Initially, thirty episodes are being taped. This is a dynamic home-based company with multitudes assisting at the house to carry on Shari's many projects.

What has fifty-seven-year-old Shari been up to in the nearly thirty years since we last saw her? Plenty. According to a *Wall Street Journal* article, she has conducted a hundred symphony orchestras, made records, and produced fifty-one children's books and eleven videos, in addition to making personal appearances around the world. She, and her husband who is book publisher Jeremy Tarcher, even wrote an episode for "Star Trek." Since most of this work was done from home, this might very well be the largest home-based studio in California.

Bill Bowerman and Philip Knight Take the Money and Run
Bill Bowerman was a coach at the University of Oregon when he decided to try to improve the shoes his athletes wore. Not impressed with the traditional running shoes of the day or enamored with the expensive German-made Adidas, he studied shoemaking with a local cobbler and set up shop in his garage. The resulting shoes were superior to anything available and so impressed was one of the athletes, Philip Knight, that he asked to be a partner. The two set up a company to have the shoes manufactured in Japan, each contributing only $500 in start-up capital.

After the first shipment of shoes arrived from the Orient, Bill kept on coaching and Philip worked as an accountant at Price-Waterhouse. The initial sales strategy was unique. Instead of attempting to go up against major shoe companies where the budgets for a single TV ad would bankrupt the fledgling company, the shoes were sold directly to high school coaches and athletes. Their first employee was Jeff Johnson, who sold the shoes in southern California. Using his apartment to warehouse the shoes, he went from school to school selling the running shoes from his trunk. Then, in 1969, as sales began to take off, Philip Knight quit his job to run the company full time.

Today this home-based start-up company has grown to be an industry giant, worth around $3 billion. The name of the shoes—you probably guessed it already—Nike!

Did You Know That These Giants Started from Home?
Many modern icons of corporate America, like Nike, began in the basement, extra bedroom, kitchen, or tool shed because then, as now, the home was the perfect way to start out. It's not only a very comfortable place to work, but the low overhead arrangement frees the up-and-coming entrepreneur from the expense of opening and maintaining a place of business, at least until the company has a product ready to sell. Here are a few more of those corporate institutions and long-standing companies that started from home.

Nervous Immigrant Writes Name Wrong and So Starts Lane Bryant
Lena Bryant was so nervous opening a savings account for the $300 she had salted away that she misspelled her name as Lane Bryant on the deposit record.

This lady, after being widowed, was left to support herself and her son. Her husband, who had died of tuberculosis a few months after their son was born, left her with little more than a pair of diamond earrings—baubles she pawned in order to buy a sewing machine.

Lena's first products were negligees and bridal gowns made for neighborhood women. From there, over several years of hard work at her sewing machine, she built the business to a $50,000 a year enterprise. (Remember that $50,000 was a princely sum of money at the turn of the century.) Marrying Albert Malsin in 1909, the company began sales of maternity wear in stores, a concept unheard of during this post-Victorian period. A single ad in the only newspaper that would carry such "risqué" advertising, sold out the store in one day. From there, through expansion, the company is one of the largest ready-to-wear garment companies in North America. All this, started from one sewing machine and a nervous mistake at the bank, is still called Lane Bryant.

The Three Davidson Brothers and Bill Harley Power Up Profits from a Backyard Shed
An offer for a free ride on a new motorcycle got Harley Davidson started. And while the company has had its ups and downs, its motorcycles are still regarded by many as the best in two-wheeled transportation.

Walter Davidson was a machinist who got a letter from his brother Art that explained that he (Art) and a friend, Bill Harley, had designed a new motorbike and invited him to ride it. The catch was that Walter had to build the new machine first. In 1903, after adding the third Davidson brother, William, the first Harleys were built in a shed in the backyard of the Davidson brothers' home and the company sped off down the road into a bright future.

Deceased industrialist Malcolm Forbes of *Forbes* magazine fame was obsessed with the massive two-wheelers. Today, the Japanese are also obsessive fans of Harley products. Japanese Harley-Davidson clubs take their expensive shiny motorcycles on tour every weekend. It seems like a paradox that the Japanese, who lead the world in the number of motor cars manufactured, prefer to ride American-made motorcycles. It just points to the quality and reputation of the product this homemade American company builds. Maybe there's a message there for other American companies trying to compete with Japan?

John Dunlap Revolutionizes the Tire with His Daughter's Tricycle
While he was already prospering in a well-established veterinary surgery practice in Scotland, John Dunlap invented the modern bicycle tire when he tried to make his daughter's tricycle smoother to ride. To make the tricycle more comfortable, he replaced the traditional solid rubber tires with air-filled rubber tubes. To adhere them to the flat wheel edges, the tubes were wrapped with Irish linen to bind them to the wheel frames. Not wanting to give up his veterinary practice, he sold his rights to the invention. But the invention went on to change the way tires were made for both bicycles and the evolving automobile tire industry. A lot of people got rich from John Dunlap's home-generated invention and the tires that still bear his name.

George Swinnerton Parker Starts a Monopoly from Home
Starting with a board game called *Banking*, which he designed at home while on a three-week vacation from school, sixteen-year-old George Swinnerton Parker sold five hundred of the games during a Christmas buying frenzy in the mid-1800s. Under the gun from his parents to take a "real job," George started out as a cub reporter after graduation from high school and worked his way up the newspaper hierarchy. Then after suffering a lingering respiratory ailment and having to cut back his activities, he went back to game making and developed a prototype for *Monopoly*, from home of course. He started Parker Brothers two years later with his brother Edward. The company is not only responsible for *Monopoly*, the world's most popular board game outside of checkers, go, and chess, but for other classic board games including *Clue* and *Risk*.

Russell Stover—A Tale of Sweet Success
As reported in Joseph and Suzy Fucini's fascinating book *Entrepreneurs—The Men and Women behind Famous Brand Names and How They Made It* (recommended reading for home-based start-up companies although you may have to make a trip to the library to find a copy because it's apparently out of print), "Unlike most husbands in the little town of Hume, Saskatchewan, Canada, who occasionally brought home a box of candy, Russell Stover surprised his wife, Clara, with a candy business. The Stovers were married for a little over a year in 1912, when Russell came home with some second-hand equipment and announced they would make and sell confections." Apparently lacking experience, through careful experimentation, the couple's chocolates developed a loyal, local following. The company hit on hard times during the sugar rationing of World War I and relocated to

Chicago, where again success was elusive. A year after the failure of their company, Russell developed the Eskimo Pie while working for another candy maker. Selling his interest in it for $30,000, he took the money and launched what is today Russell Stover Candies, Inc. with Clara Stover, who ran the business after his death in 1954. Today, few cities in the United States are without a Russell Stover candy store.

Of course, not all homemade millionaires become household names. In the next pages we'll give you an in-depth introduction to some less well-known, but equally intriguing success stories. Of course, all these people, and the ones we have just introduced to you, share the common traits of persistence, the willingness to work hard, and a drive to keep going. As we've mentioned already, these are the traits you will likely need if you want to join their ranks, unless you are lucky and come up with the idea for the next Pet Rock, and we're not going to hold our breath for that.

CHAPTER 2

Where Do the Ideas Come From?

When people ask us about starting a home-based business, they inevitably ask questions like these: Where does the idea come from? What kind of ideas work? Does the idea need to be original or can I copy what someone else has done?

In interviewing hundreds of successful home-based entrepreneurs, we have discovered that there are no predictable answers to these questions that work for everyone. The ideas for home-based businesses have no universal source and ordinary ideas seems to work as well as brilliant ones. The source of business success may be in the idea in some cases—but it is more frequently embodied in the tenacity and motivation of the entrepreneurs themselves.

In keeping with our objective of providing real-world role models, in this chapter we profile home-based businesses that were started from ideas of all kinds. You'll discover that whacky ideas can make money, like the rubber duck races promoted by Eric Schechter and George Getz and the strings of lights in the shapes of bacon and eggs sold by Sue Scott. You'll see how Tom Chapman turned the nightmare of foreclosure into the dream of a new home. You'll meet Ingrid Elsel, who turned the loopholes and bureaucracy of California's environmental regulations into a personal gold mine. There are five more entrepreneurs profiled in the chapter who had ideas as risqué as documenting the nude scenes in major motion pictures and as ordinary as imprinting bath towels to make their fortunes.

Of course, in other chapters in the book you will encounter even more sources for business ideas—some fantastic, some mundane. For example, in chapter 3 you'll see that Bill Herz's passion for magic was transformed into an innovative way to train corporate executives. In fact, you'll see that many people have transformed "hobbies" into major corporations. There are also seemingly ordinary home-based businesses that reap fortunes for the entrepreneurs that start them, like the construction firm run by Kenneth Bates, the writing business started by Dan Siemasko, and the Amway franchise started by the Mejdrich family. In this book you will find home-based business ideas to suit almost any personality or skill set.

Regardless of the idea that spawned the venture, the profiled companies bring in substantial revenue for the entrepreneurs who started them. In the profiles in this chapter, and throughout the book, you'll discover that the idea is not always as important as its long-term execution in the marketplace.

Please note: Addresses and contact numbers have been provided in this book when the people gave us permission to provide them. Feel free to contact these people for more information on their products and services. If no address or phone number is included in a profile in the book, it is because the entrepreneur did not want that information included in the profile.

✦   ✦   ✦

These Entrepreneurs Get Their Ducks in a Row for Big Bucks

Profile: Eric Schechter & George Getz

Company Name: Great American Duck Races

Year Founded: 1988

Homemade
Success Secret: Almost any quacky idea has potential.

Business Profile: Great American Duck Races arranges charity-sponsored duck races that employ thousands of yellow "rubber" ducks wearing sunglasses. They handled eight races the first year. This year they will coordinate more than a hundred races with more than $10 million generated for charity and a tidy profit of their own.

Start-up Capital: A loan to purchase the first thirty thousand ducks.

The Office: The ducks were stored in a dusty warehouse with Eric and partners calling the shots from their respective homes. Eric now has an office but stills works from home when he can because he likes it best.

Working Hours: Seventy or eighty hours a week in the early days. Today, it depends on the racing schedule.

Home Office Technology: A computer for tracking the ducks by serial number and doing the accounting.

Family Profile: Eric is married to Mitzi and they have a five-year-old daughter.

Education: Eric has an MBA from UCLA and a bachelor's degree in mechanical engineering.

Favorite Pastimes: Eric competes in tennis matches when he's not racing rubber waterfowl around the country. Eric and his wife also enjoy riding horses.

Almost all charities and not-for-profit organizations require external fund-raising to stay in operation. Some of the higher-profile colleges, museums, and medical facilities have a fairly automatic process for raising money, often including government funding and regular contributions from moneyed individuals and corporate sponsors. But for most not-for-profit enterprises, raising large amounts of money is a chore, especially during tight economic times. A successful money-raising tactic in hard times is to sponsor some kind of newsworthy event that draws large numbers of people and only requires each participant to contribute a small sum of money—at least this is how Great American Duck Races does it.

The rubber duck races typically receive widespread publicity in each city where they are held, drawing both supporters of the sponsoring charity as well as people simply interested in the absurdity of a rubber duck race and the opportunity to win the grand prize—usually a car or other substantial award provided by a local company. Media sponsors promote the race and prize sponsors donate their goods to be given away as prizes to the winning duck or ducks.

The race works as follows: Before the event is held, the sponsoring charity has participants adopt a duck or a flock of ducks. The cost is usually about five dollars a duck. Then on the day of the event, a large dump truck backs up over the river where the event is set up and releases ten thousand to fifty thousand of the four inch tall grinning plastic ducks (complete with sunglasses) into the water. The ducks just do their own thing and float effortlessly to the finish line. At the end of the designated racing area, the first duck to pop into the "Duck Trap" takes the grand prize place. Its owner is identified by the fowl's barcode printed on the bottom and the person who sponsored that duck wins the race! Ducks and their numbers are tracked by computer with a program developed for the purpose called (what else?) Quack Track.

The event varies considerably from city to city due to the nature of each area's waterways. In Chicago, in an event sponsored for the child abuse unit of Illinois Masonic Medical Center, the bright yellow ducks are dumped into the Chicago River from the Michigan Bridge. The ducks are then forced down the river by the fire department using water cannons. In a desert city like Phoenix which has no continuously flowing rivers nearby, they are run down an irrigation canal, originally dug by the Indians who settled in the area several centuries ago.

Charities love the event because thousands of people who might not otherwise have an interest in the sponsoring organization will pay to adopt a duck. It's been a strong fund-raiser for all kinds of groups. And, along with the race, special events such as "Quacker and Cheese" and VID (Very Important Duck) parties bring in additional revenue, as do duck T-shirts, rubber duck sales, and other duck memorabilia. Great American Duck Races gets paid by the duck, selling ducks in blocks by the thousand. They also make a portion of the revenue generated from other duck-related sales.

Who would come up with such an absurd, but wildly successful idea? Well, Eric H. Schechter is the head duck behind the idea. He was a real estate broker and a member of a young men's organization that wanted to put on an event to raise money for children's charities. As Eric explains, "We'd thought of the traditional golf tournament, black-tie dinners, bachelor auctions—things that really everyone else has done. Then in a 1950s fund-raising book I saw a little discussion about what they used to do in Ireland with wooden decoys. And we thought, 'Hey, we can do that with rubber ducks and put them in the canal and make ten or twenty grand.'"

Getting started was the hard part for Eric. "I must have missed a meeting or something because I was elected chairman and the next thing I know I'm running this rubber duck race trying to figure out where are we going to get the ducks from. Could we get sponsors? Could we get permission from the city? Well we did—and the event was wildly successful. We started getting requests from other charities in other cities." As a result, Eric took the business private in 1988, though there was some animosity on the part of his service club for making it into a business. Eric says it was he and his partners who personally had to get a loan to buy the ducks, not the club. His club benefited because he ran the race for free the first year for the sponsoring charity, but he confesses that some members of his old club feel angry about the loss of control of the duck race idea.

When Eric went into commercial rubber duck racing, he did it in first class style—with a colorful logo, designer rubber ducks, and a comprehensive step-by-step workbook for the charities to use to run the ultimate duck race. The races take a lot of work, so Eric tries to be selective about the groups he will take on to run the races. The ducks themselves are manufactured in China and this leads to Eric's favorite "duck tale."

Eric explains their most difficult problem was getting the ducks manufactured to be strong enough to endure shipping and multiple races. "It seemed simple enough—build a rubber duck that could withstand twenty or thirty races and could handle a drop from a hundred-foot bridge. We brought new ducks in last year in June—50,000 of them. They came across the desert. When we opened the boxes, the seams had all popped, and the ducks were flat in their boxes. They all popped because of the high heat—they were fried. We had 50,000 dead ducks. We finally had to hire an engineer to redesign the duck. Today, we have at least 150,000 durable ducks in our racing stock."

Soon after the first successful duck race, Eric started promoting the idea to other charities. He made tons of phone calls to organizations around the nation and sent out complete information packages on the concept. At first he wasn't selective with the charities he would sell the idea to—but he soon learned that he had to qualify the charities as much as they qualified him. To make money, Eric learned he had to find charities where people were willing to work to make the event a success. As Eric points out, he provides all the tools, but it is the volunteers in the charities that make the event pay off. He also looks for groups who are willing to sponsor the event on an annual basis—as an ongoing promotion. This allows Eric to grow the business in a very controlled fashion. He sells a planned number of new races each year to select groups. The new race sponsors are the most work. The second and third races offered by a charity are more profitable—because the people are already trained and they get better at it over time.

As to the future, for most of us it's probably a matter of rubbing a lucky duck and hoping for the best. But duck racing is on the rise and Eric has a couple of potential investors "egging him on." (Eric warns not to get him started on puns.) Eric explains that racing is not only increasing in popularity, it's going worldwide with races coming up in Mexico and Sweden. The Swedish races will be funded by SAS, the Swedish national airline, and Saab, makers of cars, trucks, and aircraft. He's also working at getting his ducks into toy stores and department store toy sections. He says it's a no-risk proposition because if the ducks don't sell, he'll take them back and race them.

If asked his advice for future home-based businesses, Eric is likely to say something like, "Don't count your ducks until they hatch."

If you are interested in arranging thoroughbred rubber duck racing for your not-for-profit organization, you can contact Great American Duck Races at:

3200 East Camelback, Suite 200
Phoenix, AZ 85018
Phone Number: (602) 957-DUCK

A Blazing Success with Strings of Bacon and Fried Eggs

Profile: Sue Scott

Company Name: Primal Lite and Primal Design

Year Founded: 1986

Homemade Success Secret: If you can turn an ordinary product into something unique, you can charge a lot for it. The trick is then to continue to adapt the product and be creative—or the business loses its advantage.

Business Profile: Primal Lite designs novelty string lights, night-lights, and desk lamps. Examples include strings of trout, cactus, Santa Cows, and, of course, pink flamingos. Some lights are seasonal, others are amusing, some simply strange—like the ones in the shape of bacon and fried eggs.

Start-up Capital: $25,000 cash advance on credit cards. Sue exclaims, "I also had a desk."

The Office: The office was started from a studio apartment with a loft and literally exploded out of it.

Working Hours: 7:30 A.M. to 6:00 P.M.

Home Office
    Technology: Macintosh computers, a fax, copiers, and equipment for shipping.

Family Profile: Married with children.

Education: Sue has a BFA degree in sculpture from the San Francisco Art Institute.

Favorite Pastimes: "Leisure — hmmm—what a concept—I've read about that. Actually, I have a horse."

Every Christmas a new set of tree light designs comes to market. Last year, ones that blinked in time to off-key chime music were the hot ticket in boutiques and department stores. But Sue Scott's lights are not necessarily for holidays and they show a much more artistic and inventive spirit at work than the lights from ordinary Christmas light manufacturers—who seem to be located mostly in Taiwan.

Sue explains what led up to this definitely unique home-based business. "Well, my background is fine art and I graduated from San Francisco Art Institute with a degree in sculpture. I did my work professionally for about ten years. Then I was director of an art gallery in New Mexico and that's when the idea of the business came to me." She got the idea for her innovative lights while looking at sculptures in shapes of cactus, coyotes, and other flora and fauna common in the Southwest.

She thought the idea would sell, but she realized that she needed to be in a bigger city to sell enough lights to make a living—so she borrowed money on her credit cards and moved to the San Francisco area to get started. Sue explains that she chose to start at home instead of in an office because like many entrepreneurs in this book, she couldn't afford it.

Sue started by finding a distributor for ordinary strings of Christmas lights. Sue used her art skills to design the first covers for the small bulbs in various shapes and had them molded at a local plastics factory. She brought the samples around from store to store and took orders. Later, when she had more designs (and more money) she produced a catalog and started calling on stores outside the area to stock her wares. The reception of the fun lights was outstanding, and now Sue has her own plant in nearby Emeryville for molding and assembling the lights.

Primal Lite products are now marketed under trade names such as Bunch-a-Lizards, Tin-o-Sardines, and other innovative names. Each set of lights is packaged in an attractive box—often as innovative as the lights themselves. For example, the Loads-o-Laundry lights (which resemble rows of socks and clothes drying on a line) are packed in a box in the shape of a washing machine with a see-through door. Another typical product is the Serengeti Glow which contains giraffes and zebras strung together and housed in a colorful box covered with jungle shapes and colors. According to Primal Lite literature, "Each set consists of ten molded plastic shapes on a fourteen-foot cord. The set includes two extra bulbs. The string light is double plugged and will accommodate up to six sets."

Now, in addition to strings of lights, Sue's company makes night lights. One of the first night lights was a dinosaur lamp—the perfect gift for pterodactyl-loving kids and adults with a sense of humor. In addition to selling Primal Lite products, thirty-eight-year-old Sue is the company's creative director. She invents the ideas for the lights and designs them. This is an important aspect of the business—the continuing evolution of ideas and implementation of the lights. This is what keeps the concept fresh and retailers coming back for more each year.

Sue bemuses how her business gradually encroached on her personal living space until it was either move out or let the business take a hike. "I started from the kitchen, then I lost the living room, then I lost the dining room, then I lost my bedroom. At the end, all I had was a rolled-up foam pad for sleeping stored under my desk. Getting sick was impossible. If I wanted to knock off early, I'd drive to the park and sit in my car. Then I'd wait until I thought the last employee had quit for the night before returning home." At that point the business moved into an office because there were no more rooms to expand into at home. Sue describes the biggest challenge of running her business from a studio apartment with a loft as, "the separation between work and personal life. Privacy became impossible."

Sue enjoys her role as an entrepreneur and the satisfaction of creating things that others will buy. "One of the most exciting things about running a business is when you open your mailbox and there's an order. It's wildly exciting when you get that first sale—the check for something that you sold, that you designed, created, produced, and put out in the world."

Sue gets these checks coming in through a combination of calling customers and sending out catalogs to the buyers in stores with color photos of the lights. The whimsy and humor in the designs are the keys to their success—the lights basically sell themselves. When store owners see the unique designs and bright colors, they simply have to have them. Some of Sue's customers include The Nature Company, an upscale retailer of nature-oriented books, gifts, and educational materials; The Hard Rock Cafe, major beer companies, and a variety of restaurants and clubs. Primal Lite products are also sold in upscale department stores such as Neiman Marcus, Nordstrom's, Macy's, and at Walt Disney outlets and the Museum of Modern Art.

"The situations you get into running a business from home are humorous—you're sitting there trying to have a conversation with Macy's and the cat is walking under your nose. You think to yourself, if they only knew . . . I remember when my back went out. There I was in front of my employees sitting in my chair in my bathrobe and what could I do? Those kinds of things happen all the time. At one point there were three of us and only two phone lines. We had hired a telemarketing person and he didn't have a desk or a telephone and someone would be on the phone and we'd all be sitting there waiting to use the other line and he would jump at the phone just to make a call."

Sue has great advice for start-up home-based companies. "I think you have to get real clear on what your priorities are and know when you have to move aside to get out of the way of the success of the company. I think that some entrepreneurs try to perform in all areas of the company when in fact they're not always best qualified for everything." This sentiment was echoed by several home-based entrepreneurs we talked to. Typically they attempted to handle something themselves to save a couple of bucks and then wound up having to have a professional sort out the mess at much greater cost.

Sue's company makes lights suitable for all-year amusement—and it doesn't look like she is going to run out of ideas or customers any time soon. Besides the seasonal lights for the Christmas tree and a string of pumpkin and skeleton lights for Thanksgiving and Halloween respectively, there are always the Lot-o-Lobsters lights for fish restaurant owners with a sense of humor. And what cat lover could resist Sue's Litter-o-Kittys lights . . . or why not a string of bacon and eggs in the kitchen? The possibilities are endless.

If you are interested in strings of lights in fun shapes—like the Ramblin' Road string of sporty red and white sedans alternating with streamlined 1950s-style trailers—you can contact Primal Lite and Primal Design at:

5726 Peladeau Street
Emeryville, CA 94608
Phone Number: (510) 652-7696

★ ★ ★

King of the Fixer Uppers Makes a Royal Living

Profile: Tom Chapman

Company Name: Chapman Design Concepts, Inc.

Year Founded: 1989

Homemade
Success Secret: Print up some cards and tell people you're ready to work. If you give people a quality product for less money than the competition, you'll make it.

Business Profile: The company subcontracts 250 workers to clean out, repair, and refurbish homes, townhouses, and condominiums abandoned by their owners or taken back by banks. His crews are typically working on twenty or thirty houses at a time—all directed from Tom's home-based headquarters. Once Tom's crews are done performing a "rehab," the units are clean, operational, and ready for resale.

Start-up Capital: Out of a job and nearly bankrupt, Tom had $11,000 in savings and took $1,000 of it to risk opening a new business in spite of the vocal objections of his wife. "She loves the business now."

The Office: A multi-acre ranch located in the desert. Tom raises beef cattle for his own meat. They also have several dogs, cats, and goats—even peacocks! The office is in a converted bedroom. Tom defines it as not being an office for outside visitors, but instead, "more like the cockpit of the Space Shuttle."

Working Hours: Up early to feed the animals, Tom explains, "My work ethic is to work as hard as I can Monday through Friday, and play hard on the weekends." Tom usually looks through five to seven properties a day to estimate repair and cleaning costs.

Home Office
Technology: Five phone lines, a personal computer, and a fax. Tom also has a cellular phone to keep in touch with subcontractors in case of problems.

Family Profile: Tom is married to Jan who helps out in the business.

Education: He finished high school.

Favorite Pastimes: Tom loves riding his Harley-Davidson motorcycle and recently worked in a movie with Charlie Sheen where he rode his "hog" as an extra. Meanwhile, back at the ranch, Tom and Jan have friends over frequently for cookouts.

In today's tough economic climate a greater number of people are being evicted from their residences and losing their homes to the bank due to layoffs, plant closings, and pay cuts. Usually after a bank forecloses on a residence, work has to be performed to clean up and rehabilitate the property for the bank or savings and loan to be able to market the property to new buyers.

Since the average suit-and-tie banker doesn't want to get his or her hands dirty cleaning up property, and most likely lacks the knowledge to perform repairs and reconstruction on older or damaged houses, the work is contracted out to someone who knows what to do and charges the institution a reasonable price to do it. Tom Chapman is one such man.

Running a business from his ranch with several hundred subcontractors at his disposal, he bids on blocks of "lender-owned" homes to refurbish and renews repossessed homes to make them suitable for resale. As Tom explains, "When a house sits vacant for six months problems tend to amplify." Some houses sit vacant for months or years before the lender allocates the cash to "rehab" them. During this period a small leak in a water pipe may flood a house, ruining walls and floors. This is when Tom's people get involved to perform major repairs before the home is suitable for occupancy again.

Tom's business got started after he left his management job at The Federated Group, a now defunct chain of consumer electronics stores. According to Tom, "It kind of got started by accident. I brought The Federated Group to Arizona. As Atari was in the process of buying out Federated I knew I didn't want to stay there. I had a feeling what was going to happen to them." Tom's instinct turned out to be correct. The Federated Group was shut down completely at a great loss to the parent corporation and amid a flurry of lawsuits concerning the possible misrepresentation of the chain's actual value.

While many of the entrepreneurs profiled in this book carefully selected and planned a business, Tom's choice of business was somewhat serendipitous. Looking for an alternative to another corporate job, Tom explains, "I used to wear my necktie as a headband in protest of the company dress code. I began looking at alternatives, realizing that my days at the store chain were numbered. I had an offer from one of my customers at Federated to get involved with selling land, so I got a real estate license and after pondering the land market for a year, I realized it really wasn't for me. It was more politics than selling, so I had this idea to put together backers to buy residential real estate property; I would rehab the houses and then we would sell them for a profit. Then I realized that lenders were rehabing their own properties just to recover their losses, so I thought, 'Well, I can skip the backing—I can skip everything and I can rehab property for the lender and make a profit.' Once I got some cards printed I went and knocked on some doors and then the phone started ringing immediately."

Tom's company is yet another example of how a home-based business can blow conventional competitors out of the water. Where XYZ company with a traditional office and straight-jacketed way of doing business may take a week to respond to a client's request for a bid on refurbishing a property, Tom provides an estimate on the bank's schedule instead of his. "Lenders got a whiff that I was doing renovations on properties, and they really liked the fact that my business could respond. You can fax us something today and there's a good chance that you can have your bid back tomorrow. These lenders are very impatient—they want to know what the bottom line is—immediately."

Tom's company grew without formal advertising of any kind. Word of mouth does the job for Tom. Tom's leads come from the brokers that the banks hire to sell their properties. Tom makes the broker's job that much easier—so the ones who know him always recommend him to the bank. "The broker likes us because our turnaround time is so quick. They know in two weeks that they're going to have a turn-key property that's going to be beautiful. When they open the door, new carpet, fresh paint, new appliances—whatever the property requires, it's done. The properties sell very quickly and very easily because we basically erase all the negatives. Our houses look better than new houses!"

We asked Tom to describe some of the most trashed houses his company had been asked to repair. "There have been a lot of them," he remembers. "Some of the damage is vindictive—you get people who throw dead chickens in the attic. But you also get people in $650,000 homes who have them professionally cleaned after they get foreclosed. Some of the homes have the locks sawed off. Some of the homes have transients living in them—that's always kind of startling."

Tom describes the biggest challenge of running Chapman Design Concepts as boosting the morale of the out-of-work subcontractors he trains and putting them back in the work force. "The biggest challenge is taking subcontractors who are pretty much beat up from the economy and getting them back on their feet and letting them see that there's a future in doing what we do—be they painters or roofers or whatever. A lot of these people were bummed out, worried about getting paid. The general work attitude is kind of bad. Now they're successful and earning a good living. We create a lot of jobs. I believe if I can make my subcontractors successful then the success will come back to me automatically, which it does."

Sounds like America could use a few more Tom Chapmans right now. He goes on, "With the general public being kind of bummed out all the time about the bad economy, the people who are involved with us in contrast are pretty much up and happy—people driving new cars, people buying houses."

Tom, champagne and strawberries in hand, with his wife Jan giggling in the background, describes the key to his success as, "Being honest. Maybe it's not trying to grind people for every cent." He's currently expanding his business into other states, but as he puts it, "I don't want to get so big that I have to move out of the bedroom. I like what I do—life is good."

If you need houses rehabilitated in your area, you can contact Chapman Design Concepts at:
1201 South Alma School Road, Suite 6500
Mesa, AZ 85210
Phone Number: (602) 228-9221

★   ★   ★

Entrepreneur Gets Down to the Dirt

Profile: Ingrid Elsel

Company Name: Ingrid Elsel/Associates

Year Founded: A while ago . . .

Homemade
Success Secret: Most of the time bureaucracy gets in the way of business, but sometimes an opportunity arises to create a business that helps people work around the bureaucracy.

Business Profile: Ingrid Elsel/Associates is a consulting company that works with surface mining companies. Ingrid describes her customers as mostly being sand and gravel companies.

Start-up Capital: A computer and a telephone at the beginning. Ingrid had enough savings to see her through to her first clients.

The Office: Initially located in a small bedroom, Ingrid quickly ran out of room. Today, she works out of an office added on to the back of her house by enclosing a patio. When the weather is nice, Ingrid opens a set of French doors to her backyard.

Working Hours: "Too long—I start at 8:30 or 9:00 A.M. I have a lot of meetings to go to and I am on the road a lot." Ingrid takes a midday break and then picks up the pace in the evening and stays up late in her office. She likes working at night because it's quiet and the phone doesn't ring.

Home Office Technology: Two computers, a copier, a postage meter, and a drafting table.

Family Profile: Happily "unmarried" after two marriages, Ingrid has two grown daughters.

Education: Ingrid has a master's degree in geography from California State University at Fullerton.

Favorite Pastimes: Though Ingrid has given up running marathons, she still likes to run for miles and enjoys bicycling. She likes to travel to Europe and islands in the tropics.

As you will likely notice as you continue through this book, there are two basic categories of businesses that can be made to succeed. First, there are businesses that are relatively standard, like starting a janitorial supply company or selling manufactured goods such as carpets or other items. The second kind of business is one where the entrepreneur, through an extraordinary business sense or sometimes by accident, identifies a tiny niche market that no one else knows about. By plugging into such a niche, a home-based business can become enormously successful in a market that is too small for a conventional company to bother with. Also, the home-based entrepreneur can undercut related office-based firms with superior service and/or lower prices. Ingrid Elsel's Ventura, California-based business is a company that thrives within a niche market that simply responded to another industry's need to deal with government regulations. It's a market that we didn't even know existed.

If you are familiar with California, then you have probably heard about its myriad environmental rules, regulations, and red tape. It's even a difficult place to obtain such basic building materials as sand and gravel—because of regulations restricting the mining. As a result, Ingrid Elsel founded a business that helps companies locate available materials and sort through the bureaucratic roadblocks to being able to acquire the material. In a softly accented voice Ingrid explains, "The state of California has already determined where those areas are but some of them are better in quality and more easily accessible than others." Then she goes on to explain her business, "Clients come to me when they need material. Then I usually become the project co-ordinator and obtain permits from the jurisdiction that's in charge—which in most cases is county government. One has to do an enormous amount of investigation, study, reports, and analysis. I have to hire the firms for geological analysis, hydrological analysis, and archeological and biological analysis. I even have to do a traffic pattern analysis, and analyze noise and air quality issues. Everything has to be analyzed that can possibly affect the environment and the community it's close to. It usually takes about a year and a half or two years to complete the studies." All this to dig up some gravel? Image what you must have to go through to mine gold in the Golden State!

This is just the beginning. After all this work is complete, Ingrid's company assembles the information into an application that is submitted to the county. The application contains volumes and volumes of writing. "I am also responsible for keeping everybody moving forward—that's where my role as project coordinator comes in. I make sure all pieces come together if there's a change in the project description, which frequently happens as the result of an impact that has been identified. Once that has been submitted to the county then they begin to go through their analysis. I usually wind up, depending on the jurisdiction, doing an environmental impact statement. I take my clients through the hearing process, senate commissions, and board of supervisors. So we're talking never less than three years, usually more like five years."

Ingrid came to the United States from Germany with two small children, and attended night school to get her degree. She worked as a geography teacher at Cal State Fullerton before moving into city planning and worked for the County of Ventura before starting her own company. She says, "For a very long time I had thought of a business of my own. But as everybody knows, one needs to find a place that is unique—a business that not everybody's doing." Working with applicants for permits at the county, she began to realize that the people coming in had no idea of how to go about handling the research required to secure a permit. "I began asking applicants if they would hire someone like me to help them with their projects. Each one of them said yes, and each one of them came through—so I was off and running in a month. In fact, after I asked them, they kind of pushed me into making a decision much sooner than I had anticipated."

Today, at fifty-four, Ingrid is active in both city planning and as a volunteer at the symphony. She currently is working on twenty-two projects. She explains that while this sounds like a massive workload, some of the projects go into "remission" for a period when the government is reviewing them and that lightens the load a little. She likes being of service to people and that's what she likes best about her home-based business. Ingrid says of her business, "It's a nice secure job because you take on a project and you're with it for a long, long, long time."

If you are interested in mining sand and gravel in California and can't handle the red tape, you can contact Ingrid at:

3875 Telegraph Road, Suite A-104
Ventura, CA 93003
Phone Number: (805) 658-8113

★   ★   ★

Movie Buff Tracks the Nude Scenes
for Posterity and Prosperity

Profile: Craig Hosada

Company Name: The Bare Facts

Year Founded: 1988

Homemade
Success Secret: Sex sells, even if you aren't Madonna.

Business Profile: Movies are reviewed on video cassettes to create a guidebook to nude scenes played by well-known stars in PG- to R-rated movies. The book, initially sold only through mail order, is now so popular that many bookstores carry it.

Start-up Capital: Craig started *The Bare Facts* while still working at his full-time job. Part of his salary was used to start and support the business during its early years.

The Office: Craig's research takes place in front of the living room TV in his two-bedroom condominium. His computer is located on a portable cart which Craig moves into position in the living room when he needs it. Craig's massive book inventory is kept in a mini-storage shed down the street.

Working Hours: Research is done "After the kids go to bed." Craig ships his orders and does his writing during the day, starting at about 10:00 A.M. most mornings.

Home Office Technology: Two VCRs and a television, as well as a Macintosh computer. Reviews and cross-referencing are done using Double Helix database software. Craig assembles the book in FrameMaker and then prints laserprinter output which is taken to a print shop for reproduction and binding.

Family Profile: Craig is married and has two children.

Education: A bachelor's degree in computer engineering from University of California at Berkeley.

Favorite Pastimes: Watching movies on video—what else? Craig also enjoys outings to the park with his wife and kids.

It's hard to believe that a special effects engineer would be bored with his job, but Craig was. At Industrial Light and Magic he worked on movies like *Howard the Duck*, but as a creative personality, even working for the best and brightest in special effects was still just working for someone else. Craig saw a way to amuse himself at work in a screening room while reviewing a nude scene played by a favorite actress. A colleague watching the movie asked about the other movies in which this actress had played scenes *sans* clothes. Right then and there Craig came up with the idea of cataloging nude movie scenes played by famous or at least well-known actors and actresses in mainstream movies. As Craig puts it, "The only way to get this kind of information previously was to be a collector of *Playboy* magazines. I wanted to be my own boss and not work for someone else. Of all the crazy ideas I had, this one seemed like the one with the best chance for success."

Assuming that the only reason anyone watches movies is to wait for the actors to take off their clothes, *The Bare Facts* comes with a convenient indexing system that allows viewers to fast-wind through the boring parts where the actors just recite their lines and get to what's really important—posthaste. (Example of Craig's scene descriptions: "Tom Cruise in *Top Gun*: brief flash of buns sixty-five minutes into the film.")

Instead of taking the traditional route for authors and finding a publisher to publish the book, Craig decided to write, produce, and publish his book himself. While this is probably the riskiest way to break into publishing, selling the book directly allows the writer to reap the lion's share of the book's profits—money that usually goes to the publisher instead of the author. For Craig Hosada, this approach has paid off handsomely.

With an endorsement from popular hick critic and humorist Joe Bob Briggs, "The most useful film book of the last ten years," *The Bare Facts* was first published in 1989. Printing a bare minimum of three hundred copies, each book in the first edition was scantily clad with a plastic comb binding and thin cover. Craig promoted the effort with a thirty-five-dollar ad taken out in a newspaper called *The Movie Collectors' World* and sold the book directly through mail order.

Craig was surprised when an article appeared about the book in *Video Review Magazine*. With the unique execution of the concept and the ironic humor in the idea that someone would actually go to all the work to create such a product, it wasn't long before editors from publications as diverse as *Playboy* and *Home Office Magazine* began calling Craig for more information and interviews. Craig even appeared on *The Joan Rivers Show* on request to "expose" the book. As a result of publicity and curiosity, Craig has spent very little on advertising. The virtually free publicity on TV, in tabloids, and in the many magazine and newspaper articles has generated ongoing interest in Craig's voyeuristic tome.

With the second edition nearly sold out, thirty-three-year-old Craig is busy working on the third edition. Craig does his own research by fast-winding through several movies a night to reach the salient material in each film. Data from viewing sessions is recorded in a database that eventually is used to produce the next edition of the book. Friends help out on occasion by making Craig aware of more esoteric films that contain unveiled movie stars who later went on to bigger and better things. Of course, he is also working on a second book to expand his market and *cover* his bases.

Craig has this advice for those thinking of starting a home-based business while they're still employed full-time at a regular job. "I would suggest that people get a line of credit or home equity loan *before* quitting their full-time jobs. I didn't do that and a lot of banks won't talk to you unless you've been self-employed for at least two years. Now I'm getting so successful that the printing of my book is expensive. Before I was just printing fifteen thousand copies and I would sell enough to existing customers to pay for the print run. But now, my next print run is going to cost $80,000. The printer gives me thirty-day terms, but I don't see much money from the print run for at least three months." Good advice for readers getting ready to leap full-time into a risky, or should we say risqué, home-based business like Craig's!

If you are interested in obtaining a copy of *The Bare Facts* and your bookstore is sold out, you can contact Craig Hosada in Santa Clara, California by calling:
Phone Number: (408) 249-2021

★　　★　　★

Imprinted Towels Soak Up Orders

Profile: Tom & Deborah Martin

Company Name: Custom Towels, Inc.

Year Founded: 1984

Homemade Success Secret: Never be afraid to ask for what you need—all they can say is no. Also, be consistent in your quality and delivery and people will keep coming back for more.

Business Profile: As the name implies, Custom Towels imprints towels for companies and athletic groups.

Start-up Capital: The business was actually started with a loan for $34,000 borrowed from a bank. Deborah Martin is one of the few entrepreneurs in this book who successfully borrowed money from a conventional financial institution to start a home-based business.

The Office: Starting out in a nine-by-ten-foot condominium bedroom that the business quickly outgrew ("If you can imagine four people in such a room") the

Martins eventually created a home environment more suitable to their company. "We built a home to accommodate the office."

Working Hours: "The phones can ring as early as 6:00 in the morning and sometimes ring as late as 7:00 at night." The Martins go out to lunch every day just to get out of the house.

Home Office
Technology: "We started out with one phone, one typewriter, and one calculator. Today we have two computers, a LaserJet printer, a fax machine and two-line phones. People come in here and say, 'Gosh, you really *do* have an office.'"

Family Profile: Debbie and Tom have been married "a long time." They have no children but share the house with four cats and two dogs.

Education: Debbie has a bachelor's degree in music performance and for six years was an opera singer for the San Francisco Opera and other major opera companies. Greg has a mortuary science degree and worked at a local funeral home.

Favorite Pastimes: Debbie still sings occasionally with local orchestras for fun. Greg is a drummer who plays with a big band for diversion. Debbie and Greg also enjoy gardening.

Debbie and Tom Martin run a company started from their home that imprints various kinds of towels and blankets with the name, logo, or slogan of a corporation or sports team. Working on white towels, the company can imprint with up to six colors or even reproduce color photos on the towels. Some of their more notable customers include Coca-Cola, V-8 vegetable juice, and FTD Florists. Their first big account was Apple Computer. According to Debbie, "We've put everything from a Kirby vacuum cleaner to the Space Shuttle on a towel."

The Martins run their operation completely from home and they figured out a simple solution to the problem of handling an inventory intensive business from their home: Instead of trying to jam production into their home and eventually move the business into a factory or warehouse when inventory became impossible to work with, the Martins contract their printing out to a local silkscreen shop. That way they get to work at home without having piles of towels jammed into every corner and closet. Good thing, too, because Debbie Martin explains that even during their first year of business they imprinted and shipped more than $300,000 worth of towels. That's a lot of inventory to handle!

The Martin's company is completely family based. Starting out with four employees—all family members—today three family members run and control the entire operation. Debbie's sister left the company, but her mother is still the company's general manager. Debbie is pleased to tell how the company got started: "I didn't wake up one morning and say to myself, I'll print towels. I was already in the business. I had worked for a company were I was a vice president and to make a long story short, the son inherited the business after the father died and in five years he ran it into the ground. I had been toying with the idea of my own business for a number of years because I think I knew the direction my employer was going to take. It was a matter of survival to find something I could do on my own. Then, I was fired and I thought to myself, 'Gosh I don't have a job,'—and push came to shove. People I had dealt with had always told me, 'Why don't you just go into business yourself and do this?' I knew I had a good thing, so I took my customer list and started contacting people who I had been doing business with and started from there." Debbie made calls and sent out fliers. That's how she got her first customers—she didn't spend much on advertising because she already had a network to worth with.

"Shortly after we started the business, I had a call from Apple Computer and they wanted to place a $70,000 order with me. At the time I didn't have that kind of credit at any of the textile mills. They typically had established a $5,000 line of credit for us, which isn't very much—especially when you have a $70,000 order. I remember thinking, Well what have I got to lose? So, I picked up the phone and called the appropriate people at Apple Computer and just very boldly exclaimed, 'I'm sorry, but it is the policy of Custom Towels that new customers must make a 50 percent deposit.' They didn't know how long I'd been in business. Here I was in this little bitty nine-by-ten-foot room. I'm asking them to send $35,000 and I didn't think they'd ever do it. So they said, 'Okay, that shouldn't be a problem,' and I got even bolder. I told them, 'I need you to wire that to my account,' and they wired it to my bank. I ordered the towels that day. Today I still don't believe it—I always think that was a miracle."

A lot of the Custom Towel's business comes from advertising specialty operations. These companies carry a large inventory of all sorts of imprintable items, as explained in the profile on Daryn Ross later in this book. Catering to local clients, these companies place orders with enterprises such as Debbie's and arrange for the imprinting to be handled as part of the deal by supplying the customer's artwork, such as a logo, that will print on the towel. They supervise the process and in return for their services, they mark up the manufacturer's price to earn a profit. Unlike the majority of sales incentive items that are manufactured offshore in Hong Kong or Taiwan, Debbie's company buys only quality towels from mills located in the southern United States. Her company's products are proudly American made. In addition to business coming from advertising specialty shops, forty-year-old Debbie created a brochure and catalog to make people aware of her wares.

In addition, her husband Tom, the vice president of the business (Debbie is CEO), uses desktop publishing tools to assemble their magazine ads which are placed in advertising specialty magazines. They also attend trade shows for corporate buyers. Some of their business is handled by independent reps, and word-of-mouth advertising has also been very helpful to building the business.

Debbie describes the best days in her business as being the ones when big orders come through. Some of the largest orders include 28,000 beach towels for a new liqueur being introduced by Jim Beam and 150,000 towels for Hallmark. Their biggest order to date was for 250,000 blank towels sold to the company that does the imprinting for Disney Studios. More recently they completed 10,000 custom blankets for Georgio cosmetics' department store promotions across the country. Says Debbie, "Those are always nice days—you can feel like you've accomplished a lot at the end of those days."

We asked why customers choose Debbie's company over the competition. Her answer points out just one more way that home-based businesses can compete better in their marketplace. "We've gained a reputation of doing what we do extremely well and that has earned us a very solid reputation in the industry. In addition, we work out of our home so we can give very competitive prices—there's no overhead!"

If you are interested in ordering imprinted towels or blankets for your next promotion, you can contact Custom Towels at:

24 Commodore
Belleville, IL 62223
Phone Number: (618) 398-6556

★ ★ ★

It's Not the Goodyear Blimp, But It Takes Great Photos

Profile: Dianne Blake

Company Name: Aerial Advantage Photography

Year Founded: 1990

Homemade
Success Secret: The most dependable source of advancement in the business world is yourself.

Business Profile: Dianne's company employs a remote-controlled blimp-camera system developed in Canada. There are about sixty other similar blimp-based photographers across the country who, like Dianne, use the same manufacturer's system to take aerial photographs where an airplane or helicopter would not be feasible or cost effective.

Start-up Capital: Needed about $40,000 for the start-up equipment; she used a home-equity loan and leased some of the equipment instead of buying it.

The Office: A bedroom furnished as an office; semi-cluttered; one wall is now covered with aerial photos. "It's a lot better than the five-by-five-foot cubicles most major corporations put you in."

Working Hours: Dianne usually has to be out early in the morning before the winds come up. Sometimes she works from dawn until midnight and other days she only puts in six hours or so.

Home Office
Technology: An eighteen-by-seven-foot blimp; cameras, computer, laser printer, fax modem, two-line phone, and a typewriter for invoices.

Family Profile: Married; has an eighteen-year-old son

Education: BA in business from National University.

Favorite Pastimes: A very outdoors-oriented person who likes backpacking, hiking, and of course, photography. She also does quilting and other activities.

After four years in the Air Force, Dianne went through various jobs until she ended up at NCR Corporation in San Diego, starting as a clerk typist in 1977. By 1991, she had advanced at NCR to the position of systems analyst. As NCR started downsizing, like so many corporations in the late eighties and early nineties, Dianne was asked to work sixty hours a week just to keep her job. Already bored with the work in general, the extra demands on her time were making corporate life less appealing. Knowing there was no security at NCR over the long term, Dianne started looking for opportunities where she could depend on herself.

Dianne's dad showed her an advertisement in *Entrepreneur Magazine* for mini-blimps used to take aerial photos. The system was originally developed in Canada and employs a helium-filled tethered blimp to lift a remote-controlled camera above the area to be photographed. The camera is carried underneath the blimp in a cradle-shaped apparatus and the image seen by the camera is transmitted directly to a video screen, so the photographer can adjust angles and apertures before the shots are taken. The aerial photographs can be sold to people who could benefit from having full-view photographs of a facility, building site, or home, but who normally would not go to the expense of hiring a helicopter- or airplane-based photographer. The blimp-shots are typically less than half the price of conventional aerial photographs, and the blimp can go places airplanes can't, like inside stadiums or convention halls. Potential clients for low-cost aerial photographs include real estate brokers, construction companies, architects, owners of large estates, motel and hotel chains, convention sponsors, schools, advertising agencies (who use the photos in client promotions), and a variety of individuals who use the photographs for insurance documentation, right-of-way litigation, or personal reasons.

At first amused by the idea of walking around with a blimp, Dianne thought about the concept for a while and, since she was already an accomplished amateur photographer and because she loves doing things outdoors, ultimately she became more intrigued with the possibilities. She finally paid to go to Canada to receive training on using the apparatus and leased a blimp set-up to get started.

She ventured out part-time at first. Dianne wanted to hang on to the steady income as long as possible so she could get the new business going. At thirty-eight, she'd never really been without a job before, so there was some anxiety about making it without a steady pay check. It took about twelve months until she had too much work to handle on a part-time basis.

Dianne wants to keep the business headquarters at home, even as she continues to expand her operations. "Staying at home just lets me make that much more profit. Almost no one cares about coming to see me at the office—they're only concerned about the photos. Running a business like this from home is a perfect deal. The only disadvantage of working in your own home is that the office is always there reminding you to finish the paperwork."

Dianne does find that "wearing all the hats" in a home-based business is sometimes fatiguing. "In a big corporation, there is always someone else to help. Here, I've had to do everything myself—the marketing, the delivery, the bookkeeping. It's a lot of work." In fact, the business is growing so fast that Dianne intends to hire someone to answer the phones and help with the paperwork. That will let her spend more time taking photos, which is how she makes money.

Dianne charges a basic fee of $195 for up to one hour on site. This typically gives people up to twenty four-by-six-inch proofs to choose from. If more time is required on site, "blimp" time is billed at $100 an hour. Like other professional photographers, Dianne owns the negatives. If the customers want multiple prints, they have to pay for them or buy the negatives. There are also fees charged for other photographic services, such as making enlargements. The fees and hourly rates are adjusted for larger jobs and there are multi-site discounts available. She hasn't quite made the requirements for millionaire status—but she is doing so well, she is so positive about the future, and the idea is so unique, we couldn't resist putting her profile in the book.

Promoting the business hasn't been a problem for Dianne. "No matter where I go, people want to find out what I'm doing. People see the blimp and drive over to ask about it. The blimp just markets itself." Dianne also sends out flyers to real estate agents, construction firms, and other likely prospects. She intends to do more advertising this next year to expand the business even faster. According to Dianne, "The photos are powerful tools for advertising, sales promotion, printed materials, and record keeping. Because the views are unique, the pictures have more impact than photographs taken from the ground. The market for the business is quite large, if I can just make people aware of the possibilities. I think I'll try to network some of the work out to other photographers with similar set-ups; that way I can use my potential competitors to expand the business. I might branch out into doing some artistic stuff as well, such as calendars and books."

The blimp does have its limitations, however. It is not allowed higher than two hundred feet or it is considered an aircraft. Occasionally the wind puts Dianne in some awkward, and sometimes amusing, positions as she tries to keep the balloon from running away from her. But other than that, Dianne only has good things to say about the business, the blimp, and her security in the future. Dianne puns of her possibilities: "Two hundred feet of sky is the limit." And she goes on to proclaim, "It's a lot more fun than nine-to-five in a corporate cubicle."

If you have a large home to sell or want a picture of your corporate headquarters to impress your friends, why not contact Dianne at:
Aerial Advantage
1268-B Auto Park Way, #130
Escondido, CA 92029-2230
Phone Number: (619) 741-5682

★   ★   ★

In-Store Samples Promote Partners to Prosperity

Profile: Caroline Cotton-Naaken & Sandra Cotton

Name: SPI—Sunshine Promotions, Inc., Mass Connections, and West Coast Warehouse

Year Founded: 1978

Homemade
Success Secret: There are not many good coordinators in the world. If you have this skill, you can turn it into a business. There is always someone somewhere who needs coordination of a promotion or an event.

Business Profile: SPI puts on in-store promotions for companies such as Nabisco and other large consumer product manufacturers. Their people hand out samples or demonstrate products.

Start-up Capital: Caroline relates, "I was working two jobs to pay for the people who worked during the day. When I did the promotions, I didn't get paid—that all went back into the business. Through the family we would get small loans and we would use those and to buy our business cards or get letterhead."

The Office: The company started in the home of Caroline's parents. As it grew it was moved to Sandra's home. "Our garages were full—we had coupons, we had fry pans, we had sample products. There were times when a manufacturer wanted us to produce a cake or cookies out of their ingredients and we had them all over the house!" Due to its explosive growth, now the business is housed in a ten thousand-square-foot office which Sandra explains is already getting too small. The company's demonstrators are all home-based independent contractors—and many of them make enough money to qualify for a space in this book in their own right.

Working Hours: Four days a week, but twelve hours a day to run the company, in addition to entertaining in the evenings and weekends spent at client sites.

Home Office
Technology: The company was eventually computerized because of the volume of goods and activities to be tracked. All subcontractors own fax machines for communication with the main company.

Family Profile: Both Caroline and Sandra are married. Caroline has four kids and Sandra has two.

Education: Caroline took some college courses, but didn't complete her degree. Sandra has a degree in business.

Ever wonder where those people come from who you see in grocery stores handing out lukewarm samples of frozen pizza? As you eat the tasteless square they watch your face for a reaction in hope that the cardboard texture and bland flavor will influence you to load your shopping cart with ten or twenty wheels of their culinary attempt. Handing you a stack of 50¢-off coupons, they point you (or drag you) to the refrigerator case containing the product so there's less risk of you walking away empty-handed. Where do these people come from? Are these people the relatives of the company founder? Or could they be housewives bored with *General Hospital* who do this on their own time or students who need a few extra dollars for party money?

Nope. Most of these demonstrators are professionals. There are companies that arrange these in-store promotions and this is big business for two sister-in-laws in Anaheim, California—Caroline Cotton-Naaken and Sandra Cotton. They run a company dedicated to arranging and coordinating in-store events through their Sunshine Promotions company, known in the business as SPI. On a busy weekend their company may have up to 2,800 people demonstrating products in supermarkets, stores, and warehouse outlets across the U.S., including well-known chains like Price Club. These promotions really work and SPI has the track record to prove it. The company tracks the success of each promotion through reports of store traffic, number of products sold, customer comments, and product price.

Caroline describes the demonstrators as home-based contractors, who are "for the most part, moms with kids; but not always, we have some retired men. They work out of their homes and they really run their own businesses." We asked how these contractors are paid since this kind of business was a new one to us. According to Sandra, "They get paid a flat fee and they budget out how to pay their workers."

SPI puts on events requested by the client company, or sometimes creates its own. Caroline describes her company services this way: "Sometimes the manufacturers come to us and already have a concept or know what they want to do—they just ask us to execute it. Sometimes, we actually are the creators of the programs and sell them back to the manufacturers. We also produce the point of sale material that will be used, be it coupons or whatever—we work as a clearing house for the coupons." The demonstration business has led to two more businesses that support the special promotions market. West Coast Warehouse is used to store the products, coupons, and promotional items used in the promotion which, in the case of a lengthy promotion, may amount to a large number of items. For this service, clients are charged for shipping and warehousing, as well as handling. Mass Connections is the marketing program wing of the company, and it develops programs.

SPI continues to be a family affair. Sandra is married to Caroline's brother and in addition to taking up the house with the business, the family pitched in to help on many occasions and lent money to help start the business. Sandra explains, "We had the whole family in it. They'd do things like put stamps on envelopes and tape on boxes. They actually helped make some of the stuff we used as samples." Caroline adds, "Every one of our family members had some part in it—they had to do demos, they were called upon all the time to deliver products or to make products." She jokes, "We used all of our friends too. Now we have none."

The business was started by Caroline, who was then working, as she puts it, "as the model in the booth type person" at trade shows and grand openings. One day, one of her clients asked if she had any friends who could hand out samples at a grocery store. "I said, 'I don't know, but I'll try to get some.' It was tough, I needed to find five people to go into grocery stores and out of the five, three of them showed up. It was pretty bad. I thought to myself, I don't want to do this. That was for LaPaz Cocktail Mix. Then the broker who handled that cocktail mix said, 'I need ten stores covered.' Then they needed twenty stores covered—it just started snowballing from one thing to another. So we really kind of fell into it. At the point I realized that it was starting to happen, Sandy came forward and said, 'Hey, let me help you out.' "

Partners are more common in home-based enterprises than we thought they would be. There are quite a few partnerships profiled in this book—not just husband and wife teams, but partnerships of in-laws, friends, and just casual acquaintances. The trick to partnerships seems to be a complementary skill set, which has been mentioned consistently by the profiled partners in the book. In this case, thirty-seven-year-old Caroline is good at sales and coming up with ideas. Her partner, forty-five-year-old Sandra, is especially good at juggling the company's finances and controlling the company's growth. As Caroline explains, "I couldn't balance my checkbook if my life depended on it. I can sell and Sandy's track record is financial—so we partnered up. She took all the financials—the paper end—and I did the selling." Working together brings balance to the business, as Caroline reports: "I get easily excited on new ideas and doing different things. Sandy, with her talents has a great ability to hold it all intact. I come up with these ideas or different things I want to try and Sandy has a way of making them work—I can't imagine how we would have made it without each other."

As you can imagine with such a coordination-intensive business, occasionally things go wrong. Like most mistakes, they are funnier to look back on than to experience. Some of the problems encountered by the company include hamburger patties that stuck together like they were glued or a product that the demonstrators were allergic to that caused them to break out in hives. One special nightmare was when one of Caroline's demonstrators, for reasons unknown, decided to order a pizza to be delivered to the demonstration site. With pizza in hand, he sat down in a lounge chair with his family and ate it in front of the customers. The store manager eventually threw him out. The most exciting event in the business, according to Caroline, was "getting our first client check for over a million dollars!"

Having started with no business plan or scheme for building the company, both Caroline and Sandra continue to be surprised at the explosive growth in the company. The future continues to look bright.

"Every day we're looking toward the future. We strive to be better and to make our own internal operations better." Next time you're in the market, think of Caroline and Sandy—for them free food is no gimmick, it's big business.

If you need your product demonstrated or promoted, you can contact SPI at:

720 North Valley Street, Suite M
Anaheim, CA 92801
Phone Number: (714) 535-8910

Who Needs an Office When You Live in a Dorm

Profile: Daryn Ross

Company Name: Innovative Concepts

Year Founded: 1987

Homemade
Success Secret: If you can sell something for someone else you can sell it on your own.

Business Profile: Innovative Concepts imprints T-shirts, sportswear, coffee mugs, glassware, and squeeze bottles for a market consisting primarily of fraternities and sororities. Customers order from Daryn's catalogs. "My gross sales have doubled every year," explains Daryn.

Start-up Capital: No start-up money was used. Daryn used his first orders to fund his first round of sweatshirts.

The Office: The business started in Daryn's dorm room at William Jewell College.

Working Hours: Daryn starts the day by taking phone orders and then sends them to his production facility run by his parents. He works twelve-hour days during the school year when his company is busiest.

Home Office
Technology: Today Innovative Concepts uses a custom software system and computers to track inventory and account activity. Originally, bookwork was all handled by hand, which Daryn said "was a pain."

Family Profile: Single for now.

Education: Daryn has a bachelor's degree in public relations from William Jewell College and is a member of Phi Gamma Delta fraternity.

Favorite Pastimes: Daryn loves sports including racquetball, basketball, and softball.

There is a massive market for specialty items, which include almost any kind of object that can be imprinted with the name of a company, organization, club, charity, or person. Common sales incentive items include pens, coffee mugs, T-shirts, notepad holders, and three-ring binders. There are more esoteric items as well. Some of the odder ones we've seen include a rubber chicken imprinted with the name of a chicken fast-food outfit, a coffee mug that stands on two cowboy-booted legs for a southwestern computer company, and a piece of reputed moon rock encased in cast acrylic plastic for NASA moon-mission participants. Prices range from about 2¢ for a plastic letter opener up to hundreds of dollars per item.

Most sales incentive or specialty advertising objects are manufactured in quantity by one company and then imprinted later according to the customer's specifications. Imprinting may be accomplished through silk screen printing, embossing, or other processes. If you look at your collection of pens and pencils in the kitchen drawer or at the bottom of your purse or briefcase, doubtless you will find at least one imprinted writing implement, given away by a company as a promotion for customers or employees.

Daryn's company is a little different than most companies that sell these products. He concentrates on the fraternity and sorority markets only—and soon will expand into the school market in general. These groups receive his catalogs and then choose the items they would like. Daryn has them imprinted with the organization's name, coat of arms, or slogan. He does quite well at it too. Sales are expected to break the $1 million mark for 1992 and skyrocket in 1993! That's a lot of sales incentive items for Daryn and his small staff to sell. It makes you wonder what this guy will be doing in ten years, when he's a ripe-old thirty-five. President of the United States? CEO of a major corporation? Or, wealthy and retired on his own private coral reef island in the Caribbean?

How does a twenty-five-year-old tycoon get started so early? In his soft-spoken tone with just a friendly trace of country twang, Daryn explains, "There was a sporting goods store in the town where I went to college. They were in the process of selling out and I happened to be in there when they were having a big sale. They were looking for a student to sell T-shirts for them on campus. I thought it might be an opportunity, but the price they were willing to pay me wasn't what I thought was fair, so I started doing some research on my own and found out that I could do it a lot better if I did it all on my own instead of for them. So, I started resourcing my suppliers and printers and started contacting organizations on campus. I took my samples and showed people and soon I started getting all kinds of orders. I did all this from my dorm room."

As for his formula, Daryn relates, "I'm completely goal oriented. My first sale was for $2500 for sweatshirts. From then on I knew there was some decent money to be made in this. I started expanding my ideas and talking to a lot of the organizations on campus, fraternities, and sororities and they wanted to know if I could get things other than sportswear. Could I get watches with their logos on them, glassware, and plastic cups? At that time I was going through distributors but then I found out that we could do a lot better if we did our own production."

Today, Daryn has a complete production company that he uses for most of his imprinting—it's run by his parents Don and Teresa. "My dad taught industrial arts and the time I started was about the time he was ready to retire from teaching. They basically went into business with me and they run the printing operation which is a separate company." This is the opposite of how families usually hand down businesses. In this case, the son asked the parents to join the company instead of the other way around.

But, has it all been a bed of roses for Daryn? He is jubilant in his reply: "The only disaster we had was a batch of one hundred plastic cups. Something was wrong with the ink and when the customer got it, he noticed if you put cold liquid in the cup, the ink popped off! Otherwise it's been pretty smooth sailing for us."

Daryn is planning on expanding, too. "We're planning on getting into the school market. We're getting ready with a national catalog that will be available soon that targets elementary schools. They order a lot of personalized things like bumper stickers that say things like, My child was on the honor role at . . ." When you see these stickers, think of Daryn rolling in his own honors in the profit arena.

If you are interested in obtaining Daryn's catalog, you can contact Innovative Concepts at:

8309 N Highway
Orrich, MO 64077 (that's near Kansas City by the way)
Phone Number: (816) 781-8162

CHAPTER 3

Should You Do It for Love or Money?

As you've been reading the profiles, the diverse motivations for starting a home-based enterprise are worth further analysis. Some home-made millionaires suggest that you select a business strictly by the market and income potential. Others suggest a business in a field that you are already intimately familiar with. Most, however, take a different track, and insist that you should choose a business you would do even if you weren't getting paid for it. This last idea reminded us of a cartoon of a man digging up a city street with a jack hammer. In the caption, he is explaining the romance of his job to another man, "I'm getting paid for something I'd normally be doing for fun . . . ."

Home-based literary agent Mike Snell, profiled in this chapter, put it this way: "Look into your heart and make sure that the kind of business you choose is something you would like to do—even if nobody paid you to do it. Do what you love and the money will follow." In contrast, Kyle Roth, a Los Angeles-based entrepreneur, offers less romantic advice: "Pick a field that pays the biggest hourly rate."

So, how should you choose? Should you start a business for love or money? The answer depends on your personal capabilities and your style of work. Obviously, if you have special skills that are much sought after and few others compete in the market, you can make a killing quickly, have the Brink's truck pick up your takings for a daily trip to the bank, and then settle into quiet retirement in any pursuit you choose. But, if you lack such skills or dislike the work you have done before, then the choice of possibilities is broad and it might be worth investigating your hobbies or personal interests as the basis for a money-making enterprise.

Choose a Business or Service that No One Else Wants to D

Here's another option that several people in this book made work: Consider a profession that no one else wants. A rule of thumb for considering a business or service: *The more interesting or prestigious the job, the fewer openings available and the lower the pay will be for new entrants in the field.* For that reason should you decide one morning to write novels for a living or grow your hobby as a landscape painter into a multimillion dollar home-based career, chances of success are less favorable than less sought-after careers. Keeping this in mind, business opportunities are abundant if you are willing to consider a mundane or contemptible job that no one else wants and if you do a good job at it while charging a reasonable price.

As an example of how this strategy can pay off, one couple that we interviewed operates a septic tank clean-out service high in the mountainous area of central Colorado. It was easy to tell that they were embarrassed just talking about what they did for a living, but when the subject of income came up, we found out that after only a couple of years in the business they were making over $150,000 annually—not bad when compared to the unemployment checks they had been receiving. They have steady income, work their own hours, and get to spend time with their kids.

The formula for their success was simple. They looked at the market area near their home and then searched for a service opportunity not being adequately addressed by other companies. After looking into a appliance repair business, a home-based quick print shop, and several other opportunities—they chose the septic tank clean-out service, acquiring the requisite truck for $6,500 from an elderly widow whose husband used to perform the service. After a few trips to the library to read up on septic tanks and chemicals and a couple of days spent helping a septic tank service in Denver to learn more about the mechanics of doing the dirty work, they were in business.

They charged a fair fee for each clean out and quickly built up a loyal customer base, because customers previously had been forced to pay a much higher fee to a service seventy-five miles away. While few people would argue this is a glamorous business to be in, it's paid off handsomely for this couple and it will put their three sons through college as well as comfortably support the family.

So, for Love or Money?

In this chapter we show a wide range of possibilities for businesses—some of the profiled businesses were started mostly from love and others were done strictly for the money. We recommend that you do some planning before you choose a business for either reason. Sit down and assemble the basic elements of a business plan and rough out the financials for your various ideas. Once you have gathered the financial data, have a spouse, business-savvy friend, or a bookkeeper review your numbers and determine their validity. If, after this analysis, the business idea for doing something you love shows it has the potential to make you successful, go for it! If not, keep looking.

★　　★　　★

A Corporate Magic Carpet Ride

Profile:	Bill Herz
Company Name:	Magicorp Productions
Year Founded:	1987
Homemade Success Secret:	Choose a business that makes you and others happy at the same time—that's the magic formula.
Business Profile:	Magicorp teaches executives how to use magic tricks and illusions to communicate key points in presentations. Bill also performs magic tricks at meetings and provides teams of magicians for special corporate events.
Start-up Capital:	$50,000 in loans and personal savings.
The Office:	A room with high ceilings in Bill's home, which is a loft in New York City with a view of Greenwich Village and Grace Church. "If you walked into my office, it's full of books—business books, magic books, my books. Props and apparatus are warehoused separately because Magicorp now has a large inventory of tricks up its sleeve."
Working Hours:	Bill works 7:30 A.M. to 11:00 P.M.— a very long day! Bill was on the road 322 days last year. "Does a room at Holiday Inn count as a home office?"
Home Office Technology:	Compaq personal computers and a fax machine.
Family Profile:	Bill is married to Gwenn and they have a baby girl.
Education:	Bill has an MBA from Cornell University. He insists "the degree didn't materialize from thin air."

He attended mime school for a year and has been performing magic since he was eight years old.

Favorite Pastimes: Rehearsing magic tricks and inventing new ones is Bill's entertainment as well as his work. His favorite joke is that when he comes home at four in the morning, head bowed down in disgrace, he tells his disgruntled wife that he has been out with another woman. His wife retorts, "Don't give me that—you've been off practicing card tricks again!"

If you could do anything you wanted and get paid for it, what would you do? Work at your favorite hobby, such as painting, rebuilding cars, or sewing? Sit back with a six-pack of beer in front of the squawk box? Or build yourself a millionaire's income by playing with cards? That's exactly what Bill Herz did—he built a lucrative business out of card tricks and magic.

Bill is a corporate magician. He started out by performing tricks for business audiences as part of sales meetings, promotional events, and educational seminars. Bill's clients include the largest companies in business: IBM, General Electric, and Coca-Cola, to name just a few of the more than a hundred major corporations that have commissioned his talents. Though Bill still performs, his business really took off when he started teaching CEOs and managers his art, so they could in turn perform their own magic at corporate get-togethers. For those of you interested in what he does, Bill wrote a book with author Paul Harris that was recently published by Avon Books titled, *Secrets of the Astonishing Executive*, which explains many of his tricks and how to perform them.

A former entertainment director for Club Med resorts, Bill explains how he established his enchanted business: "I had been performing at corporate events, parties, and meetings for some time. I wish I could say, 'Boy, I was a genius and I woke up one morning and thought of the idea,' but it came about completely by mistake. We were doing a big show over in England where I was performing and the CEO said, 'Hey, can you teach us some tricks and illusions that we can perform ourselves?' I said, 'Sure, but let's turn it around and make the tricks relevant to what you're talking about.' I do have a business background and I thought it would be pretty easy. And, it was a great hit—a tremendous success. I came back and I was telling a client in New York about the client in London and he said, 'Hey, what a great idea. Can you teach us too?' It still didn't dawn on me that I had a real business going and then I was doing some stuff for General Motors and I told them about these two clients and GM also said, 'Hey, great idea!' Then it finally hit us over the head that we could do this to make some real money."

Bill, who describes himself as a Type A personality with a sense of humor, also provides magicians for company special events. But rather than calling on a pool of performers as a talent agency would, he matches the magician to the task at hand. Bill explains, "We want to find out about the event you're putting on and then we match the right talent. If it's a bunch of lawyers, we'll find an attorney who's also a top notch magician or maybe an ex-judge—someone who really knows the field and can tie in jokes that are applicable." Bill is entirely devoted to his work. As he puts it, "I love my work. I eat, drink, and sleep my work. Sometimes I can't wait for the weekend to end. If I won $70 million in the lottery tomorrow I'd say, 'Oh, that's nice.' Then I'd go right back to work."

Bill's business requires special planning and adaptability. As an example, Bill remembers one event where the non-English-speaking chairman of a large Japanese consumer electronics firm was supposed to magically appear from inside a giant prop made to look like one of his company's consumer audio products. Bill had insisted on a ten-minute period to rehearse with the executive and get him ready just before his scheduled appearance. For reasons unknown, instead of showing up ten minutes early, the man appeared right at the minute he was supposed to appear on stage, completely unrehearsed and not sure what to do. But being a professional, Bill was already prepared for the worst. "My two assistants on stage were American, but both spoke fluent Japanese. This is the type of problem that we anticipate in advance. I have people who work with me and we sit there and we go through everything that can go wrong. What if he doesn't show up? What if he forgets his speech? We cover every single angle. So, when this executive was on stage, we were literally able to talk him through the act and nobody knew it hadn't been rehearsed. And, he came off as the star which is exactly how we wanted it." Bill and his people take extensive notes during the acts and after each one they sit down and review their performance. Bill demands perfection: "If they don't say afterward that it was the best meeting they ever had, I feel real bad about it."

Bill can't imagine working for someone else. "I find that I work ten times as hard but I love working for myself—then your success is in your own hands." Bill started his business from home to save money. As he explains, "It's a good way to control start-up costs by reducing risk. The biggest mistake I see people make who start up their own businesses is that they hire a secretary and they rent a space before they have any business. I see people investing in things that really aren't important. Ask yourself, 'Am I spending my time on the things that are really going to make my business grow?' "

Bill promotes his magical seminars through direct mail campaigns, though most of the customers for Bill's special magic are gleaned through word of mouth and referrals. With only these simple secrets—and more than full-time effort—the business continues to grow at an amazing rate.

As far as advice to those thinking of starting their own businesses, Bill's recommendation parallels many other entrepreneurs in this book. He assures, "I think everybody should start his or her own business. If you do what you love, you'll make money. I've been magically convinced of it."

If you are interested in the magic presence of Bill Herz, you can contact him at:

67 East 11th, Suite 522
New York, NY 10003
Phone Number: (212) 777-6807

★　★　★

A New Angle for L.A. Law

Profile: Kyle Roth

Company Name: Power of Attorney

Year Founded: 1987

Homemade
Success Secret: Sometimes business opportunities just fall in your lap. But to turn them into prosperous undertakings, you need to realize what has been handed to you and then pursue it.

Business Profile: The company designs and installs computer systems for the offices of attorneys in Southern California. One-stop shopping for law office automation, including training, customization, installation, and software.

Start-up Capital: Not much at first, some equipment and a full tank of gas.

The Office: At the beginning the garage was the warehouse and four computers, a fax machine, an answering machine, copies of software, and two desks in the spare bedroom made up the corporate headquarters. Kyle is not the most organized person in the world, and he moved out of the home office when he hooked up with Arthur Zuckerman, his current partner, "due to heckling by his wife to get out of the house." In practice, the trunk of a VW Jetta is Kyle's working office.

Working Hours: Eight in the morning until seven at night, five days a week. Spends most of the time on the road or in attorneys' offices doing the installations and training.

Home Office Technology: Multiple computers, a fax machine, cellular phones, multiline telephone system, a satellite pager hooked up to the email system in the office, and an electronic bulletin board for clients to call in on.

Family Profile: Kyle is married to Casey Collins. They have a five-year-old daughter, Galen. At first, Casey worked at home part-time answering the phone, making sales, and doing the bookkeeping while Kyle installed the systems—but now she happily does her own thing.

Education: Kyle has a bachelor's degree with honors in biocybernetics and a master's degree in computer science, both from UCLA.

Favorite Pastimes: Before Galen arrived, Kyle and Casey used to drive around Los Angles visiting theaters and looking for new hole-in-the-wall ethnic restaurants. Now they eat at home. For vacations their first passion is skiing, skiing, and more skiing. They are going to try to do Europe this year.

Until 1987, Kyle was a perpetual graduate student with a string of unrelated jobs. About the time he finally finished school, at thirty-five, he decided to marry his sweetheart of twelve years and they quickly decided it was time to have a family. The question was how to pay for life, wife, and child in Los Angeles now that grants and summer jobs were a thing of the past. He tried a brief stint as a marketing support engineer at Intel, but only lasted three months at the job. His work was okay, he just couldn't stand the lifestyle. Not suited to corporate life, Kyle found a better way to sustain himself and the new house in Westwood—set up a business at home and tap into the vast attorney's network in Los Angeles.

Kyle is demanding, brilliant, and quick-witted. His intolerance of corporate life was the main motivation to start his own business. Kyle, tongue-in-cheek, explains, "Nobody wants to bear any responsibility for anything in big businesses because each person is too busy protecting him or herself. Everything takes such a long time to get done and I have no patience with that. I don't believe in deferred gratification. I want to do it and I want to do it now. My clients want the same thing. That just doesn't happen inside big companies. I also believe that 80 percent of people in corporations are examples of the Peter Principle; they have all risen to various levels of incompetence. The amount of mediocrity in large companies is staggering."

How Kyle decided to run a business catering to lawyers is a tale of pure serendipity. Kyle hadn't taken a single course in law while at UCLA—it is one of the few subjects he missed in his fifteen-year escapade with the higher education system. After an old friend from school asked Kyle to help set up some computers for a new law office, then another lawyer and another asked Kyle to provide the same support, Kyle simply saw an opportunity in something that started out by accident. While the right computers and software for the job were readily available, few lawyers had enough computer experience to choose the right equipment and put it together. The process of setting up the offices introduced Kyle to the available technology and revealed how little attorneys really know about using personal computers and other office automation products to get their work done faster.

After Kyle was pretty well established, he met Arthur Zuckerman at a client's office. Arthur had similar expertise in computers and had been doing similar installations at attorneys' offices. They started talking, liked each other, and almost instantly decided to join forces instead of compete. They got involved with IBM and soon Power of Attorney was doing all the networking installations for IBM around the city. Then the IBM center shut down and Kyle and Arthur inherited "big blue's" clients. Later they bought an installation business from another company, and inherited their clients as well. Ultimately, they ended up with more clients than they wanted. They didn't like the work in downtown L.A., so they decided to be more selective about the clients they supported. Now their work is mostly confined to the west Los Angeles area.

After months of nonstop computer installations in practices around the city, Kyle added a new service to his burgeoning company—training. Once the office technologies were installed, most attorneys and their support staffs required several days of training to learn how to use the new machines. At over $45,000 an installation, with more than $5,000 per site in training, and another $4,000 in annual service and support fees, it isn't too hard to figure how the money adds up.

Kyle's biggest problem in keeping the business going was getting organized. He is inherently a person that does things on the spur of the moment, never thinking to put one thing away before starting another. He still basically runs the business out of the back of his car. When the car was stolen recently, the business almost came to a standstill. Since Arthur isn't any more organized than Kyle, they decided to hire an office manager who could keep things on track. According to Kyle, "She has really been responsible for keeping us on track and on schedule—and we attribute much of our financial stability to her skills."

Kyle is nothing if he isn't opinionated, and when asked about what makes his business successful, he doesn't hesitate to respond. "First, we operate in a well-defined niche market. We know our market and we do what we do better than anybody else. If we don't like a client, we don't deal with him or her. We don't have time for arrogance. We do good work and if the clients get too demanding, we let them go to someone else. There is enough business out there that we don't have to put up with nonsense from clients. Their only alternative is to go to somebody less qualified. Though this sounds egotistical—I know the competition. Like 90 percent of the world, the competition out there is pretty mediocre. If you have a tightly defined niche like we do, it is easy to become the master of that niche."

The company now has six employees and is making well over $1 million a year. Kyle has very specific expectations of his associates in the business. "As a businessperson, I expect everyone to be as competent and enthusiastic as I am. I am constantly disappointed. I am a poor manager because I don't always stay on top of my employees and they constantly take advantage of it."

As a businessperson, Kyle admits that he has not yet achieved perfection, in spite of his demanding nature. "I could be more concerned about the bottom line, but I am reasonably good at making money. I order some stuff because I like to play with it—then I have to try to figure out how to sell it for some legitimate application. Arthur is the same way. We are really hooked on the technology and the business gives us an excuse to buy things we don't really need." We figure that they need some diversion. After all, they consistently put in twelve-and-thirteen hour days to make the business work.

So, what does this self-proclaimed expert advise other entrepreneurs to do if they want to succeed as he has? Here's what Kyle advocates above all else:

1. Don't take the money out of the business. "It will kill the business if you take too much money out in perks, salaries, or whatever else."

2. Make sure you know the business you are in backwards and forwards. "I think it is suicidal to go into a business that you just think up one day. You have to learn something about it first."

3. Look at your market and find a niche that you can master. "You can always grow out of a niche into a larger market, but it is much harder to take on a wide market and shrink it down to a niche. The smaller your market, the less competition there will be, and the easier it will be to dominate the niche. Of course, whatever you do, you have to do it well."

As far as choosing a business with good potential, Kyle offers this suggestion: "Choose a business where the time value is high, where people will pay you a lot of money for the value of your time as an expert or because nobody else does the same thing as well. It's not necessarily true that you can't get rich working for an hourly rate, you just have to be able to charge enough for each hour."

Because the computer business is going to continue to change, Kyle views the future as promising for the business. According to Kyle, "People are only going to want more toys to use in the office. To keep up to date, all our clients will have to add new things and new technologies, like CD-ROM, messaging systems, and more."

What advice does Kyle have for the home entrepreneur? "Don't give up too easily. Be persistent. If you can stay at it for one year without going deeply into debt, you'll make it. If your spirits get low when business is slow, consider what you have to give up to go back to work for someone else. That will get you going again."

★　　★　　★

The "Business Book Guy"

Profile: Mike Snell

Company Name: H. Michael Snell, Inc., d.b.a. The Michael Snell Literary Agency.

Year Founded: 1975.

Homemade Success Secret: Your environment is as important as the business you choose. If you aren't happy with your surroundings, it is a struggle to make the business a success.

Business Profile: A home-based literary agency that handles approximately 125 authors writing everything from business and computer books to best-selling novels. (Literary agents work with authors to assemble salable book proposals and manuscripts and then submit them to publishers. In return they receive fees as well as a percentage of each book's profits.) Mike also writes his own books, ghostwrites other people's projects, and edits and rewrites clients' "problem" books. His wife Pat handles children's books and other "fun" book projects.

Start-up Capital: Two years of expense money tucked away and a cadre of contacts in the publishing world.

The Office: The bottom floor of a five-thousand-square foot house overlooking the sea at Cape Cod.

Working Hours: In the office at 5:30 A.M. to begin writing. This provides quiet time until the phones start ringing at 9:00 A.M. Break time is 2:00 or 3:00 P.M. with a walk on the beach. Mike and Pat return phone calls from the West Coast later in the day.

Home Office Technology: Two rotary-dial telephones and an answering machine. Mike and Pat do not use or anticipate the need for computers, fax machines, or other office technology.

Family Profile: This is the second marriage for Mike. He has two grown children from the first marriage. Mike and Pat share their spacious home with several pets including Mike's favorite, an affectionate Springer Spaniel named Holly.

Education: Mike studied English and earned his bachelor's degree at Depauw University (where Dan Quayle went to school between golf lessons). Mike earned a Phi Beta Kappa pin for his scholarship.

Favorite Pastimes: Walking on the beach with his dog, shell fishing, tennis, and gardening in their award-winning berry garden.

Mike Snell will be the first to tell you that anyone can be a literary agent by simply printing up a batch of business cards. But Mike Snell is no ordinary agent. His two-person agency represents hundreds of successful authors and he is probably the best-known agent in the publishing world for packaging business books. Mike develops ideas, not just authors—and that's what makes him unique. He spends almost half his time writing, editing, and developing book ideas for his clients—and the rest of the time he tries to sell them to publishers. Mike also takes on unpublished authors, as long as they have promise. Other agents will rarely consider representing writers without a track record.

Mike's own secret ambition, like so many English majors, is to write the great American novel. Though he hasn't managed to finish his own first novel yet, some of the authors he represents have already done that, including David James Duncan, author of *The River Why* and the newly published, *The Brothers K*, which just reached the *New York Times'* best-seller list. David has been nominated for a Pulitzer prize for both novels.

Mike didn't start out as an agent or writer. After graduating from college, he needed a job. A writer at heart and English degree in hand, he decided that working in the publishing industry would provide the right combination of relevance and gainful employment. He got his start in publishing inside Wadsworth, a small and well-regarded textbook publisher based in San Francisco. He started the day after he graduated from college. Through the college boom years of the late 1960s and early 1970s, Mike acquired and edited textbooks for publication. In his role as acquisitions editor, Mike learned to assess writing talent and negotiate deals and contracts. His tenure with Wadsworth allowed him to build useful relationships with high-ranking editors inside other major publishing houses and established authors around the nation. But, after spending several years rising through the ranks, Mike began to experience the frustrations of the nine-to-five shackles. Working under the "corporate thumb" was making him unhappy. He sought independence and the satisfaction of making his own decisions and taking on the risk and responsibility of running a business of his own. Mike explains it best: "I was never comfortable being managed by someone and on my performance reviews it often came out that people perceived me as difficult to manage. I wanted freedom, autonomy, and I wanted to call my own shots. I was just dying to get out on my own."

After proving himself at Wadsworth by building a successful catalog of computer titles, Mike needed more challenge and developed a plan to start a new business book division. The company liked the plan very much, but regarding Mike as too young and headstrong to run such an operation, management decided to bring in a veteran publisher to run the division who would then become Mike's boss. After learning of Mike's indignation in losing control of his own idea, Mike's boss offered a halfhearted concession to soothe Mike's ego by suggesting that the company would try to find another job for him. That was the last straw for Mike and he just blurted out, "Mike will take care of Mike!" as he walked out the door with authority. Mike was finally on his own.

Mike got right to work. Mike's plan was to put as little capital into the business as possible and use hard work and contacts to make the business pay off. He set up shop at home in Boston with a few used desks and a couple of phones. He had put away enough money from his days at Wadsworth to pay the mortgage, the phone bill, and live frugally for two years. Instead of wasting weeks shopping for equipment and setting up an office, he spent his time intensively calling on influential editors and contacting authors for their book ideas. Thus he started selling books and book proposals as he went. Over time he became known for handling authors who delivered quality business books on time. This helped cement relationships with the biggest and best publishers in the business.

Mike's hard work quickly paid off quickly—the Michael Snell Literary Agency achieved positive cash flow just six months after its initiation. Mike explains his philosophy of work this way: "I work a lot longer and a lot harder for myself than I ever did inside of other companies. I think that a sense of ownership is another reason that I work so hard for myself."

Today Mike and Pat share a unique home office with a view of the Atlantic Ocean from the west side hook of Cape Cod. The bottom floor of their five-thousand-square-foot home is the office. Their used wood desks are staged around the giant room, organized by the stages of book development. There is a desk for incoming ideas, a desk for editing, and a desk for developing new manuscripts.

Most agents would tell you that New York is the place to be if you are going to make it as an agent. But Mike loves working from his home and doesn't seem to suffer from his location on the Cape. As he puts it, "I spend my days talking on the telephone with editors who sit in cramped office towers in New York. While all they've got is a view of the pigeons sitting on the next building, from my home office I can watch a pair of whales mating." In our telephone interview with Mike, we can hear the distinctive cries of sea gulls gliding past his window. It's almost too idyllic.

Mike, at forty-six, plans to keep working as an agent for quite a while because he loves the work. He still has unfulfilled goals to achieve—he would like to have one of his authors' books make it to the number one spot on the prestigious *New York Times* best-seller list. Already many of his authors have charted on the list, but no one has reached number one. He would also like to see one of his writers be awarded a major literary award, such as the Pulitzer Prize. Again, his clients have come close—but still no cigar.

Mike, always articulate and confident in his approach, has very specific advice for home-based entrepreneurs: "First, whether you have to beg, borrow, or steal it, get enough money in the bank so that you can live an acceptable lifestyle while getting started. Second, live where you want to live. If you're going to work out of your house, you can pretty much live almost anywhere. Third, plan your business so that you understand the length of time you will need to get into the black. Fourth, look into your heart and make sure that the kind of business you choose is something that you would like to do even if nobody paid you to do it. Do what you love and the money will follow."

Leapin' Lizards! Former Rock and Roller Sings a Better Song for Kids

Profile: Ron (RONNO) Hiller & Judy Millar

Company Name: Song Support/RONNO Productions

Year Founded: 1989

Homemade Success Secret: If people don't like the package, they'll rarely bother to find out if they like what's inside.

Business Profile: Ron and his sister, Judy, write and produce music for children. Ron also performs his music under his performing name, RONNO.

Start-up Capital: Two VISA cards run up to the limit.

The Office: Both Ron and Judy have individual home offices. Ron's office is in the living room of his apartment and the dining room is used for storage.

Working Hours: Ron starts work at around 9:00 A.M. and works until 10:30 or 11:00 P.M. He puts in about sixty to sixty-five hours a week. RONNO performs during the day and Ron does paperwork in the evening.

Home Office Technology: Two computers, musical instruments, and recording equipment.

Family Profile: Ron is single and Judy is married and has a teenager.

Education: Ron has a bachelor's degree in English from the University of Waterloo. Judy has a bachelor's degree in English and French.

Favorite Pastimes: Ron keeps his energy up with trips to the local YMCA and Judy likes the outdoors and is a movie buff. Judy also writes verse for greeting cards and has had about 1,400 verses produced in print over the last decade.

Thirty-eight-year-old Ron Hiller is a musician who began his career playing rock and roll with a band, Copper Penny, in Canada. After several hit records, Ron found himself growing tired of the popular music scene with its marginal ethics and uncertain future. Taking on work writing jingles for commercials, Ron returned to school and completed a degree in English and was certified as a teacher.

Nearing the end of his college program and armed with writing skills and teaching experience, Ron decided to put his education to work where he felt it would do some good—he began writing and performing music for children.

Working with his sister, Judy, they created a new company called Song Support and began writing and producing music together. Once the music took shape, the siblings assembled a complete performance environment for children that included RONNO (Ron's stage name) performing live music onstage with a series of colorful puppets, providing comic relief to the delight of young audiences. The music and performances are not your ordinary "kid fare" either—Ron's songs deal with timely social issues such as protecting the environment, getting along with others, and building self-esteem.

As soft-spoken Ron explains, "We had a lot of experience to draw on because we had written songs all along, that sort of pop-rock stuff. We wanted something colorful and Judy had done some work with puppets and wrote puppet scripts some years before. It was suggested that we use puppet characters kids could really identify with. Children would hopefully learn some important values right along with the puppets. At the same time, it would be colorful, engaging, and fun. It was the sort of thing that we went back and forth with and over the weeks and months and it just sort of developed."

At this point, the business split into two halves—RONNO performed his music along with Judy's puppets, and they sold sheet music and recordings of the same songs RONNO performed in his act. Realizing that the music's messages could be used by parents and educators, they began dividing the songs by theme. They also package educational plans to go along with the music that can be used by teachers who use the songs as part of specific learning programs. The cassettes may contain a series of songs about building self-esteem, cooperation, or protecting nature. By offering a series of topical cassettes, buyers can choose exactly the kind of messages they want for their children. Ron mixes the message songs on each tape with simple fun songs, to engage the young listeners.

One of Song Support's first recordings was *Lunchbag Lizards*. Initially *Lizards* was promoted directly at performances, but to grow the business, Ron and Judy began a direct mail program to alert both Canadian and American retailers and distributors to the music and its messages. Retailers quickly jumped on the bandwagon and cassette sales soared. About this time, Golden Music (a division of Golden Books), picked up *Lunchbox Lizards* for international distribution and Ron and Judy never looked back! Today they have several cassettes of their music in distribution, a sheet music business of their songs, and Ron still performs as RONNO.

Ron finds the positive feedback from the children who visit his performances very rewarding. "We get a lot of letters from children in their own writing where they say how much the songs and concerts meant to them. When they tell us 'I loved your songs and I really do like myself,' or 'I really do want to take care of the environment,' or 'I'm going to be a better friend to someone,' it's very moving. You can tell you've really connected—you've planted a seed and put some water on it. It's going to last and bear fruit down the road. If it wasn't for the feedback we probably couldn't keep going with all the hard work and the sacrifices. The feedback from the kids is really important."

Ron is quick to relay the formula for his company's success. "We work hard and are highly motivated. We really craft our material and it seems we've kicked open the doors that have remained closed to many of our peers who have been at it longer." And that's a formula that any home-based entrepreneur can follow—or maybe even a lunchbag lizard.

If you are interested in finding out where you can get copies of the entertaining educational products produced by RONNO and friends, write to:

Station C, Box 722
Kitchener, Ontario, Canada N2G 4B6
Phone Number: (519) 744-757529

★　　★　　★

Only Out to Change the World

Profile: Hap Klopp

Company Name: Hap is best known as the founder of The North-face; now he owns HK Consulting.

Year Founded: 1967—68

Homemade
Success Secret: A happy life is ultimately the only goal worth working for—when a business flows from that center, then the money follows.

Business Profile: The Northface was a company that manufactured and retailed an entire line of outdoor products from backpacks and ski clothing to geodesic tents. HK Consulting capitalizes on Hap's knowledge of outdoor products and international distribution and completes a wide range of business consulting services for clients around the world.

Start-up Capital: The money for The Northface came from borrowing about $80,000 from friends and family. He sold The Northface for $80 million.

The Office: When putting the Northface together he used whatever space he needed in the home and quickly expanded out into retail space. HK Consulting is in a loft.

Working Hours: Starts about 5:30 A.M. and works until 6 P.M., could be longer—"I only use twelve of the 24 hours."

Home Office
Technology: "When I started, people didn't know how to spell the word computer—I had a phone and that served me well. Later we got into computers." Now he has all the technology of a modern home-based business.

Family Profile: Married, has two children.

Education: Undergraduate degree in economics and MBA from Stanford.

Favorite Pastimes: "I love life—any outdoor activities." Hap does it all—rafting, ballooning, sail gliding, and more.

Hap Klopp is a figure of legendary proportions in the world of outdoor sports. After leaving Stanford Business School, Hap couldn't see himself fitting into the corporate mold of the large business world. After all, this was the 1960s—corporate was out, natural and organic was in. So Hap went to work for a company in the outdoor business and they said they would sell the business to him if he turned the operation around. He did, in less than twelve months. And as Hap puts it, "Then they said, 'Now that it's turned around, we don't need to sell out to you any more.' So, I went off on my own and took the same concept, and started The Northface, working out of my home to develop the concept and get people involved. I acquired some retail stores and then started manufacturing the products in the back of the stores. This way, I had income from the first day until I could do what I really wanted to do, which was manufacture the goods and retail them from my own outlets. The Northface was an extension of my own lifestyle and love of the outdoors.

"I started out in my home to save money—I didn't have any money to spend on rent. I couldn't set up anywhere else. The biggest challenge running it from my home was creating momentum—there is no inertia when you start a business and you have to make an extra effort to make relationships out in the world. I don't know what the keys are to my success, but I am pernicious. I attack a market. There was also the joy in what I was doing."

Hap's success was based in part on being in touch with the times.

He developed quality products, promoted them aggressively to the people around universities who shared an interest in nature and outdoor adventures, and created a corporate environment that supported the philosophies of caring and peace that were central themes of the period. As one store was successful, he added another in planned locations. Through everything, Hap remains a businessperson—so growth was part of a strategic plan, nothing was haphazard or accidental. Hap was driven to be the best in his field.

There was hardly a university student in California in the 1960s who didn't at least pretend to be interested in backpacking and nature—and Hap was in the middle of the scene. Being a part of the outdoor movement was as important to his sucess as anything. By being involved, he was able to try new products and see what worked and what didn't. As a result of his involvement, he assembled the best products, the most variety of outdoor goods, and sponsored events that got people involved in wilderness adventures. The Northface logo was seen on the day packs of every hip, consciousness-raised young person of the 1960s, whether climbing the cliffs of Yosemite or hiking across a campus to a demonstration—it was one of the symbols of a generation that wanted to rediscover the natural world.

As the consciousness of the decades changed and interest in the outdoors moved toward fitness activities, The Northface had to change—but Hap was ready to hand the business over to someone else. Hap and the partners he had gathered along the way ultimately sold The Northface for over $80 million and Hap went on to his next career. "When I sold The Northface, I had a lot of contacts internationally and the idea of starting the consulting firm was to utilize the channels of communication I had already set up to do business across major borders. Now I operate in offices in the Pacific Rim, Berkeley, and Europe."

Hap is a crazy kind of guy with a long career as an entrepreneur, but no one who knows him would call him unbalanced. Hap is a participating, loving, and sharing person. His second career as a consultant seems well suited to his personality. His current advice to people is simply, "Have fun. There's no right or wrong, there is just you. Hug, kiss, love, and laugh—that's it."

When we spoke with him, Hap had just returned from promoting his book, *The Adventure of Leadership*, around the country. He wrote the book because, "I have an insight about what's wrong with the working world. I use adventuring to motivate big businesses to do better. It occurred to me that adventurers and entrepreneurs are excited, driven people, and business people in big companies are not. I am trying to change that.

"People aren't bringing the passion of their world into the business. People can't stand coming to work. And when you ask why they don't quit, they respond with something like, 'Well, I have fifteen more years until I can retire.' This is so opposite to what I believe in. You don't stop waiting for the perfect world—you make it."

In a life rich with adventures it's hard for Hap to decide what was most exciting about his career. He is very proud of the geodesic tent he developed at The Northface—a tent that revolutionized the market. He calls it a magical design, based on Buckminster Fuller's concept of a geodesic dome. He also has warm memories of the famous adventurers he has worked with including the Whittakers, the first people on top of Everest; Ned Gillette, who went to Antarctica; Jan Reynolds, who hot air ballooned over Everest; and Will Stieger, who explored the South Pole. Almost everybody in adventuring was a customer of the The Northface and a personal friend to Hap. In terms of clients today, Paramount, Japanese Railway Systems, and Nora, a huge Norwegian conglomerate, are among the names in his portfolio.

Hap comments that his future is going to continue to be brilliant. "These are exciting times. I have some articles going into *Inc.* and *Success*; some television appearances on *'The Today Show.'* It's different and fun. I just want to change the world. Why limit yourself to 'branch out,' when you can change the world?" Knowing Hap's determination and energy, he probably will. In some ways, he already has.

If you are interested in obtaining more information about Hap's consulting services, or if you would like to have him speak at a major conference or convention to share his wisdom about entrepreneurial management, you can contact him at:

1807 Suite B 4th Street
Berkeley, CA 94710
Phone Number: (510) 845-2715

★   ★   ★

Dreams, Rag Dolls, and Love Are Transformed into Rewards Beyond Imagination

Profile: Marty Maschino
Company Name: Attic Babies in Drumright

Year Founded: 1987

Homemade
Success Secret: If something makes people smile, you have the first ingredient for a product that will sell.

Business Profile: The first sixteen "Attic Babies" were born in 1987. Today, Attic Babies employs up to 110 workers, depending on the season, and manufactures more than nine thousand of the impish, handcrafted dolls a week, ranging from four-inch teeny, weenie babies to life-size display dolls. Marty continues to design the rag dolls herself, to keep the Attic Babies fresh and alive. The dolls are distributed across the United States and internationally.

Start-up Capital: Marty used about $10,000 saved in her previous work as an at-home designer. She borrowed money after the first big orders started coming in.

The Office: Originally she worked at home in her den where she had a sewing machine. The level of clutter was an indication of the amount of creative energy being expended. She brought on six other "home workers" to help cut, sew, stuff, and dress the first orders. After many expansions and a series of facilities, the current headquarters is a 15,000-square-foot building with a separate 2,500-square-foot office facility.

Working Hours: Five days a week. "There is no typical day at Attic Babies, but we are never bored as there is always something unexpected going on."

Home Office
Technology: Started with a sewing machine. Computers and other office equipment came after she needed to track the shipments, orders, and other business details.

Family Profile: Now divorced, Marty has five children who provided inspiration for many of the impish doll designs.

Education: One year of college; never finished because she started making more money without a degree than a college graduate would.

Favorite Pastimes: Loves to travel, plays volleyball, and goes to the lake whenever possible. Pulls weeds for therapy. But most of all, she likes to be with her kids, who are always top on her list. Very involved in community and state activities.

Marty almost always worked out of her home, starting as a freelance interior designer to bring in extra money. With five children she wanted to stay at home as much as possible, and when there wasn't a design job, Marty made extra money by creating doll designs for craft shows. She was pregnant with her fourth baby when she needed something soft and light to carry around from show to show—and thus Attic Babies were developed. When she showed the first sixteen designs at the Dallas Wholesale Gift Market in July 1987, thousands of orders rolled in. And success has just snowballed since then.

At forty-one, Marty Maschino is full of life, creativity, and wonderful ideas. Just talking to her makes you feel good. Grossing over $3 million last year, it's clear that the little rag dolls called Attic Babies, with their impish faces and engaging personalities, make thousands of other people feel good all over the world.

Marty attributes her success initially to the desperation to simply keep a good income coming in; it took two people to keep the family going at the beginning. But Marty demands that she work in something she loves, and thrives on the challenge of being creative. "Putting love and ideas into each product is what keeps us going and growing. It embarrasses me to be put on a pedestal because of my success. I design because I put my heart into it. I love the people who love Attic Babies and I love to design the dolls."

Each doll design is given an imaginative name, like Boo-Boo Betty, Choo-Choo Charlie, Happy Huck, Heavenly Heather, or other whimsical identity. At Christmastime elves and Santas appear on the scene, including Raggedy Santa, Jingle Jangle Joe the elf, Ol' Time Santa, and many more magical personalities. The Attic Babies led to an expansion into stuffed bears, rabbits, and Raggady Rag Muffins, animals that include characters like Farkle the puppy. Marty also branched into professional dolls, with Dr. and Nurse Doodles, Flakey Jake the banker, and a variety of others. Some dolls are named after Marty herself, like Fertile Mertle, because Marty has five children of her own. Fertile Mertle is an obviously pregnant doll with her hair tied up in rags holding three babies in her loving, stuffed arms. Marty retires the doll designs when she feels they have "lived their lives."

The retired dolls are replaced with new faces and mischievous characters. About forty designs are "retired" each year out of more than three hundred total, and forty new individuals are designed to take their place.

Six to eight weeks a year in spring and fall, Marty goes on doll-signing tours around the country so the babies can be autographed by Marty. There is a big following of Attic Babies collectors. Almost no one stops with just one doll—the dolls are so full of life, warmth, and personality that people just want more. On a recent tour, one lady brought in 110 Attic Babies to be signed. "The response from people makes everything worth it. You feel like what you're doing is important and worthwhile."

Marty's babies are displayed in high places as well. Barbara Bush is an avid Attic Babies collector and on invitation, Marty presented Mrs. Bush a special edition Attic Baby at the White House. The character was based on massive research on the first lady's and President Bush's preference for clothing and accessories. Every person in the factory got to put in a loving stitch or two. The carefully crafted rag doll was awarded the name "Grammy Bar" in an employee naming contest. Attic Babies are also displayed at the Oklahoma governor's mansion; it seems that the governor's wife is one of Marty's biggest fans. And Attic Babies have been used as props on television shows and movies.

Even after manufacturing thousands of the stuffed figures, Marty still revels in the joy she gets from bringing her artistic creations to life. "I love every one of these Attic Babies. They're all like little kids, all like extensions of my own children."

Marty advises home-based business owners to get informed about laws and restrictions placed on home-based companies. "You can't just do what you want. The laws are constantly changing about home-based businesses, and it's important that you know what is important as far as recordkeeping, how to handle free-lance workers, and how to organize the accounts. If you don't know the IRS and government regulations, it can cause a lot of problems. It's important to get the right facts or hire an accountant or other advisor who really knows the facts about home-based companies."

Marty doesn't have a long-range plan for the business or even one for the next six months. She doesn't believe anyone can predict the future. "Whatever you think is going to happen, that's not what will happen. I am a one-day-at-a-time type of person." Recently, the recession has slowed the growth of Attic Babies because the sales of gift items in general are significantly depressed. Still, thousands of babies are being shipped out each week and, for the future, Marty just hopes the designs continue to keep people smiling and laughing as they have in the past.

As an employer, Marty seems casual and undemanding. Her employees speak of her genuine love of people. Marty feels the same about them. "Everyone who works for me is an asset to the company and I always keep that in mind. It's very important to Attic Babies' success." But don't think Marty is set back and calm all the time. Marty is the kind of person who thrives on stress. "I do my best work just before the deadline," she muses.

With all her warmth and humor, Marty is also a focused business-person who believes in hard work and dedication. "I am driven. My goal is always to do my best and competition is good for me—it makes me do better as a designer and motivates me to be creative. I am always optimistic and feel good in what I do. I never think I can't do it or that I will fail. Life in general is a challenge, so everyone is a gambler.

"You have to have an open mind to real life. As an entrepreneur, you have to be willing to just make things happen, in spite of setbacks. I see a lot of people come and go because they give up. A person's worst enemy is usually himself. You have to have faith in yourself. You are always going to have skeptics who will say that you can't make it. Know that it isn't true. Have a positive attitude. If one thing doesn't work, then pick something else and keep trying."

Even with her optimism and positive attitude, it still surprises Marty when she receives awards for her efforts. She was named Oklahoma's Small Business Person of the Year in 1990 and has received a slew of other honors. Marty tries to remain low key, but people always find out about her—they're drawn to her love, warmth, and compassion. It's no surprise to us that this engaging person is selected for awards. We think she deserves every one she gets.

If you are interested in finding a distributor for Attic Babies in your area so you can add one of these "children" to your own brood, you can contact Attic Babies, Inc. at:

P.O. Box 912
Drumright, OK 74030
Phone Number: (918) 352-4414

"Unemployable" Homemaker Paints Her Own Path to Success

Profile: Carol Sherwood

Company Name: Red Horse Clay Company

Year Founded: 1984

Homemade Success Secret: There is always a way to transform your passions into profit.

Business Profile: To support her fine art career, Carol builds decorative pottery featuring Southwest-inspired pictographs. Her ceramics are sold by specialty stores across the United States and by major department stores including Macy's and Bloomingdale's. The business is growing by leaps and bounds as more people see Carol's work in stores or through the small ads she runs in national craft magazines.

Start-up Capital: "I hardly had any money at all." Carol used about $200 to buy some clay to create the first line of decorative pots.

The Office: Studio "A" is set up in a two-car garage. Studio "B" is located in a large spare room. Studio "C" takes up most of the back patio of Carol's house. It has been enclosed with glass doors. Thus, the work areas take up most of the house.

Working Hours: Up early to make phone calls to customers on the West Coast before her talented and modest staff of four part-timers arrives. After supper Carol does paperwork. Deadlines sometimes mean longer hours.

Home Office Technology: Computers support the billing and other business functions, but Carol prefers creating to computing.

Family Profile: Married; she has two grown children from her previous marriage.

Education: Bachelor of arts in studio art from Arizona State University, which she earned while in her thirties.

Favorite Pastimes: Reading and relaxing after a long day in the studio.

The Southwest is rich with evidence of lost tribes and cultures—remembered through their painted ruins nestled in desert highlands and their ancient irrigation canals that laid open the routes for modern highways. Some of these cultures flourished for centuries and then disappeared. Speculation is that the people interbred with other Indian cultures, starved due to climate change, or, as was suggested by an incredulous tabloid, were kidnapped by extraterrestrials and used to populate a distant desert planet. Many were the victims of westward expansion by a growing American nation.

Fortunately, their colorful and powerful symbology etched on rocks and painted on intricate woven baskets remains for modern cultures to cherish. The significance of this legacy has not been lost on modern artists in the Southwest. One of those inspired by these motifs is Carol Sherwood, who created a visual language with the forms. She has adapted the original drawings into a decorative set of symbols, including buffalo riders, pueblo dancers, power deer, and ceremonial dancers, that she paints on ceramic objects that are sold throughout the country. Her pottery has propelled her into the status of super-successful home-based entrepreneur. But, it wasn't always this way.

As a middle-aged homemaker with two children, Carol Sherwood needed self-identity and found herself obsessed with art. She decided to return to school, and after securing a scholarship to attend community college and later Arizona State University, Carol achieved a fine art degree while in her thirties. Upon completing her studies, Carol discovered that she and her husband had almost nothing in common and they agreed to split up. Carol remembers, "The only glitch was that I had been married for twenty-three years and did not have a career, a job history, or a paper trail. So when I went to an employment agency because I needed a job to support myself, the guy basically laughed in my face and said I didn't have any skills for the real world. So after crying for a couple of days, I realized I was really stuck. So I thought, what can I do? I've got a degree in art—I've got to do something."

Carol started by showing her large sculptures in well-regarded galleries in Phoenix. "I thought, this is it. My career has been validated. I'll sell lots of art and be financially secure. Very quickly I realized that this is myth number one among neophyte artists. It couldn't be farther from the truth. What I sold didn't even meet daily expenses, art supplies, and gallery commissions. So, I learned that if you love art and want to do it, you still have to figure out how to pay the rent."

So the Red Horse line was founded right at that point. "I thought I could make a lot of small Southwest pieces and I could do some drawings and sell them to tourist shops, specialty stores, and galleries. That would be the way I could make a living." Carol made some prototype pieces and began taking them around from store to store. The inspiration for the pieces came from ruins in Arizona, Colorado, Utah, and New Mexico. These first pieces merged the idea of ancient Indian symbolism into a colorful, contemporary format that would become the heart of her business. Her first sale was a $500 order from Goldwater's (now called Robinson's), an upscale department store chain in the Phoenix area where she lives. Upon receiving her merchandise in August for the Christmas season, the department store people were less than encouraging. "They said, 'Don't call us, we'll call you after Christmas to tell you how it went,' But, in less than a month, Goldwater's called back and said that they had sold the entire order!" Carol rushed to create more merchandise for the stores and soon others were asking for the Red Horse Clay Company's ceremonial pots, wall hangings, and decorative bowls.

After two years of steady orders, Carol realized the local market was too small to boost her to financial independence. She called the local office of the Service Corps of Retired Executives, known as SCORE, and asked for some advice. They advised her to plan, advertise, make better use of her space, and control her growth—which she did. Carol took out several small color ads in national publications which got orders rolling in from around the country. Where most artists sell their wares by traveling from store to store, Carol does not. Carol explains, "I used to show work in person, but it wasn't really effective for me. I've learned to eliminate what's unnecessary and only work at what's effective and produces the highest return. Selective advertising and word of mouth do the job just fine."

As for the future, Carol wants to keep her growing business home-based: "This business has major potential. I make decisions about how I want to live my life at the age of forty-two—the quality of life I want, not the amount of money I want, is important. I could take a partner, get a bank loan, and move the business into an industrial park. I could get more equipment, more people, more accounts—maybe hire reps, we could make lots and lots and lots more money—but I would probably have an ulcer."

In addition to being a businesswoman and owner of Red Horse, Carol is still a fine artist at heart, who continues to sell her serious work through regular art galleries. "My fine art is my first love, but I can profit from Red Horse, and if I stay tuned in to the trends, the sky's the limit. Occasionally I still do fine art pieces. I just received a really big commission for big ceramic car pieces McDonald's wants for their restaurants in Chicago. But, Red Horse takes up most of my time because it's growing every year."

For people thinking of starting a business at home, Carol explains how she made herself look like a bigger company than Red Horse Clay Company really was, right from the onset. "You just can't tell them that you made the pottery at home because they'll think you're some little bored housewife. They won't believe you can deliver the goods. I made sure that I dressed like a successful businessperson when I first went out. I did my homework and put together a nice presentation. I played down the fact that I made my pottery at home. Instead, I just told them I had a studio in Mesa, Arizona."

Carol feels strongly that you need to separate your home life from your home-based business. Carol also recommends, "You have to approach it like a real job. I get up every single morning, I wash my face, I brush my teeth, I get my breakfast, I get dressed, I go to work. I just don't happen to drive away to an office. If you don't get up and do it like a business, I don't think you will go anywhere!"

If you are interested in ordering Red Horse Clay Company's ceramics and gift items, you can contact Carol at the Red Horse Clay Company at:

2159 East Encanto Street
Mesa, AZ 85203
Phone Number: (602) 833-1375

★   ★   ★

Packaging Anything to Go Anywhere

Profile: Ray DaRin

Company Name: Tri-City Packaging Industries, Inc.

Year Founded: 1990

Homemade
Success Secret: There is always a better way to do things. If you can discover one, you've discovered a market niche for your business.

Business Profile: A company that provides superior quality, less costly packaging and shipping services to get any product to anyplace around the globe. Tri-City Packaging is a total solution for companies that need to ship products locally or internationally—handing the crating, customs bureaucracy, and carrier coordination for almost any shipping demand.

Start-up Capital: $100, fourteen years of shipping and packaging experience, and a lot of sweat.

The Office: Originally Dad's garage in East Rochester, New York; now it's a six thousand-square-foot warehouse in nearby Victor.

Working Hours: Ray lives the business 24 hours a day. He works whatever hours it takes to get the job done.

Home Office Technology: The expected computers, fax machines, and other standard office equipment that any shipper/exporter must have to do business.

Family Profile: He is divorced. Relationship plans are still open.

Education: Attended technical school in Rochester. Admittedly through experience and practice, however, Ray gained his real education in the packaging trade.

Favorite Pastimes: Woodworking on occasion, but boating is his first love.

Ray and his brother William, local boys who grew up in Syracuse, New York, have turned drive, ambition, experience, muscles, and some woodworking skills into a unique enterprise that will ship anything to any place. After only one year they were the premier packaging company in the Rochester, New York, area and hope to become the same for Syracuse and Buffalo soon. After that—who knows? Ray has a whole world to package. According to Ray, he ships his clients' products the "right" way—and Ray insists that this means throwing away the book on packaging to do it better. "Right" is cheaper, "right" is better protected, and "right" is there as promised.

Driven to "make it" before the age of thirty, Ray started the business when he was twenty-nine with William. Starting with only $100 for crates, Ray and William capitalized on their years of packaging and shipping experience at Taylor Instruments and started Tri-City Packaging out of Dad's garage just to make some "beer money." But the business grew so fast, they had to quit their regular jobs to meet the demand for their quality, low-cost packaging and expert shipping services.

With clients as diverse as Xerox and Ragu Foods, Ray claims to be able to ship anything, via any carrier over land, through the air, and on the sea, with better results and for less money than the competition. He does this by using his brains and "the simple rules of physics"—by looking for less-expensive materials that do a better job and by taking time to modify and customize each package so things arrive safer for less cost. Ray doesn't cheapen the packaging, he just makes things cheaper to send. He also prides himself in the personal, dedicated service he provides—he treats each contract as if it were his own products on the line. Saving money for every client is a constant goal and an ongoing challenge for Ray—and he knows this service is what keeps the customers coming back again and again.

Consider the conveyer he shipped for Xerox to England. The delivery truck dropped the package from a crane right in front of the office. The package crashed to the ground. When the client saw the crate outside, it looked like match sticks surrounding a lump. But, much to the recipients' surprise, when they opened the shattered crate, the equipment was unscathed. Ray says that's the difference experience makes when it comes to shipping.

Sending packages to exotic and hard-to-reach locales is yet another of Ray's special skills. He has been shipping to Russia long before the Soviet Union ceased to exist. Asia, Africa, or islands in the Pacific—it doesn't matter to Ray. If you need to get it there in one piece, he'll find a way to do it.

The first year of business the garage-based company grossed $140,000. In 1992, they grossed over $600,000. The size of the materials and the number of projects forced the company out of the garage and into larger facilities. Ray reckons that next year's results depend on the economy, because "you can't ship products for companies if they aren't selling products to ship." But, given Ray's determination to be rich and independent, and his special skills in getting products from place to place, we're not too worried about his continued success.

Expect to find Ray working just about any weekend and into the wee hours, putting the packages around his customer's diverse wares—especially if it's raining out. But, if it's sunny and there are no shipping and packaging challenges to solve (rare according to Ray), expect to find this packaging guru on his twenty-four-foot boat floating in the lake. After his divorce, he even lived on the boat for a while. It's his way of getting away and concentrating on the things in life that really count—like watching the sunset on the water and tossing down a brew or two.

Ray's advice for would-be entrepreneurs is simple: "If you sell tires, don't try to make donuts. Do what you know. It's only through knowledge and drive that entrepreneurs succeed. If you don't have drive and dedication, it won't matter how good your idea, product, or service is."

Other than securing his millionaire status, Ray says he doesn't want to guess about his future. According to Ray, the economy is just too fickle to predict. Asked if he would do it again, he simply said, "No way. If you won the lottery, would *you* keep working?"

If you are in the upstate New York area and need to get things from one place to another in good condition, contact Tri-City Packaging Industries at:

845 Phillips Road
Victor, NY 14564
Phone Number: (716) 742-1230

CHAPTER 4

Home-Based Businesses Are Healthy, Politically Correct, and Ecologically Sound

It's not news that ecology, political equality, and health are major concerns in the 1990s. Perhaps it's just coincidence, but many of the most successful home-based millionaires we uncovered have decided to make a difference in these areas and have started businesses that have made people healthier, animals safer, or the world a better place to live.

In fact, home-based businesses offer inherent ecological advantages over traditional businesses. They generally reduce the pollution produced when people commute between home and work. Because fewer people are involved in the business operations, the tons of wasted paper from memos, reports and other documents in large bureaucracies are replaced with efficient, personal communications, thereby significantly reducing the waste of precious natural resources. Home-based businesses are also politically correct. They give people of almost any background or economic condition the opportunity to start a business with only minimal resources. Home-based businesses are often healthier than other businesses because, as you'll see throughout this book and in this chapter in particular, the owners pay greater personal attention to the well-being and happiness of their employees than is typical of most large corporations. In addition, some home-based entrepreneurs have pointed out that their personal well-being is greatly enhanced when they can control their own destinies through their own efforts.

The profiles that follow describe a wide range of home-based businesses that were started because the entrepreneurs felt they had something important to contribute to their communities and the world. The businesses range from manufacturing natural toothpaste to designing fake fur coats, from selling weight loss formulas and organic vitamins to completing health care research for critically ill patients.

It's apparent from the diversity of ideas and the personal conviction of these entrepreneurs, that healthy, politically correct, and ecologically sound businesses are a natural for home-based prosperity. It seems that these businesses prosper simply because the entrepreneurs who started them truly care about people and the world they live in.

There are still a wealth of opportunities in these areas to be tapped by other entrepreneurs, like you. Expect to see more of these world-conscious home-based businesses flourish over the next decade. If you have a passion for protecting animals, making the world cleaner, or using resources in more ecologically-sound ways, there is probably a business in your heart that will not only make money, but can make a difference at the same time.

★   ★   ★

Fabulous Person Makes Politically Correct Faux Furs

Profile: Donna Salyers

Company Name: Donna Salyer's Fabulous-Furs

Year Founded: 1988

Homemade Success Secret: The best business ideas come from your heart—or while stuck in rush hour traffic.

Business Profile: Donna makes fake fur coats available as both finished coats or as kits that sewing enthusiasts can assemble. The business is doubling in revenue every year.

Start-up Capital: Around $15,000 in savings.

The Office: The second office was located in the family room complete with a very noisy pinball machine. This was a big improvement on Donna's first office in the furnace room. The current studio is in an old Woolworth's building in the space once occupied by a dentist. Donna and her husband have built an apartment for themselves above the "shop."

Working Hours: Up at 6:30 A.M. as Donna puts it, "to start worrying." Then out with her husband for a walk and a discussion of the crisis of the day, and the day goes on from there.

Home Office Technology: Home-style sewing machines and computers for tracking orders and sending letters.

Family Profile: Donna is married and has a son and daughter in college.

Education: One year of college.

Favorite Pastimes: Donna loves to ski and plays golf and tennis.

Professional furriers are a dying breed. The are going out of business because clients have decided that a new fur is not politically correct, because of raised consciousness, fear of reprisal by animal rights activists, or simple lack of the disposable income for a $10,000 purchase that sits in the closet most of the year. An alternative to the luxury of animal fur is now available—thanks to Donna Salyers. Formerly a syndicated sewing columnist, Donna Salyers makes synthetic fur coats that closely resemble the real thing—in cosmetic appearance, texture, and style. The coats are a result of sophisticated fabric engineering brought about through Donna's contacts at the fabric mills.

A newspaper article headline described her wares as "A Kinder and Gentler Fur Coat." Donna's "furs" don't steal the lives of animals either. There are no cold-hearted traps or questionable fur farms with tiny enclosures used to make Donna's coats.

When you think of fake furs you probably think of those tacky, washed-out artificial furs that look like a fuzzy bathroom throw-rug that's been washed one time too many. Donna's faux furs are unique. They have been carefully manufactured, shaved, and colored to take on the natural texture of the real thing. Donna's fabrics feel and look like real animal fur. Her "mink" and "sable" are soft, dense, and have rich deep color. Her "raccoon" fur is coarser, with stiffer fibers and the striations of color common in real raccoon fur. In fact, her sample fur swatches sent to our office were so authentic, Samantha (our very active Norwegian Tree cat), spent her afternoon dragging the artificial beaver pelt around the house. Of course, a fur coat is more than just fabric. Styling is key to making furs look elegant, and Donna's coats excel here as well.

The appeal of Donna's coats is obvious—you don't have to kill an animal to have a stylish, warm coat. Donna first made her creations available in kits, which included everything from fake fur fabric to the "furrier's" label to go inside. Included also are the velvet-lining, monogramming, and a special clothes hanger. Donna started advertising her high quality coat kits in small ads at first. But the beautiful designs and fabrics got attention when movie and television stars began to appear in the coats. Soon Donna found herself in the middle of a publicity blitz in national newspapers and magazines, and more people started asking about the coats. High-end fashion publications such as Vogue featured the coats, and Donna's styles really got notice when Loretta Switt of M.A.S.H. fame was seen on TV's "Entertainment Tonight" wearing a Salyer's fur.

Donna still advertises her kits in *Vogue*, *Butterick*, and *Sew News*. But more recently the business began an expansion into ready-to-wear coats for busy women who don't have time to sew or don't know how. Donna also sells patterns at the fabric stores in the *Vogue* catalog, for which she is paid royalties. As she explains, in an article in a brief profile of her products in *Women Entrepreneur* where we first discovered her, "My clients are environmentally aware. A lot of them have the money to wear real fur, but they prefer fake fur."

Donna got the idea for her line of faux furs while making regular trips to New York to tape her syndicated TV show on sewing and fashion. As she explains, "Everyone in New York wears a fur coat—everyone but me. So I decided I was not going back to New York until I also had a fur coat. But I didn't have the money. I had to go to New York and I heard about some man-made black fox fur. I got my hands on some through a friend of a friend. I made a coat and wore it to New York. I was in front of the Waldorf waiting for a taxi and the doorman came over and commented about the beautiful coat I was wearing. I wore that coat and everyone loved it—I would go out and do speaking engagements and seminars and everybody wanted to try on my coat. I would be there to talk about how to make a suit, but they wanted to talk about my beautiful fake fur coat.

"I wore it for years until it was wearing out, so I thought about it and I decided to get a real fur coat. I decided not to ask my husband— I decided just to do it. I'd worked hard. So one day I was in my car and had the car radio on. There was a commercial for someone having a fur coat sale and I decided to buy one after my meeting—I didn't need to have permission. The next thing that came on was [commentator] Paul Harvey doing his noon broadcast. He was talking about a toy manufacturer in London who would go out and collect litters of kittens and skin them and make mink teddy bears. I was aghast because we've always had cats and I love cats. What if I bought what I thought was a mink coat and it was a kitty coat? Then I thought, 'You fool, what would it matter, like the mink doesn't suffer when it's skinned, only kittens suffer?'

"It was at this moment the truth struck me—I couldn't wear fur. I just wanted a pretty coat, I didn't want to kill animals. Within days I started to make phone calls and found out about available fabrics." And that's how Donna started her faux fur business. And she has as much vision for the business now as she had on that first day. "Our products make people happy—it's not like selling cemetery plots or life insurance. It saves animals. I love this business!"

Donna started out of the sewing room in her suburban home. She designed the patterns, worked with fabric mills to manufacture the materials to her specifications, cut out the pieces, and assembled the kits. She did everything, with the help and support of her husband, of course. Eventually the business grew enough to hire other people to cut the fabrics and help her with the administration. But Donna didn't want to run a factory—she liked the family environment and flexibility of working out of her home. So, the Salyers bought the old Woolworth's building downtown and built their home on the upper floor. Now even though there is a whole crew in the manufacturing area, Donna still works at home.

Donna can't imagine not having a home-based business: "I always had a home-based business. I never saw that as a detriment or a negative in any way. I've loved working at home and I started working at home when my children were small—most of all I didn't want to be an absentee mother. I began a writing career because I could do it at home and my writing grew into a syndicated newspaper column on sewing. I gave that up six months ago because I decided that I couldn't do that and run the fur business too." Now that she's concentrating full time on the company, forty-six-year-old Donna sees big growth in her business. Assuming that real furs continue to decline in popularity and that women still want to wear elegant coats, the potential looks very warm for a home-based business like Donna's.

Donna has this advice for home-based start-up companies, "Don't be afraid. And Lord, if I can do it, anyone can do it. . . ."

If you are interested in buying or making a politically correct "fur" coat for yourself or someone you love, you can contact Donna and her company of faux furriers at:

Phone Number: (800) 848-4650 (Ask for a free catalog.)

★   ★   ★

Products that Are Good for People Are Good for Business

Profile: Tom and Kate Chappell

Company Name: Tom's of Maine

Year Founded: 1970

Homemade Success Secret: Your own concern about the people who buy your products will be rewarded in ways you can't imagine.

Business Profile: A leading producer of natural, environmentally-safe personal care products. The company now boasts over 60 employees and a sustained growth rate of 25-30% per year. Their first product was Clearlake, a non-phosphate liquid laundry detergent, but we love Tom's best for their great all-natural, fennel-flavored toothpaste.

Start-up Capital: A $5,000 loan from a friend.

The Office: Started out on the kitchen table. Today the facility is a converted train station.

Working Hours: Tom consistently puts in more than forty hours a week. Kate is at the company several times a week and also works on her art career.

Family Profile: Tom and Kate have five children, ranging in age from 9 to 26.

Education: Tom graduated from Trinity College in 1966 with a degree in English. He recently earned a Masters of Theology at Harvard Divinity School. Kate graduated with honors from the University of Southern Maine in 1983 with a degree in communications. She also studied art at the Sorbonne in Paris.

Favorite Pastimes: Kate now devotes much of her time to painting—her art is featured at the Mast Cove Gallery in Kennebunkport and at Harvard University. Tom is active in the Episcopal Church of Maine and the Maine Global Conference.

Tom Chappell had grown disenchanted with his insurance career. Like many of the people inspired by nature and driven toward a simpler life in the 1960s, Kate and Tom Chappell decided to leave corporate America and "move back to the land." They tried to use unprocessed foods and simple unadulterated products. But, when they looked for natural personal care products, like shampoos and soaps, there weren't many choices. Unable to find ones that met their criteria for quality and simplicity, they decided to make and sell their own.

With a loan from a friend, Tom and Kate began making products for home use that would not harm the environment. Tom's of Maine is a company built out of respect for humankind, the natural world, and the community. Their first manufacturing facility was the kitchen table. There they produced their first product, Clearlake, a non-phosphate liquid detergent. They asked their customers to recycle the cartons by mailing them back, postage paid, to be refilled. This gave the company a reputation for being different—more concerned about the environment than the cost of recycling the containers. Tom's office today is in a refurbished shed—a sort of "recycled" train station in Kennebunk.

The current product line has evolved significantly from those first days. Now the company concentrates on natural care products. The toothpaste, a major source of their revenue, comes in recyclable aluminum containers and the recycled-paper boxes are printed with environmentally safe soy-based inks. They are constantly adapting the packages to maximize recyclability and minimize waste. All the products are still made with the handmade care of the first ones, however, and are manufactured from the highest quality natural ingredients. The company's recyclable packaging still has homey notes from "Your friends, Tom and Kate." They didn't move into "green initiatives" as so many other companies are just to remain competitive, they started out that way.

Blonde, wide-eyed Kate continues to oversee new product development, though she is less active in the business than she was at first. The products, from baking soda toothpaste and aloe vera shampoo to deodorant made from coriander, are biodegradable, contain no preservatives, synthetic colors, animal fats, or alcohol, and are never, never tested on animals. The products are safe and pleasant to use as well—for example, a report by Indiana University's Oral Health Research Institute stated that Tom's of Maine toothpaste is less abrasive than eleven of fourteen major brands tested.

When the Chappells moved from Philadelphia to Maine, they were enchanted with the simplicity of life, in spite of the poor economic conditions. According to Kate, "There weren't any jobs here, the economy was depressed and there were a lot of houses with peeling paint." The location didn't impede Tom and Kate's goals—the business has grown steadily through the years. Last year, Tom's topped more than $16 million in sales. According to an interview in the Lynchburg, Virginia *News & Advance*, Tom remains awed at his company's growth. "When we did a million dollars, I subconsciously said, 'Maybe there is $10 million here,' and now that we have passed $10 million, I'm saying, 'Maybe there is $100 million here.' "

Today the Tom's of Maine products are distributed in more than seven thousand health goods stores in the U.S., Canada, and England. They are also distributed in twenty thousand food and drug stores. Progressive Distributors and CVS were the first major chains to agree to stock Tom's of Maine products next to the "name brands" and today several other drug and food chains show strong support for the company's vision of natural, environmentally safe, quality products. Tom's products cost a bit more, but people seem willing to pay the extra price for the quality and to protect the environment. Tom and Kate have been well-recognized for their efforts and their important contributions to their community—in 1992 they were selected as the Small Business People of the Year for the State of Maine. Tom Chappel received CNBC's 1991 Entrepreneur of the Year award and the company was given top ratings from the Council for Economic Priorities, being one of only twenty-four U.S. companies on the CEP's Honor Role. To list the other awards would fill up pages.

As successful as they've been, the company today still reflects Tom and Kate's unique integration of personal and corporate values. Social responsibility is as important as profitability to the founders, and they have been remarkably successful at proving that ethics and business are indeed compatible terms. Tom, a tall man with glasses and narrow features, is devoted to Ralph Nader consumerism and an advocate of family values and responsible management. Tom's values in business were shaped after his father's textile company failed. Though bitter, homeless, and hurt after the collapse of the business, Tom learned that business must make money to survive, but can also be a benefit to society. According to Tom, "If I am going to be in business, I'm going to be responsible and ethical about it and I'm also going to be shrewd."

Kate and Tom continue to prosper because ecologically sound business is good business, not just a marketing ploy. Tom says it this way, "I believe we have been able to, at Tom's, expand upon the historical point of view that business is just for making money to a broader view that business is about doing good for others in the process of getting financial gain." Tom's of Maine is one of the rare companies where the founders actually live the values they promulgate in their mission statements.

If you want to find out where you can buy Tom's of Maine products in your area, please write or call:
Lafayette Center
P.O. Box 710
Kennebunk, ME 04043
Phone Number: (207) 985-2944

★   ★   ★

Dollars and Flowers Blowing in the Wind

Profile: Catherine Engel and Carol Fagan

Company Name: Wind Related, Inc. of Hamilton, Montana— "home of blue skies and unlimited opportunities for those willing to work for their dreams . . ."

Year Founded: 1985

Homemade
Success Secret: When partners (or sisters) can combine their skills in creative ways, new opportunities bloom.

Business Profile: Manufacturers of wind art—an art form utilizing fabric to catch the breeze and the sunlight. Wind Related creates beautiful windsocks in forms inspired from nature that are a pleasure to look at and listen to.

Start-up Capital: Started with "zip." Their only resources were four generations of family labor and a desperate desire to succeed. The bank wouldn't talk to them seriously and the SBA turned them down because they didn't ask for enough money. Eventually Grandmother gave them a line of credit on a $10,000 CD she had put away.

The Office: Catherine drew the designs in her drawing room, they cut the fabric in their parent's basement, and Carol sewed the windsocks in her kitchen. Two years later they moved to an office because they needed more space for manufacturing. Their current facility is about five thousand square feet.

Working Hours: Now they work normal hours and get weekends off, but they started by working seven days a week.

Home Office
Technology: Sewing machines, a special band saw and knife blade developed by their father, but no fax machine because Catherine doesn't think it's cost effective yet. "When it's cost effective, we'll get one."

Family Profile: Carol has two children. She is engaged. Catherine recently remarried and has no children.

Education: Carol, a Fulbright-Hays scholar, has a Ph.D. in biology from the University of California at Santa Barbara and is a self-taught artist who has shown her work internationally in group and solo shows. Catherine also worked as a research biologist for fourteen years. Carol attended a junior college, and in the "school of life," has a master's in child rearing, housekeeping, and wifery. She worked for eighteen years making custom-designed outdoor products, including airbrushed clothing, hang glider sails, and paintings.

Favorite Pastimes: Catherine, a real outdoor person, rides a mountain bike or does gardening. Carol works on remodeling old Victorian houses. They are both active in community organizations and spend time encouraging would-be entrepreneurs to get started.

Desperation sometimes leads to inspiration—and Wind Related, Inc. is such a story. Carol's husband was dying of brain cancer and she had children to support. The transplanted Californians wanted to stay in western Montana's Bitterroot Valley, which they cherished as home, in spite of the depressed local economy. Carol asked Catherine, who didn't have a job at the time either, to help her come up with an idea to make a living at home. Catherine, as always, had a lot of ideas. Catherine's first choice was making flavored, herbal goat cheeses—a trendy food gaining favor in specialty and gourmet markets in upscale neighborhoods around the U.S. But Carol said she didn't like the idea. Carol said she could relate to working with fabrics more than working with goats. So, Caroline considered their two areas of expertise, sewing and biology, and came up with the idea of making three-dimensional, biologically correct windsocks from ripstop nylon.

The sisters found the concept for the product was easier than the initial execution. Executing the first designs was agonizing. The first idea was to make wildflowers of the western United States. Trying to transform the complex biological forms into beautiful windsocks was initially a trial of balancing form, color, texture, and, most important, manufacturability. Some of the first attempts were flops—and then they worked it out. The results were stunning. The first design was a pink bitterroot with green streamers. Finally, twelve flower windsocks were developed. They bought another sewing machine and some fabric and made samples. Then Catherine hit the road, driving across the western United States. In the first month they earned $1,000 and they finally felt like they had a real business.

The whole family was involved at first. They helped with developing manufacturing techniques, giving business advice, and building the work tables—whatever it took to get the product out the door. Even their grandmother, who was almost blind, would count parts for the wind socks, which gave her a purpose in life. Wind Related now employs an in-house staff of ten to twenty people, depending on the season, independent contract sewers, and sales representatives. This makes the company a major economic force in a place like Hamilton.

The designs caught on quickly. The company started out as Wind Works, and they changed the name to Wind Related a year later. It wasn't long before the business really prospered. When they started there weren't any similar designs and now there are a number of companies that try to copy the streamer-laden works of art. "You know you're successful when you're being copied right and left. But no one has been able to copy our proprietary production methods. We try to stay ahead with the designs of our products, but if it weren't for our production method, we wouldn't be where we are today."

Catherine logged more than thirty thousand miles in less than four months to promote the products—and as a result of the vibrating steering wheel, had to have surgery. But that hasn't stopped her creativity or her initiative—she still gets on the road to get the word out for more than two months every year. Now the products are sold in more than three thousand outlets, all over the world. Stars like Glenn Close, Christopher Lloyd, and others own Wind Related windsocks. Some large chains carry the products, including Penney's and Neiman Marcus—but the company's real strength is in smaller galleries, handcrafts shops, nurseries, garden centers, and interior decorating salons.

Being able to adapt is important in a business like Wind Related. The products were originally targeted toward museums, airport gift shops, and national park gift shops. Quickly they found that airport gift shops didn't work, because they need to mark up the wholesale price five or six times—which made the wind art too expensive. Catherine also discovered that museums at that time needed educational material with the items they sold to maintain their not-for-profit status, so they put educational inserts about the flowers and other designs in the package with the wind art. This flexibility and creativity has allowed the company to keep on top of the market. "People are always looking for something different in the market—which is one of the advantages of being a smaller company. We are constantly thinking of new ideas, formats, and concepts. We just did some gorgeous butterflies for the San Diego Zoo."

One of the most intriguing ideas the duo had was talking to the manufacturers of headstones and convincing them to drill a hole to hold a windsock stand so the delightful creations wouldn't interfere with the maintenance of the cemetery grounds. As a result, the Wind Related pieces are being used more frequently to adorn gravesites, to make a loved one's final resting place stand out from all the others.

The Wind Related products appeal to the senses with brightly colored, three-dimensional forms that twirl, flutter, float and wave in the winds. Streamers rustle in the breeze and create a restful, meditative sound. The designs are primarily flowers and birds. They also make dinosaurs, sea creatures, farm animals, and a variety of seasonal, holiday, and sporting designs. Catherine's knowledge of plant and animal forms, coupled with her natural artistic traits, allows her to develop the innovative windsocks. The designs are airy, translucent interpretations based on the actual shape and color of the flower or animal the windsock represents.

Catherine, forty-three, creates the designs and handles most of the sales. She attends the wholesale gift shows and makes contact with outlets and store owners. Carol, forty, handles the manufacturing end of the business. Catherine and Carol believe in being good role models for other entrepreneurs and spend many hours encouraging would-be business owners in seminars and community organizations. "If we would have had good role models when we started, we would have made fewer mistakes. Now we can be the role models for others. For example, instead of just interviewing accountants and then hiring someone based on gut feeling, go and ask similar businesses about the accountants they use. It's important that the accountant and lawyer you hire understand your type of business, otherwise you can get into all sorts of problems. We also got a patent attorney very early on—and that was very important to us. We don't have money to sue people for infringement, but just one letter is usually enough to stop a company from copying your work. But if you don't file the patent or copyright, you have no way to protect yourself and your intellectual property. It's also important to know your competition and your marketplace. You constantly have to look at new ideas. Being small let's us adapt quickly."

The sister team also encourages other entrepreneurs to complete a five-year business plan before they get too far along—something their parents encouraged them to do. Catherine comments, "So many businesses have good ideas and tons of enthusiasm and they put lots of time in, but they don't have a plan on which to focus their energy and no path to follow toward their goals. They end up going off in a million directions and accomplishing nothing as a result. You also have to believe in your business. You need energy to get you through the tough times. When you find yourself doubting your business, it's time to get out."

Catherine also warns other entrepreneurs to watch out for the people who let you down. For example, they've had accounts that lied about receiving the goods so they could get additional shipments for free. "We trust a lot of people and some of them simply let you down. But we continue to trust people anyway."

Sustained success does not come without challenges. Along with the day-to-day chores of keeping things on track, getting new designs out, and making sure that orders are shipped on time, the recession is a major obstacle to deal with. "Sales were down 60 percent during the height of the current recession. It was rough for a while, because the product is a totally discretionary item and people are going to buy food and clothes before they go and buy a windsock. We prosper in good times; in bad times we have to be more creative." Still, the sisters have high hopes for the future. The company is back on the growth path and expansion is predicted. According to Catherine, "People will become more centered on their homes in the future and they will look for unique items to decorate them—and because people are more environmentally conscious, the products will continue to appeal to more and more people."

Though they are now a company with national distribution, the home-based personal roots are still central to the company's philosophy. Sensitive, creative people, the sisters care about their employees. They can't afford expensive benefits, so they try to do little things to make the employees feel important and appreciated. For example, every week they have a "Power Hour" for their employees. The employees determine the topic for the presentation, which might be a class in emergency medical procedures, lessons in quilt making, or a parenting seminar.

In 1990, Catherine and Carol were selected as Montana Small Business Persons of the Year in recognition of their achievements. They even got to meet former President Bush in a special meeting of entrepreneurs from around the U.S. Wind Related's strong sense of innovation and community have produced a profitable company that's trying to make the world a better place at the same time. In creating things of beauty, and in supporting the economy of their community, they are doing a good job of meeting their goals.

If you are interested in distributing or buying Wind Related products to enhance the beauty of your world, you can contact the company at:

P.O. Box 1006
Hamilton, MT 59840

★   ★   ★

Plant Entrepreneur Grows Plenty of the Green Stuff

Profile: Carolyn W. Grant

Company Name: Plants by Grant

Year Founded: 1976

Homemade Business Secret: If you can make people's work environment more pleasant, you will have customers for life. If your service includes ongoing maintenance, your revenue base will expand exponentially.

Business Profile: Plants by Grant specializes in the design, installation, and maintenance of interior plantscapes. Plants are sold, rented, or leased to corporations, offices, hotels, and shopping malls. The business has grown to forty-four employees and cares for forty-five thousand plants a week.

Start-up Capital: $950 from a savings account.

The Office: Starting in her home with a small greenhouse in back, four years later the budding business blossomed into a warehouse after her husband could no longer move through the house without whacking a swath through the indoor jungle with a machete. "We were doing Christmas plants and my husband came home. There were five hundred poinsettias all over the house. He couldn't even get to the bathroom."

Working Hours: Fifteen-hour days at first. "You have to do what you have to do."

Home Office Technology: Nothing special—though they do keep a database of information on all the plants and the maintenance routines, which is critical to the ongoing profitability of the company.

Family Profile: Carolyn is married to Will and they have a thirteen-year-old son.

Education: Carolyn has a degree in home economics from the University of Georgia and special studies in "the school of hard knocks."

Favorite Pastimes: Reading, skiing, and traveling to the Caribbean and Europe.

In the last twenty years, indoor plants have become an enormous growth industry. Where indoor plants were once rare in homes and even less frequently found in businesses, today companies use plants to make their corporate offices more homey and shopping mall designers add indoor plants and even full-grown trees to make the modern mega-malls more appealing.

A daughter of a tobacco and peanut farmer, Carolyn Grant started her plant business just in time to ride the wave of interest in indoor plants. Carolyn started a plant store after her husband was relocated. She had been promised a job with the Dairy Board, her employer before she moved, but it failed to materialize and so she sold plants with a partner for a year. After selling the business, when her partner's husband was relocated, Carolyn decided to open Plants by Grant from her home rather than encumber the business with the overhead of a conventional storefront or warehouse.

With an engaging Georgian drawl Carolyn explains, "I've always liked plants. In the mid-1970s when lots of people were buying house plants, we had our plant boutique and we'd have corporate people come in and say, 'I'd like some plants in my office.' I've always had the attitude of, sure I'll do it. I didn't know how to do it at first, but I figured it out along the way and so we had three corporate accounts by the end of the year." Carolyn explains that companies became interested in plants when, "In the 1960s, The Ford Foundation in New York started doing plants, and then IBM started doing plants in their corporate buildings."

When she first got started, it took fifteen-hour work days to find clients and handle the plants. She talks about the early days of the company with retrospective amusement: "I went out and hit the street. I would have three sets of clothes in the car—I'd have the sales clothes and the work clothes and I'd change clothes as I went. In the mid-1970s not many people had plants, and not only did I have to convince them that they needed my product, I had to convince them that they needed plants at all."

Most of Plants by Grant's business involves selling plants with a maintenance agreement. Carolyn's staff is off watering and looking after the purchased greenery on a weekly basis following delivery. This is a great arrangement for corporate clients who may lack the manpower, knowledge, and experience to maintain an army of plants. Since each plant variety has different care requirements, only a horticulturist can be sure how to care for each kind and bring drooping or bug-infested charges back to life. In addition to selling and maintaining plants, Plants by Grant leases plants, though this is a much smaller part of the business.

Forty-two-year-old Carolyn was initially turned down for a bank loan for her company because as she puts it, "Banks had a lot of trouble loaning money on a product they viewed as perishable." She overcame this obstacle with small loans from her family and plowing the company's earnings back into the business to build her company. Not surprisingly, Carolyn notes that "the most interesting thing about the company is to watch it grow." And grow it has. From one employee (Carolyn) and a small greenhouse in the backyard, now Plants by Grant is located in a nine thousand-square-foot warehouse and employs forty-four people!

Occasionally, even at Plants by Grant, a tree falls in the forest. Carolyn relates this story as a typical example: "We installed plants in this hotel and also installed the trees. Unfortunately we did not get the job until all the doors were put up and there were four twenty-five-foot trees that we had to put into this lobby. So we get there and the trees are like forty inches wide and they have to go through a thirty-six-inch opening. So we get these trees to this door and this trucker says, 'Lady these trees are never going through this door.' And I said, 'Man, these trees are going through this door!' So we put them through the door and put these trees in. But, on the third day one of these trees dropped every single leaf on it—no leaves left. I mean, we have killed things, but not that quickly. The manager of the hotel said, 'Oh it's all right, it'll probably come back in a few days.' But it didn't, and the manager called just before the hotel's grand opening. We had to go in at four o'clock in the morning and you have to understand that this is not just putting a tree in—this tree weighs about three thousand pounds! So we pushed, shoved, pulled, and wrestled the thing until we got it in. That's the kind of responsibility that keeps you in business. You have to do these extra things to succeed."

Now a member of Raleigh Chamber of Commerce, Carolyn talks about a recent discovery that her company contributed to. "We are finding that plants clean the air. They do take toxins out of an office environment—a lot of buildings have the sick building syndrome—and plants help make the air better. We did some studies last year with NASA to determine what to put into Earth stations and to see if they wanted to put plants in there. They did a two-year study which said that plants take toxins out of the air." According to the research with aloe vera and elephant-ear philodendrons, low levels of formaldehyde, a common pollutant emitted by furnishings, were scrubbed almost completely from the air in only twenty-four hours. Of course, in a large room or office a number of plants must be used to fully cleanse the air—one tiny aloe plant is not enough.

Still, these findings make Carolyn feel even better about what she does. Her plants are not only making company environments nicer places to work in and shopping malls and hotels more attractive, but they are making commercial spaces a healthier place to be. She also believes that the workplace should be a pleasant place to work in and strives to make Plants by Grant a pleasant place for her employees. "I believe it's not how rich you are but it's the work environment you provide for your people. I don't want any employees to be unhappy in their jobs. Life's too short to be unhappy where you work."

Carolyn has practical advice for the sprouting home-based business. "The basic thing that you need to remember when you're starting out is that you have to keep your overhead as low as possible. You need to start out small and you need to build from there. You need to be realistic in your goals and be conservative in your forecasts. Then you can have wonderful dreams come true on down the road."

If you are interested in greening up your business and are located in or near North Carolina, you can contact Plants by Grant at:

8109 Ebenezer Church Road
Raleigh, NC 27612
Phone Number: (800) 782-0965

★　★　★

Turning Fat into Dollars

Profile: Kay and Don Lubecke

Company Name: Health Plus, a Division of Lubecke Enterprises.

Year Founded: 1988

Homemade Success Secret: Healthy products are popular—but it's the perseverance of the entrepreneur that sells them.

Business Profile: A networking business, also known as a multilevel marketing business, that promotes the nutritional and weight management products of The NANCI Corporation. The NANCI Corporation International is a five-year-old, $40-million network marketing company in Tulsa, Oklahoma founded by the well-publicized entrepreneurs Eli and Nanci Masso. The fiber-packed NANCI products were endorsed in Robert E. Kowalski's best-selling book, *The 8-Week Cholesterol Cure.*

Start-up Capital: $3,000 from Don's boat fund to set up the office.

The Office: The living room was the original office and now a separate office and new living room have been built by Don. Kay is very well organized at all times to minimize stress, and the view of the desert hills and their five-acre estate from the office window sustains their feeling of well-being.

Working Hours: When home, they work from 8 to 6—but they don't have to work that hard all the time and hours are flexible. Both travel sixteen weeks a year all over the world for business and pleasure to complete networking necessary to promote the business.

Home Office

Technology: Two computers, fax machine, copier, and three phone lines. Voice mail has been an important technological addition for the Lubecke's networking program because they can leave longer messages for prospects.

Family Profile: Married for a long time, Kay and Don are partners in life as well as in the business. They have two grown children and three grandchildren.

Education: Kay has a bachelor's degree with honors from Knox College, Illinois and a master's degree in education from Arizona State University. Fourteen years experience as a Lamaze instructor in methods of natural childbirth. Also has experience raising dairy goats.

Favorite Pastimes: Don and Kay play golf now whenever possible. Kay is going to start taking golf lessons, since she's sure that Don is going to keep spending more time on the course. They travel a lot now, so the goats are gone. But mostly they love to talk to people about the business—every activity is an opportunity for Don and Kay to network with someone new—and that means more money coming in the door.

When Kay's kids started college, the reality of life set in. Kay realized she had only the dreary prospect of social security to look forward to in her retirement. They hadn't saved anything for the future—just getting by and feeding the kids had seemed like a major accomplishment. To make things worse, the recession was eating into Don's remodeling business. Kay Lubeke felt the future was bleak.

To help out, Kay decided to look for a networking opportunity—otherwise known as a multilevel marketing program. The start-up costs are low in networking programs and there are no long-term financial commitments like there are in a franchised business. Kay had represented products before, but the big bucks didn't come in as promised. The programs Kay had tried just weren't set up for people in the field to make money—and this is true of many of the multilevel marketing schemes out there. Many of the programs are established to make the company owners rich, not the people in the trenches making the sales. But, because of her teaching background and because Kay finds it easy to talk to people, the networking concept continued to appeal to her, in spite of the lackluster results the last time around. "Networking is more like teaching than selling," Kay declares. "It's a natural for someone like me."

Kay wanted to represent a nutrition-oriented product—because it was something she could relate to. She had been a nutritional counselor for thirteen years when she was involved training pregnant women in Lamaze natural childbirth techniques. Kay would only represent a healthy, proven product—but she also wanted a program that would really pay out on her networking activities. For two years an acquaintance had been bugging Kay to try representing the NANCI products, but the timing hadn't been right. Now Kay was ready to listen.

The NANCI products include a nutritional supplement called Luv-it, a weight loss product called Lose-it, and a variety of fiber-rich foods, including nutritional candy bars, cookies, and fruit drink mixes. Because Kay was open to finding another way to make some money, she tried the products and liked the results. She analyzed the program and it seemed feasible, at least on paper, that a significant income was possible if she worked hard.

Kay was convinced about the opportunity, but Don really didn't think she could make more than a few hundred dollars a month in any networking scheme—but he agreed to let her use his boat fund to get going. Kay started in business by turning the living room into a working office. She got on the phone and started talking to people. Soon people were trying the products and Kay was bringing in money. When the checks started rolling in, Don finally started taking the business seriously. Don even tried the NANCI products and lost over sixty pounds in a year. He used to take naps every afternoon, but now he has enough energy to remodel the house and even finds time to play a round of golf or two.

Kay made this observation about her experience in the networking world: "Many times the networking businesses are started by women as a sideline to make some extra money. The husbands don't get involved until the money materializes. It didn't take me long to start making more than Don. Now he is an important part of the business. When Don got involved, things really started to happen. With both of us working at it, the potential seems unlimited." In their third year of networking, Kay and Don grossed a quarter of a million dollars. They expect to make over $400,000 this year and are still growing. In addition, they get other rewards, such as luxury cars and cruise vacations, for being top performers in the corporation.

Kay and Don have kept the operation in their home to keep overhead low and because it gives them flexibility and freedom they wouldn't have in an office. Kay comments that it is important to hold regular office hours at home and to let other people know when the "office is closed." "It's a challenge to make people understand that a home office is not open twenty-four hours a day. We need our free time and it's important to separate business and personal life." Initially, Kay had to learn to manage her spare time. She loves the business so much, at first she would go to bed thinking about it and wake up still thinking about it. Now she plans personal activities and scheduled time off during the week so she has some balance in her life.

Goal setting is another important part of Kay's daily regime. She sets many goals for herself and is constantly evaluating those goals and adjusting her activities to meet them. Don says, "The only thing that is constant in our life now is change. The flexibility to change and adapt is key to our prosperity."

Kay is eager to tell others how to make things work in a multilevel marketing business. "I go to work every day and have a regular schedule. We don't treat this as a casual business just because it's in our home. We treat it like a real business, which it is. Someone is always here during business hours. This business requires faxes, mail, telephones, and most important, dedication. Every day we do what it takes to remain successful. Some people go to play for themselves instead of going to work for themselves. You can't be successful that way."

Proud of her achievements, Kay wonders why more people don't try to make it on their own. "We have gone from poverty to total independence, have a beautiful home in the mountains, and won't have to worry about retirement. That feeling of security is wonderful. In the three years we have represented the NANCI line, we've had four luxury automobiles, two cruises to Hawaii, and the income to buy a first and a second home. It amazes me that people are commuting to work every day—it amazes me when there is such freedom out there."

The future for the company continues to be promising as NANCI distribution is expanding into other countries, including Japan and Mexico. According to Kay, "Networking is great because you ultimately get 'overrides,' which are commissions of sorts, on sales made by people you contact through networking." Kay and Don are now getting a significant "override" from the president of the Japanese subsidiary of The NANCI Corporation, because they are the ones who originally sponsored him.

According to Kay, another aspect to the company's ongoing success is the personalized service that networking provides, which isn't commonly available from retail stores. "We provide a great program with personal service and, as a result, most of the people want to represent the products and let their friends know about them. We get paid down through seven levels in the network. It's really a people-helping-people business."

Though Kay thinks working at home is the best way to go, she warns would-be homeworkers to evaluate if they are really good at being their own bosses. "A lot of people fail because they need someone to tell them what to do. People tend to lose sight of the priorities. One of my couples who went into the business makes about $4,000 a month now—which is good because they don't really work very much. One day they didn't show up at an important company meeting, because of a family crisis. If they had been working for IBM, one of them would have gone to work and the other would have solved the crisis at home. But people forget when they work for themselves that it is still work. If they were salaried they wouldn't have both missed the meeting—they would have worried about keeping their jobs. That's the double-edged sword of working for yourself—it gives you the freedom to succeed or the freedom to slough off. It's always up to you to make the choice." Only fifty now, it looks like Kay has been making the right choices in her own business. Because of their vision and hard work, the Lubecke's future has been transformed from bleak to brilliant.

If you are interested in trying the NANCI products or obtaining information on becoming an independent distributor for the company, you can contact the Lubeckes at
 33211 North 55th Street
 Cave Creek, AZ 85331
 Phone Number: (602) 252-6627

"Your Research Findings Have Brought Us Much Hope"

Profile: Janice R. Guthrie

Company Name: The Health Resource, Inc.

Year Founded: 1984

Homemade

Success Secret: There is always a market for information.

Business Profile: The company collects medical information on specific maladies suffered by clients. The collected information may reveal new information that the patient's doctor is unaware of. Like other electronic information brokerages, the business is growing rapidly.

Start-up Capital: Janice's husband's full-time job supported the business until it could stand on its own.

The Office: The office is in a converted garage in Janice's suburban home.

Working Hours: Days are spent interviewing clients. Nights are spent on the computer searching databases and other sources for information. "We do most of our computer searching at night because the rates are lower; we have long distance calls as well as computer connect time to consider."

Home Office

Technology: Computers for research and assembling reports. Faxes for receiving articles from medical libraries.

Family Profile: Janice is married and has two grown children.

Education: Janice has two master's degrees in education from the University of Central Arkansas.

Favorite Pastimes: She runs three times a week and reads medical textbooks in her "off" hours.

What would you do if you were diagnosed with a life-threatening illness? Take the savings account and blow it on a world tour? Hole up in a clinic in Mexico that offers unorthodox medical treatments? Or follow the traditional route through the medical establishment, allowing a doctor you barely know to diagnose and treat you? Janice Guthrie found herself in just such a dilemma when she was diagnosed with a rare type of ovarian cancer. Worried that her doctor's treatment was not necessarily the best or the only option available, she chose not to put all her eggs in one basket and went out to learn about her illness on her own. Janice explains, "To educate myself about the condition and try to make the very best decision, I went to a medical school library and read everything I could about my particular kind of cancer.

The information that I gleaned led me to a specialist who was interested in treating my type of tumor and who treated it successfully. I found that the search for the information and the actual utilization of that information empowered me in eradicating my fear and the uncertainty of living the future with cancer. It also helped me to regain a sense of control over my own health."

Between surgeries, Janice began to reflect on her life. She had already resigned her teaching and administrative job at the university because she couldn't keep up with it physically. In her sonorous Southern accent, she speaks candidly about a tough time in her life and how she turned a personal nightmare into a business that's both personally and materially rewarding. "I began to ask myself, 'If I could do anything in the world, what would it be?' and then I worked through *What Color Is Your Parachute?* It became clear to me that I loved research and that was my profession—I liked working with people on an in-depth level, going beyond a superficial, social relationship. It began to occur to me that I could do for others what I had done for myself and provide them with information on their medical conditions. So, I launched the business in 1984, and I was right, there was a need for it."

Why don't doctors provide this potentially life-saving knowledge on their own? Simple. There's just too much to read and learn for any human being. Maybe a huge central computer could track all of the information and provide a single source to doctors who want to track the latest information on a particular illness. But because of a plethora of professional journal articles derived from research, studies, and discoveries, there's no way for a doctor to stay really current in his or her field—there's just far too much information. For this reason, an individual doctor's treatment of a serious medical problem may occasionally be incorrect, outdated, or even harmful, because no single human can know everything there is to know about medicine.

Janice Guthrie and her partners in The Health Resource, including Julie H. Smith, attempt to fill this knowledge gap in medical treatment options. Upon a request for information on a specific illness by an afflicted individual or his or her family, Janice and her staff begin searching medical journals, databases, and other publications for the latest information. They look for data on treatments and research that the average doctor may not be aware of. For a moderate fee, patients can have The Health Resource research their symptoms and diagnosis and compile a 20- to 150-page report of all recent data on the illness. Using this information, the patient can then take control of the healing process and better understand the treatment options available. The information also helps patients locate leading-edge researchers and doctors who may know more about a particular problem than a doctor or specialist culled from the phone book or the recommendation of a family doctor.

Typical of the appreciation of their clients is a woman who asked for help with her two-year-old son, who suffered from a painful stomach condition for which her doctors had prescribed surgery. The woman wrote this in her letter to The Health Resource: "The information on my son's stomach disorder literally gave me the confidence and strength to postpone surgical correction. We gave the medicine a bit longer to work and it did. Without a doubt our son would have had to have unnecessary major surgery if I had not received the report from the medical information service."

This business, unlike some of the *Cinderella* stories profiled in the book, took time to get off the ground, but it was important to Janice because her efforts helped prolong lives and saved lives, so she kept at it. "I had this wonderful idea and I wanted to be involved with people doing this research for them. I literally sat here and waited for the phone to ring. The first three years were very tough and I am always grateful that I happen to be married to someone who is gainfully employed, who could support me through those first three years. I didn't pay myself a salary—any profit I turned directly back into the business. After five years we really turned the corner and it became very profitable."

Forty-eight-year-old Janice had to overcome some obstacles at first as well to maintain concentration on her work. "It requires a lot of discipline. I tried an earlier home-based business, and I wasn't quite able to separate the business from my family responsibilities. So, my husband enclosed a part of the garage and I had to walk outside the front door and through a door into the office. For me, that separation of the office from the home really sets the mood. When I walk into the office every day it is basically a separate place for me. At first I had to be very firm with neighbors and friends, telling them that I *work* from eight to five—otherwise I'd find myself wasting my time in conversations."

Janice gets many rewards, besides the financial security, from her business. "Many of our clients stay in touch with us. We really become friends with many of our clients. The work is truly a source of deep feeling for us. I've had a lot of offers to make this into a really big company. A venture capital firm flew me to New York and wanted to invest money in the company. But, as long as I'm in control of the business it will continue to be small and it will be a home-based business—that's the way I like to work!"

If you are interested in an affordable, in-depth analysis of an illness or medical problem, you can contact The Health Resource at:

209 Katherine Drive
Conway, AK 72032
Phone Number: (501) 329-5272

★　★　★

The First Wealth Is Health

Profile: Kristine & Gene Hughes

Company Name: Nature's Sunshine Products

Year Founded: 1972

Homemade Success Secret: If it's hard for you to find something you need, you can bet it is just as difficult for someone else to find it. If you can make this product easily available to all the people who need it, then you have discovered an opportunity.

Business Profile: Nature's Sunshine Products is a multilevel marketing company with seven thousand distributors that manufactures health supplements, vitamins, homeopathic medicines, and a water purifier. This originally home-based company is now publicly traded on NASDAQ.

Start-up Capital: Seven families each contributed $150 in capital.

The Office: The company was started on the kitchen table at home. The "healthiness" of the business forced it into larger quarters.

Working Hours: Whatever it takes.

Home Office Technology: Nothing initially, even the capsules were stuffed with herbs by hand. Today, the company uses such esoteric instruments as gas chromatographs to analyze herbs, as part of the efforts to maintain the high level of quality control.

Family Profile: Kristine is married to Gene and they have seven children.

Favorite Pastimes: Spending time with the family.

Maintaining good health through the use of herbal remedies is an ancient art. The practice of herbal medicine is even seen in animals. Chimpanzees suffering from parasites have been seen to carefully choose cleansing plants when they are ill. When healthy, they don't include these herbs as part of their normal foraging diet.

A quote from Ralph Waldo Emerson on their brochure/catalog states, "The first wealth is health." Nature's Sunshine Products makes herbal products that are designed to keep people healthy, feeling good, and revitalized. The product line includes vitamins, herbs, and weight-management formulas. When we asked how they were doing during the interview, soft-spoken Chairperson of the Board Kristine Hughes replied, "Wonderfully well, thank-you." Good thing too, because this is this company's raison d'être!

Kristine had the idea for the company because of an illness in her own family: "My husband had a bleeding ulcer. He had been to the hospital and wasn't getting well. One of our neighbors said to try a special herb and he did and he got better. We then tried to find that herb in the health food stores in a capsule and we couldn't find it. At that time you could find herbs in bulk or in tablets but not in capsules and this particular herb wasn't even in a tablet, so we decided to encapsulate the herb and try to sell the product to the health food stores. My husband and his nephew took ten bottles to a health food store and they were just so thrilled to see them because no one in the whole country had done that yet. Reorders kept coming in and we sat around the kitchen table encapsulating by hand and stuffing the capsules into bottles."

After talking to some friends, the Nature's Sunshine folks decided to go into multilevel marketing to grow the business faster. This would eliminate the need of borrowing money for expansion. Kristine explains, "We were working at home selling to the health food stores and after two years we decided to go multilevel. We had friends who were in Shaklee, another multilevel marketing company. Shaklee had vitamins but they didn't have herbs. They said this would work very well multilevel and multilevel's better because you don't have the cash flow problems you do selling to health food stores. You get some strong customers who believe in the products and they talk to their friends and neighbors and it goes like that."

Today the products are sold exclusively through multilevel marketing because, as Kristine puts it, "We don't want to compete with our customers." Nature's Sunshine now offers more than five hundred products, sold exclusively through a network of seven thousand distributors. Fifty-three-year-old Kristine is unassuming and confident as she describes the strategy: "The people who sell our products are mostly people who themselves have been ill. They use the herbs and like them and they tell their neighbors and friends. It's just the herbs in the bottles—we don't do any advertising, it's all word of mouth. It's not a high-pressure type of thing. Our people aren't in it for the money necessarily—they're in it to help other people."

The company was started through a cooperative arrangement with seven families. Starting out with a contribution of $150 per family, Nature's Sunshine Products is one of the most astounding success stories in this book from a financial point of view. From the tiny amount of start-up capital, publicly traded Nature's Sunshine Products sold over $72 million worth of products last year. Tranquil Kristine's insights for those starting a home-based business include, "Find a need, a lot of it is timing."

The company's amazing growth from kitchen table to big business is something that just happened, according to Kristine: "It happened just slowly and gradually and it was just fun to watch it. My husband was a school teacher and we have seven children and we just didn't have a heck of a lot of money. The first time that I was able to spend money and not feel bad about it was when we went down and bought some lawn chairs. It was the first time I didn't have to watch what I spent and that was the best feeling."

If you are interested in Nature's Sunshine Products, and would like the name of a local distributor who handles the line, or if you would like to become a distributor yourself, you can contact them at:

P.O. Box 1000
1655 North Main
Spanish Fork, UT 84660

Ballooning School Profits Soar Over Rockies

Profile: Mike and Joyce Bundgaard
Company Name: Lifecycle Balloon School, Ltd.

Year Founded: 1972

Homemade
Success Secret: Look around your environment. If there is something you love to do or see in that environment, there are others like you who would enjoy the same thing.

Business Profile: Lifecycle Ballooning sells hot air balloons and trains would-be balloon pilots so they can get their licenses from the FAA. Lifecycle also offers balloon rides.

Start-up Capital: A used hot air balloon bought for advertising purposes.

The Office: Two bedrooms of a three-bedroom house are used as offices for Mike and Joyce respectively.

Working Hours: Up at 3:00 A.M. for sunrise balloon flights. Up at 5:00 A.M. for a day in the office during off-season. Mike says that with these hours he's learned the value of going to bed early.

Home Office
Technology: A fax machine and several older Kaypro computers which were bought used for pennies on the dollar.

Family Profile: Mike and Joyce are married and have no children, but they have one cat named Hot Air Henry, after the cat in a children's book that takes a balloon ride.

Education: Mike has a bachelor's degree in physics and a master's degree in architecture from the University of Colorado. Joyce completed two years of college at the University of Nebraska.

Favorite Pastimes: Ballooning, of course, including traveling to Japan for balloon races. They also enjoy bike riding, camping, and sailing on a local reservoir.

Forty-eight-year-old ex-Marine Mike Bundgaard fell into hot air ballooning almost by accident. Running a marginally profitable bicycle sales and repair shop in the early 1970s, Mike decided to buy a hot air balloon to advertise and promote his struggling enterprise. Mike participated in a number of ballooning events and mastered the art of lighter-than-air flight. As his proficiency improved Mike began participating in ballooning regattas where several balloons are launched at one time. It was at one of these events that he met his soon-to-be business partner, Joyce, who he would later marry on the balloon field. Once Mike had learned to pilot his new purchase he decided to leave his landlocked bicycle business and sell (or as Mike puts it, "give away") the business to some friends who were employees at the shop.

As Mike recounts, "I enjoyed flying the balloon more than I enjoyed retailing the bicycles. I took the balloon business and developed it out of my home. I guess it was an economic decision because I couldn't afford anything else. We couldn't afford to rent or lease any space. For several years it was sort of meager but then the publicity on the transatlantic attempt developed a lot of interest in balloons. By the late 1970s it started booming and we were selling twenty-five balloons a year and of course we had to train all the people as well." The business rode the updrafts to profitability as more people became interested in ballooning. The beautiful, brightly colored balloons float gracefully in the wind, attracting riders everywhere. Today, Mike says that the interest in pilot training has declined somewhat over the boom years, but the demand for balloon rides is growing rapidly, especially in the pristine Colorado Rockies. What better way to experience the snow-covered peaks without disturbing the silence and solitude of the environment?

Mike and Joyce have piloted balloons for a large number of famous and not-so-famous passengers, including Congresswoman Pat Shroeder on her fortieth birthday celebration. Mike and Joyce promote their business through ballooning groups, in small local newspaper ads, and through flyers distributed at local businesses. But most of the growth comes from word of mouth from other people who have taken rides or taken lessons.

The growth in ballooning was fueled in part by improvements in balloon materials. Unlike the barely-governable balloons of the nineteenth century, depicted in the movie *Around the World in Eighty Days*, today's propane-driven balloons are better built and lighter. Ballooning professionals only take their craft aloft near sunrise or sunset and only in the right kind of weather. This keeps Mike and Joyce out of the air for part of the year—and they use this time for personal interests.

Piloting a balloon is relatively simple compared to other forms of aerial travel. Modern balloons offer a sea of digital readouts that track altitude, temperature, and other salient measurements, but according to Mike, "There are basically only two controls—you can put heat into a balloon or you can valve off hot air from the balloon. To give you a comparison of complexity, the FAA requires minimum flight hours in an airplane of around forty to get a license, but a hot air balloon pilot only needs ten hours."

While Mike was forced to start his company from home, we asked him if he would prefer to move the business out of his house. His comment, "I wouldn't have it any place but home." Mike and Joyce have a unique home office arrangement. Each has a bedroom converted into an office. Mike describes his office as neat and organized and Joyce's as cluttered. Furniture is bare bones—desks made from doors mounted on top of filing cabinets and brick and board bookshelves. In addition to Mike and Joyce's offices, they have a busy office manager who works out of an office in her own house down the street. Thus, this is a two-home business.

Mike and Joyce's success secrets are almost as simple as operating the balloon. When asked about them, Joyce replied authoritatively, "The answer is hard work. In the early days we were teaching ground school five nights a week and flying almost every day. We would finish ground school at 9:00 P.M. and then be up again at 3:30 A.M. the next morning to fly. It was a lot of hard work up front, but it was a lot of fun." Mike adds, "To a lot of people ballooning is like a lifetime fantasy and when you sell a balloon, you have to train the owner. It's not like selling an automobile. We helped a lot of people realize their lifetime dreams of flying a balloon, owning a balloon, or becoming balloon pilots. There have been a number of individual cases where we've known the people over a long period of time and we could see how their characters changed when they realized they could fly themselves." Though the financial rewards are in the stratosphere for Mike and Joyce, it seems that the future rewards remain in the clouds.

If you are interested in learning more about the hot air balloon experience, you can contact the Bundgaards at:
2540 South Steele Street
Denver, CO 80210
Phone Number: (303) 759-3907

CHAPTER 5

Do You Really Need Home-Office Technology to Make a Million?

All but a handful of the people profiled in this book own and use computers, copiers, and fax machines. One couple actively dislikes technology and refuses to even consider using a fax machine—considered by most to be the handiest piece of home office equipment. While it's not necessary to use technology in a home-based business, most people think it really helps.

What you specifically need for your company depends entirely on the kind of business and your own style of working. Of course it also depends on how much money you have to spend. If you take your $2,000 start-up capital and blow it on a computer, fax machine, and two-line speaker phones, you'll be out of business quickly unless you can find more money or have an outside job to keep your enterprise afloat.

When we asked most of the homemade millionaires to give their advice for other people starting a business, a frequent comment ran like this: "Start small, don't spend any more money than you absolutely have to. Then as the business grows reinvest the money in it to grow the business but avoid buying expensive equipment and furniture. Buy only things that pay for themselves." While you could argue that a computerized billing program will pay for itself by saving you time, if you blow all of your start-up money on a computer for such a program, then you'll have no clients to bill. Wait until you have clients, then worry about billing them.

Technology Is a Poor Investment, So Only Buy What You Need
Never look at technology as a tangible asset that you can always sell if you need the cash. Resale on technology products is usually pennies

on the dollar. Instead, buy only the equipment that will directly help you make money now. Keep in mind that the longer you put off the purchase, the cheaper the technology will become. Prices on machines such as computers, phones, and faxes are spiraling downward while power and features are improving. Buy a basic phone now and upgrade later. Purchase a used or bottom-of-the-line computer if you must have one and an ink jet printer rather than a laser printer. This set-up is perfect for writing letters, billing clients, and tracking a modest inventory. Then as your business grows, replace or upgrade your equipment as you can afford the expense. Keep in mind that technology, like office furniture, depreciates instantaneously. Less than a year after purchasing your $4,000 computer and printer system it may fetch only $1,000 on the used equipment market. In four or five years you may have to pay someone to haul it away. If you wait that year, you can buy the same thing for $1,000 or choose from superior new equipment which also will have come down in price. The average business doesn't really need powerful computers—almost any personal computer can handle word processing for letters, proposals, and spreadsheets for simple accounting, and that's what most entrepreneurs do with the computers anyway.

Of course, there are some home-based businesses like desktop publishing or presentation development companies that demand the best equipment and state-of-the-art technology. If your home-based business is one of these, then lease the equipment instead of buying it, if you can get the credit. That way you can keep your technology up to date without investing too much cash.

Avoid Boondoggle Technologies

By the time you equip a home office with furniture and equipment, if you buy the best and spend your money unwisely, it would be easy to drop $20,000 or $30,000 almost overnight. But by being careful, you can probably start your company with little more than a single line telephone, a used desk and chair, and a desk light of sorts. But, it's easy to be tempted to waste money on unnecessary purchases or increase your monthly overhead with a lease on an expensive photocopier or postage meter that you really don't need. Pitney Bowes, makers of both copiers and postage systems, had a program in the 1980s where they would go through an office building to find small businesses without copiers. Locating one, they would make an irresistible offer: A brand new full-size office copier free for up to thirty days as long as the business would sign a three-year lease for the copier if the company decided to keep it. This meant copier payments of around $300 a month for any company that kept the copier. And it was a hard offer to refuse because behind the salesperson making it, two burly delivery men would be busy setting up the copier. We, the authors, know because we still have the copier!

Few companies will roll copiers into your home-based business, but it's tempting to swoon for a $1300 plain paper fax or six two-line phones so you're ready to "expand" when the time comes. Copiers can be very easy to buy if you have good credit because copier sales-people will call you five times a day if you apply for a business license in or near a big city. The pressure to buy one can be compelling—especially if you are trudging through the snow to your nearby copy store on a daily basis.

The way to avoid making inappropriate purchases is to promise yourself to think about the purchase for a full seven days before you decide to buy. At the end of the seven days you'll probably think to yourself, Why was I even thinking about buying that? I can't afford it and I don't really need it. If, on the other hand, the purchase still makes business and economic sense after seven days, then it's probably something you need.

Some Home-Based Businesses Depend on Technology

Because almost all the businesses profiled in this book use home-based computer technology in some way, the businesses presented in this chapter are those businesses that depend on technology for their existence. These include businesses like Michael Boom's writing business, which develops documentation for technology companies and Dan Siemasko's business that depends on computer technologies for developing the multimedia presentations used by his clients. Of course, there are other companies in this book that depend on technology as well. For example, in the last chapter you read about Janice Guthrie, who is one of the new information brokers who accesses on-line databases to create new products for the masses. In Janice's case, computer technology is used to create detailed reports that help medical professionals and individuals who are trying to determine the correct course of treatment for illnesses and injuries—but the opportunities for similar information brokerages in other domains seem endless.

There are so many computer-based business prospects for home-based entrepreneurs, including accounting businesses, tax preparation businesses, online help services, desktop publishing agencies, and computerized training programs—it's impossible to cover all of them in one book. The people in this chapter represent only a handful of the possibilities. As technology continues to develop, there will be even more.

★　　★　　★

From Underground Comics to Aboveboard Businessman

Profile: David Tatelman

Company Name: Homestead Book Company

Year Founded: 1972

Homemade Success Secret: It is important to change with the times. You can't keep doing things the same way forever and expect to grow.

Business Profile: Homestead is a book distributor that also handles underground comics and publishes restaurant and food guides. The company also sells books direct through a mail-order catalog.

Start-up Capital: $500 saved from a failed bookstore venture. The capital was used to buy underground comics to sell to bookstores and specialty shops.

The Office: Homestead started in a basement with David, then its sole proprietor, carrying his inventory around in the back of his Vega station wagon. (You *do* remember the Vega station wagon don't you?) After several years in business, the growing book inventory eventually overwhelmed David's basement and the company moved into a converted corner grocery store.

Working Hours: "Where I used to drive my books around all day and do my accounting at night, I get weekends off now and I get vacations."

Home Office Technology: David relies on a computer system to manage his massive inventory and juggle his more than six hundred customer accounts. He computerized early—he's had his networked system in place since 1987.

Family Profile: He's still single, but he does have two cats for company.

Education: David has a bachelor's degree in psychology from the University of South Florida.

Favorite Pastimes: David enjoys travel, scubadiving, good food, and jogging.

Can you start a successful company out of the back of your car? Yes, as long as you don't drive a Mazda Miata. David Tatelman started his book distributorship out of a station wagon, after a bookstore venture he established went belly-up in the early 1970s. Taking the last $500 from the business ("The last $500 I had . . ."), David bought an inventory of underground comic books which he drove around town and sold from the back of his Vega station wagon to local book stores and specialty and magazine shops that carried comics. He initially focused on one line of adult comic books known then as "underground comics."

These intricately illustrated comic books included adult themes and oddball characters such as Mr. Natural, Flakey Foont, and The Fabulous Furry Freak Brothers, created by offbeat cartoonists including R. Crumb, Gilbert Sheldon, S. Clay Wilson, and a host of others who mostly lived in the San Francisco-Berkeley area of California. Those of you who grew up in the 1960s probably remember these names and characters—the underground comics were immensely popular during the hippy heyday. Sometimes graphically portraying sex and employing weighty titles such as *Big Ass Comics*, more than one bookstore owner got in trouble with the law for handling these controversial wares. For the most part, this chapter in comic book history closed at the end of the 1970s and the only underground comic artist from this period to go mainstream (sort of) was Bill Griffith, who today draws the strange-but-true syndicated strip *Zippy the Pinhead*. But by that time David had expanded into distributing traditional books and was working a part-time job in another bookstore to pay the bills.

In the beginning, it was at the urging of a girlfriend that he reluctantly decided to run Homestead full-time and dump the bookstore job. Soft-spoken David explains, "I had a girlfriend who had a waterbed store. She said, 'Go for it. That's the only way you're ever going to do it, and do it full-time, otherwise you're never going to make it.' She inspired me. I don't think I could have done it without her pushing me to do it."

David continued expanding his distribution business aggressively, and also decided to try publishing on his own as a sideline. David's first effort as publisher was the *Complete Guide to Growing Marijuana* (remember, this was in the early 1970s so people still did things like that) and he began handling *High Times*, a magazine for smokers of "alternative" substances. David describes the magazine as so popular during this period that none of his dealers ever returned a copy; in fact the magazine ended up reprinting its back issues because there was so much demand.

The sales of the magazine were a real boost to David's business and he did so well with it that the publisher made him the sole distributor for Washington State and then later they gave him Oregon as a territory as well. With the increased stream of revenue, David began adding more and more conventional book titles to his inventory and during this period, Homestead evolved from a one-man operation into a successful company carrying a variety of products and working with a growing number of clients. David sends out a mail-order catalog now, and continues to distribute titles to bookstores and other retail outlets. He publishes one or two books a year, usually something of personal interest or about food. (We've always been thankful that David published our first book in 1988, titled *Eastside Eats*, a restaurant review guide that we wrote about the east side suburbs of Seattle.)

Not surprisingly, forty-five-year-old David is active in the Democratic Party and the American Civil Liberties Union. In contrast he expounds a hard-nosed business philosophy that seems almost out of place compared to his liberal politics: "I try to make it a philosophy never to sell something I can't make money selling and I stick by my guns." He goes on to illustrate the tough side of book distribution. "That sounds kind of simple but, in the book business, people are always trying to get you to buy things at the worst price and sell them at the worst price—and they try to get you to pay for things before you can tell if they are really going to sell." He says that he has to be constantly on guard about purchasing risky or overpriced inventory; something he tracks with a computer to keep a weather eye on the company's finances and by signing all the checks for payables personally.

David remembers the most memorable day in his business as "the first time I could pay myself!" Talking from the porch of his house overlooking Puget Sound with the seagulls squawking overhead, he explains what has made him successful. "The main thing in any business is just sticking with it and never giving up. You have to be devoted and determined not to work for anyone else. You have to be willing to put in long hours for no pay. You have to use technology in smart ways. I think the biggest motivation for most successful entrepreneurs is to not want to work for someone else. They work doubly hard to avoid that." He has this advice for budding homemade millionaires who haven't quite got down to starting their ventures: "Never give up, the main thing is sticking with it. Remember the trite but true adage: If at first you don't succeed, try again. Just keep bouncing back. You have to take chances, but they should be *calculated* chances."

If you are interested in obtaining back issues of underground comics or a catalog of popular books handled by Homestead, you can contact Homestead Book Company at:

P.O. Box 31608

Seattle, WA 98103

Phone Number: (206) 782-4532

While you're at it, why not order a copy of *Eastside Eats*, if you're interested in the authors' first foray into publishing—there are still a few copies available and we're sure David would love to get them out of the inventory.

★   ★   ★

Video Script Writer Opens His Own Show at Home

Profile: Jim Hatfield

Company Name: Jim Hatfield Productions

Year Founded: 1988

Homemade Business Secret: If you like what you do, you can start a business based on the skills you have already developed in other jobs. There is no need to do something new unless you want to.

Business Profile: Jim writes scripts and produces videos for PBS (Public Broadcasting System) and for organizations and companies. He also trains people to look and sound good during their television appearances.

Start-up Capital: $10,000 from his first job with PBS and a severance package from his last employer. Most of this was spent on computer equipment.

The Office: Initially started in a spare bedroom. As the business grew, an addition was made to the house, funded with a home-equity loan. Jim describes his office as highly organized, thanks to the endless efforts of his wife.

Working Hours: Jim adjusts his working hours depending on the work load. Some of his time is spent shooting informational videos on location. He works all night when the business demands it.

Home Office
Technology: Initially resistant to using so much as an electronic typewriter, Jim now employs a Macintosh computer with a fax modem.

Family Profile: Married and has two sons—one a senior in high school and the other a cadet at West Point.

Education: Jim has a bachelor's degree from Grinell College in Iowa and a master's degree in journalism from Columbia Graduate School in New York.

Favorite Pastimes: Jim plays the trumpet for several bands. Trumpet practice is a regular part of his business day.

It's difficult to make it through a week's worth of the *Wall Street Journal* or a single issue of *FORTUNE* without a company or corporation spokesperson decrying how American workers aren't loyal to their companies. Of course, these industry pundits rarely look at the issue from an employee's point of view. Workers know that the all-too-common reward for years of loyalty and dedication is an unceremonious layoff whenever the economy tumbles or the company's fortunes take a turn for the worse. But there are remedies for the suddenly pink-slipped employee who has not only served his or her company well but has used that time to hone skills and build a trade or field of expertise. Jim Hatfield is just such a guy.

Jim took the skills he had developed through years in the television broadcast industry and put them to work for himself. Like many successful home-based entrepreneurs, it was a sudden layoff that got him thinking about working for himself. Jim was initially surprised at the cancellation of his weekly documentary "Two on Two," which Jim describes as a "baby Sixty Minutes," created for Chicago's TV Channel 2. As Jim puts it, "It's something I should have seen coming. Along with a change in the station's marketing, our station became particularly concerned with profits." Once his show was canceled, Jim found himself without a job, and he already knew from his year's experience in broadcast TV that getting a new job with another station would take time and likely force him to relocate to another town or city—something that neither he nor his wife wanted to do.

Then—a lucky break: One of Jim's contacts from CBS offered him a scripting job! He was asked to create the script for a PBS episode of *On the Waterway*. This, along with a small severance package from his broadcast job, gave Jim enough money to start his own business. But what to do next—rent an office or work at home? "I'd always wanted to start a business in my home. I decided that commuting two hours a day or more by train takes an awful lot out of your life. I think that for people starting out on their own, the fewer financial obligations they have the better off they're going to be."

To get his business off the ground, Jim began building on the network of people he already knew in the industry. Calling everyone he knew who might have work for him, Jim let his peers know that he was in business for himself and that his word processor was for hire. Worrying that his start-up capital would not sustain him until work came in, Jim's persistent marketing efforts began to pay off. As he explains, "One of the things you quickly find out is that it's very important to start contacting friends and associates who are in an area you want to go into. I did that right away and rather quickly developed relationships for writing."

As his business grew, in addition to script writing on his Macintosh computer, Jim began taking on other projects. He sold consulting time to teach people the techniques for looking good on TV and video. He also began taking on complete production jobs where he called all the shots and hired free-lance talent and contractors to carry out the nuts and bolts of assembling the video.

At fifty, Jim attributes his success to being good at what he does. This, along with his persistent efforts to build a network of contacts, has paid off handsomely. To ensure that his network is maintained and enlarged, Jim makes account contact a regular part of every business day. After reading the daily newspapers over a cup of coffee to keep up on trends and events in business, Jim spends part of every morning making calls and keeping in touch with clients and potential customers as part of his marketing push. Jim declares, "I still think the biggest mistake is to stop marketing yourself. One day you wake up and and realize you don't have anything to do today. You don't have anything to do tomorrow or even next week. Then you get on the phone and line up new work. But, my kind of work doesn't happen overnight. You have to be kind of relentless about it and devote some time to maintaining contacts and building new ones."

With Jim's success has come some interesting jobs for interesting people. He has written for stars including former CBS News anchorman Bill Kurta, actor Jason Robards, Mason Adams from the *Lou Grant* show, and travel guru Arthur Frommer. What does Jim think the future holds? "I thought about what would happen if somebody called me and said, 'We're starting up a national TV-based magazine. Do you want to come to LA?' I would say, 'No. We're living pretty comfortably right now and I would like to see my sons through school. I think we'll stay pretty small.'"

If you are interested in getting a script written for your company or group, you can contact Jim in Glen Ellyn, Illinois, at:
Phone Number: (708) 469-5690

★ ★ ★

Former Oboist Writes His Way to Success

Profile: Michael Boom

Company Name: Toxic Screen Dump, Inc.

Year Founded: 1984

Homemade Success Secret: It's appropriate to give up your first career if there is something else you want to do more. Just because you spent a lot of time learning how to do something doesn't mean you have to do it the rest of your life.

Business Profile: Michael divides his time between writing computer books and contracting computer manual writing to Silicon Valley firms.

Start-up Capital: The purchase of a computer and the time to learn how to use it.

The Office: In a room with an attached bathroom on the bottom floor of Michael's two-story house. Michael's office has a view of a golf course from two large front windows.

Working Hours: Up early to log onto computer networks and make phone calls. Michael visits clients at least once a week to assure them that even though they don't see him much, he's hard at work.

Home Office
Technology: A Macintosh IICI for writing projects and a fax machine. Michael also has two workstations on loan from companies he writes for, including a Sun SPARC Station and a Silicon Graphics Personal IRIS machine.

Family Profile: Michael is married to a ballerina, Lynn Morton, who runs a ballet school. Children figure important in their future, though they have none right now.

Education: Michael has an MFA in music, specializing in oboe performance, from California Institute of the Arts. (Mike hangs his diploma above his toilet.)

Favorite Pastimes: Bicycling and mushroom hunting in the Oakland hills.

Toxic Screen Dump, Inc. wins our award for the most uniquely named company in this book, and the company's thirty-seven-year-old founder, Michael Boom, gets the best title award by referring to himself as "Head Honcho" on his business cards. Mike authors product manuals for companies located in California's Silicon Valley. Computer books that explain how to use software packages or ways to put computers to work are a growing genre, and can be lucrative for writers who can bring life and accessibility to technical topics.

The initial growth in computer books began in the early 1980s with many publishers jumping on the bandwagon to get as much on the shelves as possible. The result was a glut of poorly written, poorly researched books. After a considerable weeding out toward the end of the 1980s, the publishers were demanding better written and more organized manuscripts from authors. Michael is one of the new generation of computer book authors who believe in careful explanation of topics and attention to detail. While this may seem like an obvious approach to writing "how-to" books, many of the tomes of the 1980s were poorly written, full of errors, and missed their mark when trying to explain "computerese" to novice users.

In addition to writing books, Michael produces quality manuals for major technology companies, including Electronic Arts, Silicon Graphics, Sun Microsystems, Amiga, computer game and graphics software manufacturer Broderbund Software, and Unicode, Inc., a not-for-profit industry association. As Michael explains, "The trick is not finding work, the trick is finding interesting projects."

Trained as a classical musician, Michael had a fair career with major orchestras—but classical music is a hard way to make a living. While playing the oboe with the Los Angeles Chamber Orchestra, Michael started writing some freelance articles to make a few extra dollars. He purchased his first computer and began writing articles for computer magazines. "I got hooked on computers. After looking at some of the computer magazines, I realized that I could write better than they could—they were really atrocious." His first sale was made to *Compute Magazine* for which he received the handsome compensation of thirty-five dollars for his effort. Because the magazine paid (oddly) by the printed page, Michael decided to write a really long article so he could improve his compensation scale with the magazine. "I wrote a big thing on programming graphics on an Atari computer which was, of course, too long for any magazine to publish, but I happened to meet some guy at a party who was starting up a computer publishing line who agreed to publish it."

Michael moved to the San Francisco Bay area around the time this first book was published and decided he would rather write than play the oboe: "I love the music but it's very political and people get very personal in freelance music. Instead, I enjoy writing about computers and when you're a home-based business owner, you don't get involved in all the office politics." Upon arriving in the Bay area, Michael started sending letters to firms in the Silicon Valley and jobs writing computer manuals began to come in.

We asked Michael what the biggest reward is in running his home-based publishing empire: "I love technology and I love learning about it. I love learning new things. The biggest reward for me is working with the people who are developing new technology and being right on the front line of new developments. The projects that are the most exciting for me involve some radical new technology that I know is going to have a big effect on the way people lead their lives. The engineers I work with are very intelligent and have great ideas. I love talking to them about new technology."

Michael's advice to people starting up a home-based business is, "If you are in business for yourself, it should be something you truly love and are truly fascinated and challenged by, because if you aren't, you're not going to able to drive yourself to have the self-discipline to make a successful business out of it. If you're just doing it to make money or to get by, I think it will be very hard to have the inspiration to make it work."

Michael has sold a number of books to several major publishers and worked for a year as a columnist for *Computer Currents*. Michael's books include *Music through MIDI* and *Learn Microsoft Word for the Macintosh Now* written for Microsoft Press, and *Introduction to Windows 3.1*, coauthored with best-selling computer author Van Wolverton and published by Random House Electronic Publishing. We asked him how many manuals he has written and his response was, "Oh God— I've lost count."

If you have an interesting new technology that needs good documentation, you can contact Toxic Screen Dump, Inc. in Oakland, California by calling:

Phone Number: (510) 635-7723

★   ★   ★

Teaching Math a Better Way Adds Up to Profit and Independence

Profile:	Robert Codner
Company Name:	MCC Publications
Year Founded:	1988
Homemade Success Secret:	There are often innovations that people use in their jobs that can be turned into businesses on the side. Sometimes these side businesses can turn out to be more profitable than the regular job.
Business Profile:	Produces curriculum materials for high school and college teachers. The materials are sold direct to teachers and schools.
Start-up Capital:	$1,000 from a settlement of an auto accident. Instead of using the money to repair the damaged car, he used it to do some advertising for his products. Thus according to Bob, his business began "by accident."
The Office:	Initially started in an extra bedroom, but it got too small. A year ago he extended the house with a nine hundred-square-foot office. "If your office environment is too small, it's stultifying to the business."

Working Hours: Bob still teaches at Evanston High School, because he loves it. He teaches from 7 A.M. until 1 P.M., then goes home and works until about 10 P.M.

Home Office Technology: Computers, laser printer, photocopier, CD-ROM reader, and standard office equipment.

Family Profile: Married; has a son and a daughter.

Education: Received his bachelor of science degree from University of Sydney, Australia with majors in mathematics and education. He started teaching in 1974.

Favorite Pastimes: He enjoys what he does so much that his work is his entertainment as well his livelihood. He also plays racquetball, a little tennis, and likes to run.

When Bob moved from Sydney, Australia to the United States because the country needed high school teachers, he started looking for better materials to use in the classroom to inspire the kids' interest in math. He found an abundance of materials at the lower levels, but a void of good examples, tests, and workbooks at the high-school and college level. So, he started writing materials for his calculus and pre-calculus classes himself. After a while, he realized that there were probably other teachers in the same situation. Bob figured they could use more good materials and once he extrapolated that, he just went ahead to see if he could sell the materials. He did a little research and learned about how to package the materials and advertise them. His beliefs were justified when the orders started coming in—indeed, there was a strong need for materials at the high-school and college level across the country.

Bob's goal in starting the company was to reduce the daily work load for math teachers so they can spend more time teaching and less time fumbling through files looking for sample questions, tests, and worksheets. Bob's motto: Ease=MC^2. Bob's teacher resource packages, student workbooks, multiple choice test packages, and complete solutions manuals are now being used by teachers in all fifty states, and in Canada.

Though his business is prospering, Bob still teaches high school full time. After talking with him for a while, it's clear why Bob's students warm up to him—he sounds like a regular Crocodile Dundee of mathematics, with a rich Australian accent and the dry sense of humor to match. Someday Bob wants to have a home in Sydney again—as well as a home in the United States. Bob could expand the product line into Australia as well—he'd call it the "Down Under Section."

Bob regularly used the spare room to grade papers—so it was natural to start up a business in that room. He began writing the materials in the summer of 1987, continued through 1988, and didn't make any real sales until 1989. Bob comments on his home working environment, "There aren't many millionaire teachers, so I started in my home because it's expensive to rent office space. I'm committed to organization in my mind, but my desk doesn't look too great—but I do know where everything is. I like my office at home. I have a UPS box by my door and shipping is done right from the house. It's very convenient. But you have to be careful when you have an office in your home that you don't spend your whole life there. There's always something to do, but you need to find time of your own as well."

The bulk of the orders for the training materials are seasonal, based on the academic calendar. When the orders are slower, Bob is developing new ideas and more products. With more than twenty products now, which are updated regularly, Bob is planning to expand to new subjects and additional media. He's negotiating with other teachers to publish some of their materials on the sciences to expand the line beyond mathematics, and he plans on developing video training materials in the near future. Originally called Mathematics Criterion Center, he now calls the business MCC Publications to reflect the diversity of his product line.

Bob also wrote a book called *From Teacher to Tycoon*, which he published and sells through the same 800 number he uses to market the teaching materials. The book was written to inspire teachers to expand their horizons and their incomes. Bob's biggest phobia is that he'll end up like so many teachers who become "fossilized" in their careers. According to Bob, "It is all they see, all they do. They have no practical experience—and can't, or won't, do other things to expand their horizons and possibilities. I want to be someone who can do and I want other teachers to know they can do it too."

As the business expands, it's harder for Bob to be the one-man operation he used to be. "My role has changed a lot since the business first started. I started with a little Apple computer, which was actually quite primitive by today's standards. Now I have automated as much as possible, with the ordering, invoicing, and packaging. I designed the computer programs myself to make them efficient. I used to package all the orders every day after school and then drive them down to UPS. Now I delegate that work to others. I have students help me package and mail materials and I arranged to have the UPS people come to my house to pick up the packages. Now I am diverting more of my energy to creating new products and dreaming up new things. I enjoy thinking of new things that will make classroom teaching more effective and efficient."

Each year the business has grown at a surprising rate. Bob ponders this for a moment. "I think it goes to show that you can discover a niche that makes sense for you, no matter what area, something you like yourself, and you can be successful if you just hang in there. Even if it doesn't take off at first, if you stay with it, you can make it after four or five years."

In the final analysis, Bob doesn't view success as a destination, but as a journey. "There is no such place as success. You never get to the destination, so you have to enjoy the journey." According to Bob there are three key elements to anyone's success, that he describes in his book, *From Teacher to Tycoon*: First you have to have a plan. It doesn't have to be typed up, but you need to know where you are going. Second, you have to have passion for what you are doing. If you don't like what you are doing, you'll never succeed. And third, you have to have perseverance. You have to be willing to learn new things. For example, Bob's skills in advertising were almost nonexistent when he started. He had to learn to write the promotional materials and produce them in such a way that would compel people to buy his products.

Bob is convinced that anyone with the three P's of plan, passion, and perseverance will ultimately prosper. "It doesn't matter if you work at home or an office, it's your willingness to try things and take some risks that count. Most people fail because they don't take the first step to get started and they aren't willing to make a few mistakes along the way. I really didn't know what I was doing at first, but I was willing to learn from my mistakes."

At some level Bob is still surprised that the business actually worked and is still thrilled with the feeling of satisfaction that comes from building something of your own and selling it to others. As Bob points out, "It takes a lot of work. Others see me and think, 'Oh, he must be lucky.' But it's really just a lot of work." Bob also gets great gratification from going to conferences and meeting teachers from all over the country, from Hawaii to Massachusetts, who come up and tell him how much they appreciate the materials. "It's impossible to describe how gratifying that is, to be known and recognized. The business is not just the money. The gratification makes me want to continue even more."

Even through the recession, Bob anticipates a lot of growth for MCC Publications. "We had a drop in sales over the first few months this year, for example, but I just worked harder and this year we will still do even better than last. We'll just keep adding more products and more media to keep things going."

Bob gets many of his product ideas from being in the classroom. He sees his role as a practicing teacher as an important part of the success of his products. He actually uses the materials he sells. Bob complains that the big publishing houses have people who write their materials who haven't even stepped into a classroom as an instructor, or it's been years since they have. "Without direct experience in the classroom, you just can't tell what will work."

As a businessperson, Bob has a desire to continue to learn more about business and marketing. Marketing is key to Bob. He is constantly reading about new marketing approaches and asking people about better ways to do things. He ultimately plans on giving seminars for small businesses to share what he has learned with others—once a teacher, always a teacher. Bob's first advice for new entrepreneurs is simple, "Go for it. Do it. So many people have brilliant ideas, but they don't get off their tails to do anything. They are just too afraid. Take some chances—you'll be rewarded more than tenfold."

Bob believes many people have just given up on the American Dream today. For all the doubters out there, Bob wants people to know that it's still possible to start with nothing and make it on your own. We concur with Bob. In Evanstan, Wyoming, the proof is alive and doing well.

If you are interested in obtaining a catalog of MCC's products or if you'd like to order a copy of *From Teacher to Tycoon*, you can contact the company at:

MCC Publications
P.O. Box 2061
Evanston, WY 82931-2061
Phone Number: (800) 334-3173—24 hours a day

In Search of a "Real" Job, a Genuine Opportunity Is Discovered

Profile: Dan Siemasko

Company Name: Siemasko Program Development

Year Founded: 1989

Homemade
Success Secret: The side jobs people take on while looking for full-time employment can often be the source of a full-time business. It's just a matter of changing your perspective from being an employee to being the boss.

Business Profile: Develops and produces training, employee development, sales promotional programs, and other prepared media communications for a wide range of companies. One of his newest products is "video newsletters." Dan also teaches script writing and program development at Duquesne University.

Start-up Capital: Just a few thousand dollars saved from some freelance jobs that kept him going while he still thought he wanted a corporate job.

The Office: Two small bedrooms upstairs have been converted to a homey program development headquarters.

Working Hours: Whatever it takes to get the work done.

Home Office
Technology: Fully-equipped windows-based computer and lots of software for writing, drawing, designing, and producing program materials.

Family Profile: Married; has a son and daughter, both grown and on their own. Also has a cat who is regarded as a business partner.

Education: At thirty-six, finished his bachelor's degree in communication and went on to get a master's in communication from the University of Pittsburgh. Also had technical training while in the military.

Favorite Pastimes: Enjoys spending time with his wife the most and travels a little, when he can.

Though Dan isn't quite a full-fledged millionaire yet, he clearly demonstrates that workaday skills can reap big profits—and because his concept (and income) is growing so quickly, we decided to include him in the book to inspire unemployed people with corporate mentalities that they can transform their ordinary business skills into profitable enterprises—and many of the victims of downsizing and reorganizations are being forced to do just that.

Now forty-nine, Dan Siemasko turned a mid-life crisis into major potential. But it wasn't planned that way. A long-term staff employee of Fisher Scientific in a media department, Dan was on the streets after they eliminated a one hundred and twenty-person communication department and reduced it to eighteen people. Dan recalls, "They eliminated the entire video section, of which I was part, and put us all on the street. Like an addict I went looking for another organization to work for, because in my mind people who worked on their own were second-class citizens, not good enough to find a real job. I left with that bias and therefore ran around looking for work and taking some part-time assignments in my search for another full-time position. People would say, 'Well, we don't have a job for you, but we do have this project we are working on, would you be interested? Can you help us with it?' So I would do the project, still waiting to find a 'real' job. I was appreciating working on my own, but didn't realize it.

"Then I did find a real job, and it was working for a small ad agency—I felt like I was stepping down. The job seemed temporary. After ten months, I realized I would be better off on my own. In the back of my mind I was still looking for a bigger, better job. I was merely making some money in order to fill the space."

When asked when he knew he had a real job on his own, Dan recounts this story. "I had always relished this one corporate position here in town and the script I was playing in my own head was that I lost that job, but eventually this international company, DDI, a large training company in Pittsburgh would hire me. I was working free-lance and they tried me out on some free-lance assignments. I sacrificed my rates with them, and did everything I could to get them to notice—but they did not have an opening at first. I was courting the position there for a while, meanwhile working free-lance, and then the dream position opened. I went through an extensive interview process, and that day while they toured me around and showed me the cubicles and pointed to the cubicle that would be mine, I got visions of Charleton Heston in the movie Ben Hur, being down in the galleys with his legs chained to them, just rowing. On the spot I realized I couldn't do it. The feeling rose from deep inside and by the middle of the interview the man across the table said, 'Are you sure you want this job?' He nearly said, 'You seem to be wasting my time.' And from my gut it just came out, and it was odd to hear from this Catholic boy, 'I'm not wasting your time any more than you are mine!' at which time I knew the interview was over. And when I walked out of that building, I knew I was on my own.

"I've had no doubt thereafter. I didn't want a job in a corporation anymore. Once I put my mind to it, I grossed $50,000 the first year, then $80,000 the second year, and now much more. I charge $65 an hour and I offer a discount for long-term projects. A typical job is about $3,000. The game when you charge by the hour is to see how many billable hours you can add up in the day. I promote my work, but most of my jobs are repeat business."

Dan has found working out of the home easy and natural. His two children have grown and moved out. His only complaint is when company comes: "It's hard when guests come to visit, because the people expect to come to someone's home and instead they are staying in my office. That's the only trouble. I find it very natural to get lost in my work here at home. I don't have the trouble others seem to mention about managing time or the temptation to just kick back and take a day off. My compulsive nature and greed keep me going."

Dan specializes today in "program development." According to Dan, program development is something very special and unique to his approach. A program in Dan's definition is a well-prepared communication event. "Program development means I help design and write prepared corporate communication, such as video scripts, audio tapes, computer courses, articles, brochures, and live speeches. My clients include biggies like Alcoa, PPG, and Westinghouse, and more modest organizations like Carnegie Mellon University and the University of Pittsburgh. Basically, I serve local executives, managers, educators, and media people interested in constructing solid communication, education, and sales promotion presentations." As examples of his program development successes, Dan cites the scripting of a series of quarterly video newsletters, a program that shows physicians how to most sensitively tell family members of the death of a loved one, a capabilities brochure developed for a high-tech firm, and a leadership development program for Aetna Life and Casualty.

Dan is quick to point out that he is not a writer. "Today I focus on program development and subsume writing. That is, while my competition may continue to offer writing services, my attention goes to all those wider questions involved in turning ideas into effective programs, such as, Are we really doing the right things? Are we doing it as well as we can? Are we spending our resources wisely?—that sort of thing."

If there is one word that makes Dan's approach different than other writers or producers it is *collaboration*. "People call me back because what I did worked. I am finding through collaboration and working closely with someone that what that person gains is another pair of hands and company—so a project goes smoother. The job needs to get done fast and well, and my success has something to do with being able to help these people get the things done fast and well—but also with keeping them involved in the process at the same time. That is a new dynamic in the relationship with clients. People want to be part of the creative process and to work with you on it. I think it's because companies are more team-oriented than they once were."

Dan's ability to use desktop technology to his advantage is another factor in his prosperity: "I'm convinced my success is in large part due to the presentation of my products. In the presentation business, looking good seems as important as being good. While most of my physical scripts are never seen by the more public audiences I serve, my behind-the-scenes script drafts are my products to my clients, so I jazz up all my documents. How can anyone in the business ignore the ease and power of desktop publishing their paper items? I produce most of my business stationery on my system. I designed the logo, scanned it in, and use it on nearly all my laserprinted products."

Technology also facilitates the collaboration and responsiveness Dan attributes to his success. Here's an example in his own words: "Last week, for instance, a banking officer who knows he can rely on me in a pinch called to see what I could do overnight. Templates I've developed in my word processor made it a cinch. The next morning I faxed him my work and he was able to review it and make changes in the minutes he had before going into a meeting. His secretary faxed me and I faxed her back. The revised sheets were ready for my client when he got out during a break. He walked into the next half of his meeting standing tall with a handful of handouts, published up-to-the-minute."

Dan's growth is due in large part to word-of-mouth accolades and return clients, though he does send out a brochure and information packet that explains the program development process and he frequents technology trade shows and meetings of professional training organizations, where he meets new contacts. Dan's wife will soon be joining the business to handle the growth. In the future, Dan intends to expand the types of programs he works on, and to be more selective in his choice of assignments. The goal is to do fewer ready-made assignments and to spend more time initiating projects that he personally considers important. Dan is already developing a program on program development—a product he hopes to sell in the near future.

It's Dan's hope that "program development" is one day a major in some college or university curriculum. He wants to share what he has learned with others, and to this end he teaches courses in script writing and program development. "Working with students forces me to articulate my notions. There's a book growing in the notes I'm taking."

Dan is now one happy, satisfied corporate dropout with a secure future and lots of new opportunities. "More than ever before, I'm doing what I like and what I like to do is useful to others." Whether you make a million or not, that sounds like a "real" job to us.

If you need help with a training program, brochure, video, or speech, you can contact Dan at:

5636 Pocusset Street
Pittsburgh, PA 15217
Phone Number: (412) 421-6717

CHAPTER 6

Should You Stay Home-Based or Expand to an Outside Facility?

For inventory-intensive companies such as Ben & Jerry's Ice Cream or The Office Furniture Broker, or manufacturing-intensive companies such as Blooming Cookies and Baskets, staying in a house or apartment would have seriously limited the future growth of the business or constrained the kinds of products or services that could be sold.

For these reasons, some of the people in this book were forced to leave the home office for larger quarters. In most cases, the transition was a positive experience. By opening a store or moving into a factory or office, it made them feel like they'd finally made it. Or, for others, moving out made their lives easier because the business was taking over their lives and domiciles. One entrepreneur finally gave up the home office because she realized that to attract really large corporate clients the company needed an office with a prestigious address. As she put it, "Big companies know that an address in the seven thousand block is not exactly the Gulf+Western Building." For her the move brought larger companies with deeper pockets and the transition from home-based to office-based business was essential to growing the company from the million-dollar mark to multimillion-dollar mark where it is today.

For the majority of the homemade millionaires who left home, the move was not made out of choice but because their business ventures grew at a fiery pace that made transplanting the businesses to bigger quarters an inevitable consequence of success. Bob Wallace (Arizona Sun): "My entire living, dining, and family areas were just packed with boxes, a labeling machine, caps, and whatnot—you could hardly move around our house." One entrepreneur who experienced this kind of growth was genuinely pained at the prospect of leaving her comfortable New York loft in which her organization had blossomed from a one-woman enterprise to a million-dollar business in just a couple of years. Her success meant she could no longer fit the eight people, computers, and enough telephones in her ten-by-ten-foot office to meet the demand for her services. In fact, so comfortable with the home office were she and her staff, that they spent *nine months* looking for an office that still had feelings of home.

But what of the companies that choose to stay at home? Most people started their businesses at home for a simple reason—they couldn't afford an office, storefront, warehouse, or manufacturing plant. Most people contemplate moving out of the house at some point, but many decide to stay at home because they simply like working there. These people don't want to give up the flexibility of their home offices. For the businesses that require more room as time goes on, some entrepreneurs just build additions to their houses or, in some cases, build new houses to accommodate the office requirements. Others control the growth of their businesses to be able to stay at home.

As one former *FORTUNE* 500 executive who is now a homemade multimillionaire explained to us, "I already pay a mortgage payment and a phone bill and a heating bill, why pay all these bills twice so I can sit in an office all day? I bought my house because I like it and my wife and I made it as comfortable as possible—we raised our kids here, too. So, I want to work here, play here, sleep here, maybe die here. I drove to work twenty-six miles each way for fourteen and a half years before I was laid off. Nobody's going to make me rent an office and force me to commute again, even if the commute is around the corner. Besides, I get to go home for lunch when I walk down the hall." Attention office brokers and leasing agents: You can skip this guy when you're soliciting new business!

Home offices have distinct advantages for many businesses— though it is important that the home office is ultimately large enough and fully functional. Consider the fellow who lives in a modest two-bedroom townhouse which he shares with his wife and young children. His company easily made enough money last year for inclusion in this book. He runs the business out of his dining room which is open to the living room and the kitchen. He likes working at home to be near the family, but he has no space and little privacy. He can't afford to buy a bigger house yet (he lives in a very expensive city, where an ordinary tract home is more than $500,000). Besides, in his current house, his family and his wife's family all live nearby and the close presence of both families is an important component to their lifestyle (and the family baby-sits sometimes when work stacks up). Considering the limitations the home is placing on his work, and we love working at home as much as anyone in this book, we'd recommend an office on the outside—at least until he can afford that house he wants to build.

★ ★ ★

Arizona Entrepreneur Makes Money Under the Sun

Profile: Bob and Ellen Wallace

Company Name: Arizona Sun

Year Founded: Research into Indian sunscreen aids commenced in 1980. The company was incorporated in 1982 and the products began shipping in 1983.

Homemade Success Secret: Never say quit, no matter how impossible the problems may seem. There is always a solution if you put your mind to it.

Business Profile: Arizona Sun makes specialty suntan lotions, moisturizers, sunblocks, sunscreens, shampoos, hair conditioners, an entire line of outdoor clothing, beach bags, and earrings.

Start-up Capital: $4,000 in savings. "We went to get a $5,000 loan but were turned down by twenty-seven banks. The twenty-eighth bank finally loaned us $1,000. We're still with that bank today because we're very thankful that they were there to help us start."

The Office: The company was started in a five-foot-square space in a lawnmower shop. As soon as possible, the business was moved into the house as a respite from the greasy lawnmower parts. "Our entire living, dining, and family areas were just packed with boxes, a labeling machine, and caps and whatnot—you could hardly move around our house."

Today, the finances, payroll, and employee scheduling for the company are still handled at home but because of the sheer volume of products being bottled, the manufacturing is completed in a plant.

Working Hours: Appointments at 6:00 or 7:00 A.M. and into the office by 7:30. The day runs as late as 9:00 P.M. seven days a week. "Whatever it takes to move the thing forward."

Home Office
Technology: Faxes, copiers, and computers with accounting programs to manage payroll, receivables, and inventory. A second computer is used to manage Arizona Sun's mail-order program.

Family Profile: Bob and Ellen are married and have two children. They have a dog, a soft-coated Wheaton, and their daughter has a pet rat named Lucky: "Lucky to be alive because he didn't get used by someone as snake food."

Education: Bob has a bachelor's degree in communications from Michigan State University and "almost a master's in marine biology and almost a master's in entomology." Ellen has a master's degree in education from Michigan State University.

Favorite Pastimes: Hiking in the desert and Bob loves sailing and snorkeling.

One of the most intimidating aspects of opening a home-based business is wondering how you can possibly compete against large, established competitors. From the outside, it looks like the big guys have all the advantages: established products with market recognition, entrenched distribution channels, and more money than you have to promote the products. The heavier the competition, the more overwhelming the prospect of failure—because in many markets, there are already more goods and services available than the market really needs, so adding one more product is a ticket for a trip to the bankruptcy court.

This didn't stop insurance salesperson Bob Wallace, however. He entered a market that is one of the most difficult and overcrowded of any we can think of—skincare and sunscreen products. While it's true that concern about damage to the skin from ozone layer depletion has people scrambling for such products in greater numbers than ever, the competition includes everyone from huge multinationals such as Revlon and Cheeseborough Ponds to boutique product companies that sell their wares in upscale department stores and specialty shops. Of course, it may have helped that Bob got started on his kitchen table and sold his very unique sun and skincare products in sun-bleached Arizona, known by armies of tourists for its warm, sunny winters and swanky resorts.

But we're getting ahead of ourselves. Let's let Bob explain how the business got started as a way to make some extra money on the side: "The original purpose was to give my wife $100 a month in extra income through selling bottles of lotion to the tourists and the resorts. Ellen was a teacher of emotionally impaired children and we were expecting our first child. Ellen wanted to stay home but she also wanted a part-time job. One night we were having a couple of beers around the kitchen table and I told Ellen, 'I'll set it up for you and you go ahead and service the thing and you can make $100 a month on it.' That's all we needed at the time."

Well, it made a lot more than a hundred dollars a month. Today Arizona Sun is big business—but how did Bob and Ellen deal with the competition mentioned earlier? They took a time-proven approach: Make a product that's superior to the competition and concentrate sales in a niche area that sells a lot of expensive skin products. The Arizona resorts were perfect for this because they house a lot of upper-class sun worshippers who visit during the winter.

As forty-one-year-old Bob explains about his enterprise's unique suncare products, "Our products are made from plants and cacti of the Southwest. It took me a number of years to learn what the Indians used to protect their skin. I figured that several thousand years ago they couldn't drive their ponies up to Osco Drugs and so my products are basically made with plants and cacti and that makes them unique. The artwork on the front of the labels makes them probably the most beautifully packaged products in the world. It's done by Steven Morath—he's a very famous southwestern artist with galleries all over the United States. The fragrance used in the products is actually from the plants and cacti that are in the product and it is a very different fragrance than other products on the market. Between the logo and the fragrance, by the time they get it on their bodies, people get hooked. Then they find out how good the product really is." Now that's how to establish a beachhead in a market full of competitors!

Once the products were formulated, Bob tested variations of the mixture in conjunction with a chemist and other professionals. After he verified its safety and effectiveness, he would do some hands-on market research to see what people really liked. As he explains, "Every week I'd go out to grocery and other kinds of stores and men and women would come walking out and I would run up to them and stick our product in their faces and say, 'What do you think of this?' No billion dollar marketing research program!"

One other positive attribute we've heard over and over from the people in this book is a drive to succeed and overcome problems no matter how insurmountable they may initially appear. Where some people would throw up their hands, the homemade millionaires just get going and fix the problem. If they have to stay up all night for a week to devise or implement a solution, they'll do it—just like that. And Bob Wallace is no exception. He once received a huge and potentially very profitable order, but thought it would be impossible to fulfill. Then he sat down and came up with a method to hand-label 500,000 bottles of his product in just eight hours.

Here's his story. "I came in the office one day and we got an order in for a half a million bottles to the tune of about $200,000 and at the time I couldn't even borrow $5,000—so that was an incredible amount of money. I moved very quickly because the order had to be filled in a total of a few weeks. If I didn't fulfill the order I would owe them $200,000 and I would also owe everyone else for the ingredients and packaging. But without any credit I talked my manufacturer into getting trucks ready to go. I talked my label-making guy from Texas with no credit at all into getting a half million labels shipped in by air freight. In other words, he stopped his presses to get me my stuff. I got my bottle guy, my cap guy—everybody stopped what they were doing to get me stuff just on my say so, which to this day I find to be incredible. And then I didn't know how I was going to get that many labels on the bottles because I didn't have the money for a machine at the time. So, I came up with an idea of having a little wooden platform for attaching the labels to the bottles.

"There's a big church near here and I figured they had hundreds of kids in their social group. I called this guy and I said, 'Listen do you have two hundred teenagers down there? If you can have them ready at eight o'clock this weekend in your social hall, I'll come down and provide a disc jockey and pizzas and subs and I'll give you a check at the end of the day for $1,000. Would you like that?' This guy thought I was a call from heaven. His comment was, 'Do you realize how many carwashes we would have to have for years to make that kind of money?'

"Everything arrived that Saturday morning as planned. I sat up on a platform and showed the kids what I wanted them to do. By five o'clock, they had finished up the order. Saturday the truck drove the bottles to the manufacturer and in two weeks he had the entire 500,000-piece order filled, capped, and boxed, I had my check in for $200,000, and I paid everybody off. That original big order kind of launched the company to the next level."

Though the first story seems remarkable enough, with another 500,000-bottle order, the labels began peeling off because of defective glue. Bob and Ellen worked twenty-four hours a day "until we couldn't see anymore" on a cardboard table at home repairing all 500,000 labels "so we wouldn't lose any money."

It's no wonder that in 1991 Arizona Sun was designated by the SBA as Arizona's Small Business of the Year and honored at a ceremony at the White House by President Bush. With the kind of dedication the company exhibits and its phenomenal growth, it's easy to see why Bob explains the formula for success this way: "Just put one foot in front of the other. Just keep walking and walking and walking—no running. Like I tell everyone, if you lift up enough rocks, under one of them, there's going to be gold."

If you are interested in obtaining an Arizona Sun catalog (and a free trial-size bottle of their moisturizer), you can contact the company at:

Phone Number: (800) 442-4786

★   ★   ★

Two Former Execs Get Off the Ladder to Take Control of Their Destiny

Profile: Janis Best & Ruth Kintzer

Company Name: Best & Kintzer

Year Founded: 1988

Homemade Success Secret: Do business like a business person, even when you work out of your dining room.

Business Profile: The company is a full-service catalog production house that creates catalogs for the fashion industry. Their clients include department stores, manufacturers, and mail-order clothing companies. The company continues to double its revenues each year.

Start-up Capital: No money was used to start the company. Instead Janis and Ruth used their savings for living money until the business "found its feet." "When we began, we had to think about how many pencils we were going to buy. There was literally no help from anybody."

The Office: The first office was the dining room table in Ruth's apartment with a filing cabinet stored in the living room. Recently the office moved into an office in downtown Manhattan after finally outgrowing the apartment. The office still has the feeling of an elegant home, however, with living area and comfy furniture.

Working Hours: 10:00 A.M. to 6:00 P.M. Ruth says, "Corporately I personally worked a seventeen-hour day, six or seven days a week and I don't want that any more. Because we're small, don't have meetings, and don't waste time, we find that we do much more work during the day than when we worked corporately."

Home Office Technology: Fax machines, copier, and computers for writing, and financial analysis.

Family Profile: Both Janis and Ruth are single.

Education: Ruth has an MBA in marketing and advertising and Janis has a bachelor's degree in marketing.

Favorite Pastimes: Janis and Ruth have similar interests, including working out, reading, and taking in an occasional movie.

Janis Best and Ruth Kintzer had the kind of jobs most people would die for—six-figure corporate positions as executives in high-profile industries. They directed an army of busy assistants and scurrying secretaries from their plush offices right in the heart of Manhattan. Nice clothes, perfect grooming—they were a part of the highest ranks of the American corporate elite, positions that probably fewer than one in ten thousand American women reach in a lifetime of inching up the corporate ladder. Then, as so many Americans in all levels of management have found themselves in the last few years, Janis and

Ruth were on the streets heading for the unemployment office. Ruth was "let go" from her senior marketing job in the cosmetics industry after a management shakeout. Janis lost her job as a manager in a catalog company in the beginning of the most recent economic downturn when the fashion industry started cutting back on promotions.

New York is often pictured in the movies as a tough city in which to survive. The person at the top one day is holding out his hat the next day looking for spare change. At least that's how it goes in the movies. But the passion of these two women is contagious. Their energy even bounds over the telephone lines as you speak with them. New York could never get them down.

Neither forty-five-year-old Ruth or forty-four-year-old Janis were very excited about going back to work in corporate America. Like many of the entrepreneurs in this book, neither Ruth or Janis worked very well inside of corporations even though they were extraordinarily good at it. Ruth explains, "I was very talented and everybody loved me, but I was very naughty because I can't put up with the corporate environment—I needed to be in charge. I couldn't take direction well—I don't like to, it annoys me. I want to do what I want to do." Not wanting to deal with bosses again and established in an industry that was eliminating people right and left to make up for eroding sales and revenues, Ruth and Janis felt the chance of promotions to the top were increasingly remote.

Both unemployed and feeling dejected, they met again accidentally when Ruth began writing resumes on the side to make money. Janis, who needed a resume assembled, called Ruth. The old sorority sisters hadn't seen each other in seventeen years. After an hour of discussing the resume and an unpromising future, Janis suggested to Ruth that they go into business with each other. As Ruth explains when Janis asked her to set up shop, "I said, 'Oh okay, doing what?' Janis replied, 'I don't know, I'll think about it.' " Returning about a week later to pick up a draft of her resume, Janis told Ruth, "I know what we're going to do—we're going to do catalogs!"

Janis explains that she and Ruth had become so accustomed to hard work leading to success, that failure never really occurred to them. Once they had decided to commit to a business they just dug in and started work. As Janis related, "We'd been in business so long and we just never felt that we couldn't do anything that anyone else could do. So the two of us didn't know that we couldn't do it. We have such incredible perseverance that we don't know to give up—it's just not in our makeup."

So, Best & Kintzer was born. Ruth explains the idea behind the company. "There was a need for a promotional company that came from the client side, that didn't just do nice graphics and pretty pictures, but could actually help because they understood the fashion business." The business got started from Ruth's Manhatten townhouse because as she explains, "Janis felt that she needed to have a place to go every day. She had to make that adjustment from working corporately and having an office to go to. She needed to know she was going some place."

Initially business was slow and it was hard to drop the corporate lifestyle. "The first day we sat at the dining room table looking at each other. Well what are we going to do now?" Janis elaborates on what initially stalled the fledgling company. "We look back at it now and we can't firgure out what we did that first year. We don't know what we did but we did it everyday. We did it like we were reporting to work. We were so corporate we couldn't do anything else. We started to work on a business plan and a list of who we were going to contact, and began putting together mailings and making phone calls. We figured out the legal part of it and incorporated, and we got an attorney and an accountant."

But it took a year and a half to acquire a major client, one that Best & Kintzer still has today. This first big break came from a chain of fashions for larger-size women owned by an entrepreneurial women who supports other women in business. Starting out creating newspaper ads for the company, within a few months Janis and Ruth convinced their inaugural client to take a chance and let them assemble a catalog.

That first catalog was a huge success—and the client came back for more. Others saw the results—and soon Best & Kintzer had a portfolio of catalogs for premier names in the fashion industry. Today they produce quality, fashion catalogs for a wide variety of customers. With their intimate knowledge of the business and the market, they bring much more than just graphic design skills to their projects. Instead, they take the entire project off the hands of a busy client company and deliver a one-stop service that frees the client company from the intricacies of a catalog project. Clients appreciate that. As vibrant Janis explains, "Our clients tell us wonderful things—how much they appreciate us—how we turn on a dime and how we listen to everything they say. See, to us these are just normal business practices. But clients tell us that other people don't give that service. The people that we work with love to work with us!"

Janis and Ruth started the business in Ruth's dining room. After working with a few clients they realized they needed presence downtown to make the business grow. The fashion industry is built on image, and Best & Kintzer needed to develop one that reflected their talent and their success. Still, they had become accustomed to the comfort and freedom of the townhouse and wanted to keep the homey feeling they enjoyed. So, they leased a space on Fifth Avenue, and had the front room decorated like a fashionable home—complete with chandeliers and a sitting area. It isn't a home-based business any more—but it still seems like one when you walk into the elegant surroundings and settle into the comfortable sofa.

Their advice for prospective home-based entrepreneurs? Ruth chirps in, "First, they need to be sure that they're capitalized to the point that they can give themselves a fair shot. Most businesses fail not because it's not a good idea but because the people go into business without enough capital to weather the storms and to last until the money kicks in. Second, make sure that you're emotionally stable because there are tremendous mood swings when starting any business. You have to learn about that before you start the business and then you'll have a sense of what to expect. If you don't anticipate the hard times, you're going to give up before you should." Janis adds, "Try to seek out other people who are doing what you're doing, people who can help you through it. Otherwise, it can be kind of lonely at first." Well, it isn't lonely for Ruth and Janis any more—they have plenty of visitors in their swank office on Fifth Avenue and plenty of alternatives for the future. The "corporately" ways they follow are now their own.

If you need a quality catalog assembled, you can contact Best & Kintzer at:
156 Fifth Avenue, Suite 715
New York, NY 10010
Phone Number: (212) 229-0500

Former Flight Attendants Build a Million Dollar Cookie Monster

Profile: Ann King & Ashley Ghegan
Company Name: Blooming Cookies, Flowers, and Baskets
Location: Atlanta, Georgia

Year Founded: 1984 (though Ann started experimenting with the now-famous chocolate chip cookie recipe in 1974)

Homemade Success Secret: The first thing is to never give up. Then it's important to know who to listen to for advice—not everyone has your best interests at heart. After that, you must know when to expand your product line in order to prosper.

Business Profile: Blooming Cookies makes gift baskets of cookies and flowers.

Start-up Capital: The only start-up dough was the kind you make cookies with.

The Office: The business was started in Ann's bedroom with the help of her mother. The first cookies were baked in an old, unpredictable gas oven. In later years, the cookie business eventually flowered to the point that it left home for a regular plant.

Working Hours: Baking started at 4:00 A.M. in the early years to meet orders from Nieman Marcus department stores.

Home Office Technology: An 800 number for order processing and computers for bookkeeping.

Family Profile: Ann's single and has a dog named Alfred for whom they bake dog biscuit cookies on his birthday and Christmas. Ashley is also single.

Education: Ann has an BA in journalism with a minor in marketing. Ashley has a bachelor's degree in marketing.

Favorite Pastimes: Ann enjoys golf, tennis, and swimming.

You might say they are cookie-makers to the stars. The customers for Ann and Ashley's unique cookie flower displays include Madonna, Neal Simon, Bill Moyers, Emilio Estavez, Barbara Streisand, and the prestigious Neiman Marcus department stores. Orders for cookies come from as far away as Japan and the Union of Commonwealth States (previously the Soviet Union). Former flight attendants Ann King and Ashley Ghegan made a fortune this year selling custom cookie displays and cookie flower arrangements—and that's not exactly cookie crumbs!

Security as a flight attendant is a thing of the past. Layoffs in the airline industry are now the norm, not the exception. Ann, a veteran flight attendant with six years of on-again, off-again employment, felt she needed another source of income to back her up. She also felt that the job was boring. "The biggest challenge for a flight attendant is making sure that everyone has enough Coke or 7-Up." She started her first business on the side, writing a travel newsletter that was distributed to travel agencies for free. The travel agents paid her a commission for trips resulting from ads or promotions in the newsletter. With the success of the newsletter, she decided that a book was next on the agenda. She thought she'd use her newsletter profits to self-publish a guide to hidden honeymoon hideaways. Unfortunately, the person who printed the book incorporated a lot of mistakes and left off a Library of Congress number. As Ann explains in her gentle Southern accent, "The book was doomed—we lost about $70,000 or $80,000 on that. At that point I was basically broke, having gone from having whatever I wanted to not being able to go out to dinner with friends."

In the waning days of the failed book project, Ann saw what she thought were stemmed roses made of cookies in a store. She liked the idea and thought she'd try to make some of her own. But, as it turned out, the roses were really made of chocolate. "By the time I found out they were really chocolate roses, I'd already gone to the store and got the ingredients for cookie dough. So, I made some flower cookies anyway. I showed them to a friend of mine who was a buyer for Nieman Marcus. She said they were great and ordered them for the store, and that's how we got started."

The first commercial design was a bouquet of cookie flowers. Flower "stems" were created with wire and green tape and the cookie blooms were mounted at the top. Her friend ordered twenty dozen cookie bouquets for Valentine's Day without even tasting them. They sold so well that the store placed a perpetual order for ten dozen cookie bouquets a week.

Ann turned her home into a cookie factory overnight. "I put a board over my bed during the day and made cookie dough. I cooked on this antiquated gas stove that sometimes took seven minutes to cook the cookies and sometimes twelve. If I got an order from Nieman Marcus, I'd have to get up at four in the morning and start cooking. Sometimes they'd burn on the bottom and I couldn't afford to throw them away so I'd have to scrape off the bottoms. It was very creative. I didn't know where to get supplies from—I'd staple bags together cause I didn't know where to buy cellophane. It was a tough beginning."

And so it went as months turned to years. Working with an old oven, only three cookie sheets, and inadequate lighting at first, Ann often needed a flashlight to judge when the cookies were done. While making the cookies for Neiman Marcus, Ann started making extra bouquets and put a small ad in the Yellow Pages in the florists section. Then Ann began delivering her cookie bouquets door to door like a florist delivers flowers. As the orders grew, Ann moved from her home into a rented space and hired people to bake cookies from her recipes, because she couldn't afford a commercial oven.

In spite of the continuing growth in orders, Ann faced a major cash flow crisis in 1987 after a partner left who had been handling much of the financial side of the business. Finding herself about $100,000 in the hole, Ann begged her long-time friend Ashley to quit her job as a flight attendant to help her sort through the mess. Ashley, who had just finished a degree in business, was reluctant at first, but later jumped into the dough with two feet.

Ann and Ashley started by meeting with a series of lawyers and accountants who recommended the company go bankrupt and change its name. They noted that they had only been in the business four years and felt there was no way to pull out of the cash flow problems. According to Ashley, "We decided on the way back that we weren't going to go bankrupt. We made a list of suppliers, called and wrote each one, and made up a schedule for repayment. Finally we paid everyone off and the business just really began to take off after that." Once a decision had been reached to stay in business, Ashley began taking care of the bookkeeping, contracts with suppliers, and distribution services, leaving Ann to create new varieties of cookies and gift baskets.

Tenacity is one of the common characteristics of the homemade success stories in this book, as illustrated in this story from Ann: "This woman called from Simi Valley, California. She wanted ten baskets for the next morning but we were already cleaned up and closed for the night. Still, I want back and baked the cookies and we put everything together. A delivery service picked it up at eight o'clock at night and they were on their way. By ten o'clock the next morning, the people who had received the cookies called Ashley and said these were the best they'd ever seen (or tasted)."

Tenacity paid off for Ann and Ashley. A series of breaks came beginning in 1988, when word of mouth brought in several major show-business clients and the dollar volume of individual orders began to soar. Their clients just keep telling other people about the cookies and the more they charged for custom cookies, the more people seemed to come back for more. Clients started requesting diverse cookie shapes, displays, and new flavors as well. Ann recreated in $\frac{1}{8}$ scale, the Tara estate from *Gone with the Wind* in cookie dough for a Japanese studio executive. To add impact to the presentation, they lined the driveway of the house with edible Magnolia cookie trees. Another cookie basket was done at the request of Warner Brothers for Madonna's agent who was turning forty at the time. Ann explains, "They wanted a two-foot-high white cross with chocolate chip cookies. I went out and bought Madonna's album and made the white cross and then painted the album cover on a ceramic pot. The white cross then grew out of the pot. They literally fell over when they saw it."

As the company grew, Ann and Ashley were forced into larger quarters. They have expanded a number of times since Ann and Ashley got together in 1987. They now manage a complete cookie-basket factory with a responsive telemarketing team and corporate offices. Their latest twelve-thousand-square-foot facility allows them to turn out more than sixteen thousand cookies daily.

As part of their strategic plans, Blooming Cookies, Flowers, and Baskets now offers national delivery. You can order arrangements created in a variety of holiday and gift themes that will be shipped overnight in a special box. For example, there's Blooming Boxers, cookie-filled boxer shorts for every occasion, a spa basket containing natural bath products and cookies, and Potted Greetings, hand-painted flower pots filled with cookies (or real flowers) in holiday motifs. The arrangements are packaged with festive bows, ribbons, and cellophane. The cookie-basket combinations can be ordered for almost any theme or personal interest. They are also creating a new line of environmental gifts with natural cosmetics and ecology-minded packaging, designed to make people more aware of the earth's resources. And of course, there are still bouquets that resemble the traditional dozen roses in a gold box with red ribbon.

Ann and Ashley have recently signed an agreement with the New York-based 800-FLOWERS gift-by-telephone network to ship all their basket orders almost anywhere, overnight. All the orders are shipped from their Atlanta headquarters. You can also place orders by calling 800-BASKETS and 800-GOODIES, which are subsidiary numbers for the 800-FLOWERS network.

Ann and Ashley offer this advice for budding homemade millionaires: "Start off slowly and do as much research on whatever you're going into as possible. Then just keep at it until it works. And don't ask so many people for advice that you get confused. Others may not know what's best for you. You need to make it your own business."

Afternote: Ann called us to report that an arsonist torched their facility only a few days after our interview with them. But like the typically persistent entrepreneurs in this book, Ann reports that they have already hooked up their phone lines and are temporarily making cookies with another baker. Since many of the TV news people in Atlanta buy their cookies, the fire gained a lot of local press coverage. That resulted in a rapid increase in sales as sympathetic viewers sought to help the company out and more people learned of the incredible, edible arrangements. In fact, they have expanded their telemarketing efforts again—and are looking at another expansion to keep up with the growth.

If you want to order delightful and tasty cookie-flower baskets for your friends and family, you can contact Blooming Cookies, Flowers, and Baskets direct at:

502 Amsterdam Ave.
Atlanta, GA 30306
Phone Number: (800) 331-9141

Entrepreneur Saves Company By Chasing Truck!

Profile:	Nora Mulholland
Company Name:	The Office Furniture Broker, Inc.
Year Founded:	1982
Homemade Success Secret:	Avoid owning inventory when you start out.
Business Profile:	"We buy, sell, and rent quality office furniture and systems. We specialize in Herman Miller Systems."
Start-up Capital:	"There wasn't any!" Nora believes that the people who work for her are her best asset.
The Office:	Sharing a 950-square-foot condo with her sister, Nora used an "old cheap roll top desk" as her home-based office that was placed in her sleeping quarters. The company quickly outgrew the bedroom arrangement and moved into more conventional quarters in a warehouse.

Working Hours: 7:30 A.M. to 6:30 P.M.

Home Office
  Technology: Originally, the business included only a telephone and a calculator. Today the business has several computers, a copier, and a fax.

Family Profile: She is single.

Education: Nora has a BS from the University of Ohio in business management. She keeps up with business through a continual program of reading and seminars.

Favorite Pastimes: Golf and learning the piano. Nora has also chased a truck or two in her lifetime!

Nora got started after getting fired at her last job in July of 1982 at a new furniture dealership. As she puts it, "I had been fired for an entirely political reason and I was in the middle of installing a $300,000 order the day I got canned. I didn't see it coming—it threw me for a loop completely. I didn't see why it would be different in any other dealership environment." But rather than laying down and feeling bad about it, she decided to get even by bouncing back and laughing all the way to the bank. Nora decided that she didn't want to be an employee again and decided to set up shop on her own.

Nora started her business this way. With the model of her parents' real estate business in mind, she chose to open her business as an agent rather then as a buyer or seller of high-ticket goods. "My parents were both in real estate and I used that concept to start this business because I didn't have any money." Her approach allowed her to start her company with less than $30 in start-up capital. The money was used to purchase a Polaroid camera for $29.95 with which she opened her company.

Camera in hand, she went around to people with office furniture to sell and photographed their goods, mounting the resulting instant photos into a photo album which Nora describes as her "traveling showcase." Nora marched the album around town to people looking for a good deal on office furniture. If a prospective buyer was interested in any of the pieces, Nora then arranged a meeting between buyer and seller where the buyer could see the actual piece of furniture before purchase. She explains, "The whole business was started on a consignment type basis where I didn't buy any of the product. I merely acted as a broker." This was the humble start of a million-dollar business!

Nora discovered that one of the lowest risk ways to open a business is to avoid purchasing any inventory. She simply arranged for buyer to meet seller and then took a percentage of the resulting sale. This is an especially effective method for keeping costs down when selling high-ticket items such as cars, pianos, furniture, and houses—because all of the risk is in the hands of the owners rather than the person who puts the deal together.

Today the business has changed into a more conventional used furniture company where Nora owns most of her inventory. "That consignment is how it all got started. In today's market the consignment part of our business accounts for less than 3 percent of our overall sales—we buy it all now."

Thirty-nine-year-old Nora describes the qualities that she feels made her successful and how she "rethought" the industry to come up with a new approach. "I think that I have really strong leadership capabilities and I don't know where that came from. I have both feet very well planted—I'm very logical and use a lot of common sense. I started in the used furniture business in a completely professional way. At that point there was nobody in the business—the concept of used office furniture was a broken down metal desk in the back of someone's warehouse with two inches of dust on it. Today we have people walk into our showroom every day and say, 'No, we want to see *used* furniture—they can't believe that the furniture we have is used."

But for a fortunate few in this book, the path to success was not usually paved with gold, and it hasn't all been a bed of roses for Nora from Day One either. With two unsuccessful partnership arrangements and an office manager who accidentally erased all the company's records from the computers, Nora has been through several serious crises that, as she explains, would have put anyone with more sense out of business. A fighter at heart, Nora successfully picked up the pieces and put Humpty Dumpty together again.

In another misfortune, a client tried to make a midnight move of furniture acquired but not paid for because as Nora puts it, "I failed to cross the Ts and dot the Is in the contract." After hearing rumors that this person planned to pull a fast one and leave town, Nora sped down in time to see the truck containing her furniture leaving the warehouse. Speeding after it in her tiny Honda, running red lights through downtown Denver, she knew that if she lost sight of the truck her money and probably her business were gone. She finally caught the truck at the company where the shady client had sold the furniture. Screaming at two burly truck drivers, with the help of the second purchaser who, as it turned out, had bought the furniture in good faith, Nora finally extracted payment from the original "purchaser." Another victory for Nora!

Nora has this advice for those who would like to follow in her footsteps by turning nothing into something big. "The most important thing is not to be afraid to ask questions and get advice. It's amazing how many people in all different walks of life are really willing to help an entrepreneur."

So if you lose your job, instead of feeling low and beaten up, do as they did in the movie *Network*, and yell, "I'm mad as hell and I'm not going to take it anymore!" Then, like Nora, go off and build a business so successful that it makes your old company seem like a hotdog stand in comparison.

If you are looking for a good deal on office furniture, you can contact Nora at:
4905 Nome
Denver, CO 80239
Phone Number: (303) 371-4542

★   ★   ★

How Can You Start a Garage-based Business if You Don't Have a Garage?

Profile: Marian and Richard Levy

Company Name: Pac Expediters

Year Founded: During the 1970's

Homemade Success Secret: Go where your customers are and do the things they do. Only in this way can you understand their needs.

Business Profile: Pac Expediters packs and ships fine art for galleries, museums, and corporations.

Start-up Capital: $200, and some leftover lumber and nails.

The Office: The business was started in a carport. With its immense success and the lack of expansion possibilities from the carport, the Levys now run the business from an ordinary warehouse.

Working Hours: "As long as it takes—we're open 9:00 A.M. to 4:00 P.M. officially, but during the art season, we work twelve hours a day."

Home Office Technology: The regular office equipment, including a computer to track shipments and customers.

Family Profile: The Levys are married and they have four kids. One of their daughters is now a principal in the company.

Education: Marian has a bachelor's degree in special education from Brooklyn College and Richard has a bachelor's degree in traffic management.

Favorite Pastimes: "We enjoy art and Richard is a golfer." Marian enjoys music and travel as well.

One of the amazing aspects of the businesses profiled in this book is that when we asked the founders how they got their start and where the ideas came from, more often than not, fate, chance, circumstance, and fortune appear to have played only a minor part. But in the case of the Levys, fortune appears to have stage-managed the entire affair. Marian and Richard came to Arizona largely by chance and they stumbled on the idea for their very successful business when acting on a whim.

Originally living and working in Brooklyn, New York, the Levys and their four children decided they needed a change. Fifty-year-old Marian explains with just a hint of the Brooklyn twang left in her voice, "We just had to get out, no matter what. My husband was going to California to look for a home. The car broke down in Arizona and I was still in New York with the kids. New York people have heard of California—the only other places besides New York are Florida and California. So the car broke down in Arizona and that's basically how we ended up there. He just fell in love with it once he saw it."

The Levy's enterprise, Pac Expediters, packs and ships art for major galleries, museums, and a handful of corporate clients, including semiconductor giant, Motorola. But like many of the other success stories in this book, the Levys got started on a shoestring. As Marian explains, "We started in the carport—we didn't even have a garage. We were real happy but we were real poor. My husband would make the crates and put them on top of the car. He'd then take them to the galleries and pack the goods in the gallery. Before we came along, each gallery did things its own way. Some of them would save and reuse crates. Others would have some guy come in and build crates. My husband, who worked in package transport in New York, began walking around the galleries and started asking, just out of curiosity, 'When you ship something, how do you do it? What if one person came in and handled the whole thing for you?' Their response was great! We picked up our first client that day, and they're still with us."

Why couldn't Mailboxes, Etc. do what the Levys do? Well for one thing, the company was just starting up when the Levys began their business, and for another, fine art requires special expertise to ship it safely. Many of the pieces are extremely valuable. Shipments of artwork require special tracking to ensure that the packages arrive promptly at their destinations. Replacing a priceless Van Gogh lost in shipping is not only an insurance company nightmare but also a consequential tragedy within the art world. While paintings are not extremely fragile unless they have glass used in their frames, damage by heat, pressure, and water can ruin them. Other kinds of art, such as sculptures, may be made from fragile materials such as blown glass or ceramic or be oddly shaped, requiring a sophisticated custom crate for safe shipment. Marian names some of the artists' work that her company has shipped. "Last week we shipped Monets, Cezannes, Renoirs, Rembrandts, and a Degas—all in one collection. We're insured through Lloyd's of London. It's a fascinating business!"

We asked how they price their services assuming that the bill for dispatching a Gauguin would be quite a bit more than shipping the work of an unknown Sunday painter, but Marian explains that the fee is based simply on the size and weight of the object. "Our price remains the same—it goes by the size and packing prices and the weight for shipping. We pack Grandma's painting that she made for her grandchildren the same way we pack a Renoir. The most unique piece of art we ever packed was a full-size papier maché cow. We've also packed for the FBI. We shipped Indian pots that were obtained illegally from digs to a trial in Santa Fe. We've shipped guns that were used in murder trials. We also ship for a lot of movie stars: Robin Williams, Robert Redford, Gregory Peck, Goldie Hawn, and we've shipped to the Pope and two presidents. Oh, and Mother Teresa, a lot of embassies, and the Smithsonian." When we asked how she packs a full-size cow, Marian replies, "Very carefully!"

What is the key to success as an art exporter? "We promote ourselves heavily. We go to art shows and meet the artists. We send flowers to each new gallery opening—one of our customers opened his third big gallery so we sent a violinist to the opening—a 'violinogram' if you will. Since it's a Western gallery, the musician played Western tunes all night. This business is a labor of love for us—it's a business of course—but we love what we do and we love the artwork." When Marian was asked if she'd ever quit the business she retorted, "When I die!"

If you are interested in shipping your art collection you can contact Pac Expediters at:

3020B Ashby North Scottsdale Road
Scottsdale, AZ 85251
Phone Number: (602) 946-5004

★   ★   ★

Her Stuffed Animals Are Not Toys

Profile: Kaylee Nilan

Company Name: Beaver Valley

Year Founded: 1982

Homemade Success Secret: If you can turn your skilled crafts into collectibles, you can charge more for the goods. In the same vein, you can turn a bad situation into an opportunity if you learn to depend on your own skills.

Business Profile: Beaver Valley makes high-quality stuffed animals priced from $600 to $2000. Each creature is unique and hand-made, making them very collectable. The business grew 42 percent last year alone.

Start-up Capital: A sewing machine, $200 left after a recent divorce, and motivation to support her two kids.

The Office: The business was started in an apartment living room. Today Kaylee still works from her home designing and managing the company, but she has two small production facilities with several employees to help her assemble her beasties.

Working Hours: Kaylee bemoans, "Long days, sometimes 8:00 A.M. until 11:00 P.M. in the early years."

Home Office
Technology: In addition to the sewing machines and related equipment, the business employs a fax, photocopier, and a light table.

Family Profile: Married again; Kaylee has two children from a previous marriage.

Education: Two years at the University of Washington and flight training to get a license as a helicopter pilot.

Favorite Pastimes: "I used to play tennis until I started to build this business."

The creation of stuffed toys was once the domain of loving mothers and grandmothers making huggable pets and dolls from their sewing rooms across the country. Stuffed toys became major business when the teddy bear, named after President Teddy Roosevelt, became a national passion after its introduction early this century. Two notable firms, Steif of Germany and Ideal Toy Company of the United States were fueled by the sales of stuffed bears. For many years, the stuffed toy industry was the province of major toy companies who produced their huggable animals in plants in the United States and Germany and later sent much of their manufacturing overseas to countries such as Taiwan and Hong Kong, where the labor was cheap and abundant. But a few dedicated seamstresses and stuffed toy lovers keep the craft alive, assembling superior animal designs from the comfort of their homes. These stuffed animal aficionados create their own patterns and add elaborate costumes and accessories, like eye glasses, umbrellas, and jewelry.

Today, Kaylee Nilan is the successful proprietor of such a home-based business—where she designs and produces collectable stuffed toys. Her business has grown so fast and been so successful, that while she still designs her critters and runs the business from home, she has had to hire several employees and open two small production facilities to keep up with demand.

But, it wasn't that way when she started. After her marriage ended in 1982, Kaylee found herself broke and alone with two children to support. While the average person caught in such a situation might head for the welfare lines or take a serious look at a low-paying job at a fast food outlet, Kaylee chose to open her own company. With only a couple of hundred dollars (all she had left) and her sewing machine, she decided to start a business designing and producing stuffed animals. Setting up shop in the living room of a small apartment, she began designing and tailoring her unique line of animals. As Kaylee explains, "The biggest challenge of running this business from my apartment was a constant lack of space." She describes her apartment home office as very cluttered. We asked Kaylee why she decided to run her business from her home instead of from a conventional office or factory. Like the answers from many of the successful entrepreneurs in this book who started on a shoestring, "I couldn't afford an office," was her reply.

Kaylee's first break came when she was offered the opportunity to share space in a booth at a wholesale gift trade show for toys. The space cost $80—and this small fee gave her instant access to a large market. Hundreds of distributors looking for wares would be in attendance. She signed up a distributor at the show and set to work in earnest creating her creatures. Kay says, "Each animal takes a full day to create. Bryant Gumble bought one of our bears—he's a collector of American folk art. We call our product stuffed American folk art and a picture of the animals appeared with him on the cover of *USA Today*.

Kaylee continued to show her wares at wholesale trade shows and sent out flyers to likely buyers in retail outlets of all kinds. Eventually the designs started getting a reputation all their own and people asked for the animals. Actress Whoopi Goldberg, Jenny Craig of diet-business fame, and rock-and-roll stars own Beaver Valley critters. Kaylee explains, "Everybody has a line of bears, but we make stuffed animals of all kinds. They are expensive because of the amount of work. They are priced at more than $200 each, sometimes ten times as much. The quality and uniqueness makes them collectable."

As more and more outlets began selling her wares, Kaylee decided to open production facilities outside her home because she had outgrown the apartment a long time before. Kaylee opened her first outside facility in 1986, but kept design under her control at home while delegating the production to a handful of carefully selected employees. "The kids have been great as well. They have ideas all the time. My son had an idea for a piece so we gave him a percentage of what we made on the design. A business consultant I work with told me about a study that looked for the qualities that made people successful in business. It turned out that it wasn't the amount of education people had or the amount of money—it was whether their parents had been successful in business." Not surprisingly, Kaylee's parents also owned a successful business.

What does the immediate future hold for Kaylee's Beaver Valley?

"We have a distributor lined up in Europe but it will take a while to set up all the import/export paperwork. This is really a critical year for us because we've grown so much. We finally got a line of credit from the bank—but it was like pulling teeth. All of our growth has been self-funded. We are talking about adding a full line of more popularly priced animals and going into other kinds of merchandise lines to grow the business in other directions."

Kaylee has this advice for budding home-based businesses: "There are so many ways to do something without much money. Find out as much as possible about others who are doing what you're doing. Find out how they are doing it—get as much information as you can—so you're not reinventing the wheel or making something that is already being made cheaper somewhere else that you can't possibly compete with."

If you are interested in learning more about Beaver Valley stuffed animals, you can contact Kaylee and her company at:

Beaver Valley
P.O. Box 678
Etna, CA 96027
Phone Number: (800) 397-5147

★ ★ ★

Houses for Equestrians Is Not Horse Play

Profile: Ron and Michele Johnson

Company Name: RJohnson MD Barns, Trailers and Equipment, Inc.

Year Founded: 1989

Homemade Success Secret: Respect your customers. If you want your customers to keep coming back, the Golden Rule is always the first order of business.

Business Profile: The company designs and builds complete animal containment and exercise facilities, from dirt work to the buildings. They market a modular barn and custom facilities that can be adapted for anything from a backyard horse facility to professional stables. They also build enclosures for dogs, llamas, and ostriches.

Start-up Capital: Ron sold his twenty-three-foot motor boat to finance the company. "It was either that or starve to death."

The Office: Converted a bedroom into an office, with two desks, a phone, some file cabinets, and a typewriter. A year later, opened up a sales office to display products and supplies and because the business needed more presence with the customers. "We would have liked to stay at home, but the customers wanted to see our work."

Working Hours: Seven days a week they start at 7:00 A.M. Office hours are 9:00 A.M. to 6:00 P.M. Either Michele or Ron is in the office every day of the week.

Home Office Technology: Just got their first computer and are trying to get the records on the system.

Family Profile: Married. They have a grown son who is not involved in the business.

Education: They graduated from high school.

Favorite Pastimes: Camping and riding. "I don't have time for a boat now, but we'll get another one someday."

Ron and Michele sell enclosures and design facilities for horses and they couldn't imagine doing anything else. The business is simply in their blood. Ron grew up on a family farm in Ohio. When he wanted to make a move in 1972, he came out to Arizona to check things out and made the Scottsdale area his home. Scottsdale is an upscale community known for its opulent resorts and winter sunshine—but there is still plenty of open land and lots of horse acreage around the city. In fact, there are still hitching posts in downtown Scottsdale for the avid riders to tie up their steeds—just like the Old West we see in movies.

When Ron came to Arizona he hooked up with a company similar to the one he owns today. He stayed with that company for seventeen years, but ultimately did not agree with the company's philosophy regarding marketing and service. Because the business was a closely-held, family affair, Ron felt stymied. One day he just decided to do it on his own so he could do things the way he wanted, without the bosses over his head.

Ron, fifty-four, has deeply-felt, country pride in what he does. He is happiest when he is delivering a quality product to his customers. "There's nothing really exciting about the work. I build a quality product and deliver it on time. I just love what I do. When I left the other company four years ago, it never occurred to me to try anything else."

Though the horse supply market is dormant, maybe even shrinking in Arizona, due to the recession, Ron's business is strong and still growing. The Johnsons attribute their success to the service they provide. According to Ron, "Our service supersedes anybody—on delivery dates, completion dates, and personal service. We do what we say we're going to do." Ron also points out that they offer a quality product that is superior to anything else on the market. The modular enclosure systems they represent provide a safe environment for the animals and are priced competitively. Most of the components for their modular enclosures are bought from outside sources. Ron then uses his years of experience and deep-felt love of animals to configure the best, most affordable enclosures possible.

Speaking in the slow, intentional manner of a midwestern farmer, Ron explains how he got started. "I advertised in some tabloid magazines that cater to the horse people in the area and announced the new venture. Then we attended horse shows and handed out cards, flyers, and did whatever was needed to let people know about us." Ron's first customers were people who already knew his reputation for service and delivery from the other business. Things just took off from there, because the Johnsons worked seven days a week and any hours necessary to make things happen.

The business is definitely a family operation, and Ron and Michele have a well-defined routine. Michele mostly handles the books and Ron handles the sales, though Ron is quick to note that Michele can sell a product as well as he can if she has to. The respect the two have for each other comes through loud and clear.

Ron and Michele started their business at home to save the overhead. "We had space and were already making the payment, so it made a lot of sense to start at home. The only difficult thing, the thing that I was uncomfortable with, was that people needed a direct view of the products. When you build buildings, you can't very well show them the product from a back bedroom or in a photograph. The first thing our customers said was, 'Where's your office?' We heard this so many times, we got a larger facility outside the home. I wouldn't have got an office outside at the start anyway—it just costs too much. I still think what we did was best, even though it caused some problems and embarrassment at first. Working at home is ideal, as long as you and your partner get along, like we do and you have the self-discipline to make things happen. There are days I believe we should have stayed in the house, for the convenience and lower overhead, but we wouldn't be as far along as we are if we hadn't made the move to a larger facility."

For the few hours when the Johnsons aren't working, they have three horses for pleasure riding. They don't show or train horses, because Ron doesn't want to alienate people with specific breeds. They just ride the trails around the area and enjoy the horses. "You can't sell to the equestrian marketplace if you don't love horses yourself." Ron is one with his market and knows what his customers want. "Animal lovers have a different outlook on life and different feelings inside. The kinds of customers I have have more heart than other people, and they expect honesty and integrity in the people they deal with."

Always deliberate and considerate in his tone, Ron is one of those steady people rooted with basic values. He is an uncomplicated, straight businessperson who avoids trickery in favor of service and integrity. If there is one thing that the Johnsons are all about, it is about doing things the right way. There are no corners cut in any aspect of the business, whether it's paperwork, licenses, insurance, or the product itself. As Ron points out, "It costs more to do things right, but I'd rather do it that way than take a chance of losing a customer or hurting an animal." Ron's success formula is consistent with the rest of his commonsense approach to business. "There are no gimmicks to success. It just takes plain hard work, believing in your product, and enjoying it."

Ron delivers buildings and furnishings around the West and Southwest. Though equestrian facilities and horse furnishings are the mainstay of the business, Ron and Michele have recently branched out into other types of animal facilities, including dog, llama, and now ostrich enclosures. There are growing numbers of people speculating in ostriches. Right now, the birds are just being bred to increase the numbers. Ultimately the breeders intend to sell feathers for decorative purposes and skins for shoes and boots. Ostrich meat is supposed to be good eating as well. According to Ron, "It's getting to be big business and our enclosures are very appropriate because of the competitive price and safety features for the animals."

Ponderous in his response when we asked him about the future, Ron takes a conservative look at his business and it's potential. "I'm not overly optimistic about the future, but I think we'll continue to grow. I would like to get involved in more off-the-shelf products. I would like to be the person people think about when they think of horse furnishings and enclosures."

Ron and Michele offer plain, time-proven advice for others who want to start their own businesses. "Throw your clock away and forget about resting on the seventh day. Don't wait for the phone to ring—you've got to go out and kick the bushes to make things happen. Ten years ago, if you had any product, you could succeed. It's like mining gold. It used to be if you went out to mine gold, you could find it laying on top of the ground. In today's market you have to dig for gold, and maybe you'll find some. That's the difference the economy makes on the way entrepreneurs have to approach their businesses." In 1992, Ron and Michele grossed more than $1.2 million—so it looks like they have a pretty good sense of where to dig for the gold in their own business.

If you have horses, llamas, or ostriches that need a barn or enclosure, you can contact Ron and Michele at:

P.O. Box 14887

Scottsdale, AZ 85267

Phone Number: (602) 465-9000

The Ultimate Iced Tea Makes a Very Cool Business

Profile: John S. Martinson and Daniel Schweiker

Company Name: Restaurant Tea Service, Inc., d.b.a. China Mist Tea Company

Year Founded: 1983

Homemade Success Secret: Find something that nobody else does and then do it so well that no one else can compete.

Business Profile: The company blends and packages China Mist iced tea, a gourmet iced tea for hotels, restaurants, and other food service operations. The tea is formulated to be brewed in fresh iced tea brewing machines, which are also designed and distributed by the company. A line of specialty, flavored teas is also available. They plan to take their teas to the retail marketplace in the near future.

Start-up Capital: They each put in $300 to get started and had some leftover equipment from Dan's coffee roasting business, including a triple-beam balance scale and a small packaging machine.

The Office: They started on the kitchen table, moved to the garage, and are now growing out of a five-thousand-square-foot office and warehouse facility.

Working Hours: Now it's five days a week and normal working hours; but it was whatever was needed when they first started out—sometimes that meant part-time and sometimes it meant twenty-four-hours a day.

Home Office Technology: Packaging machines, fax machines, a business computer for the accounting, and a Macintosh for doing all the advertising and promotional material.

Family Profile: Both partners were married within a few months of each other just last year. Coincidentally, both their wives are named Suzanne.

Education: John dropped out of college twice. Dan didn't complete his undergraduate degree, but he went to law school and received his law degree. He briefly had a practice in Iowa, but didn't like practicing law.

Favorite Pastimes: Dan is a fly fisherman and does most of the traveling for this business, including about thirty-one trade shows a year—that allows him to get in a bit of fishing on the side. John enjoys bicycling and plays tennis. Both are actively involved in the community.

In the South, West, and Southwest, iced tea is an important refreshment. In fact, iced tea is now the most popular beverage served in American restaurants. An alternative to coffee that has grown in popularity, iced tea is typically served in giant glasses, garnished with lemon, and endlessly refilled just like the coffee cups in an East Coast diner. Now, because of John, thirty-eight, and Dan, forty-three, people don't have to drink the bitter massmarket iced tea produced by Lipton and Red Rose—there is a smooth, fragrant alternative that is always refreshing.

Dan and John had both been in the coffee business and started the tea business out of desperation. Dan was losing his gourmet coffee roasting company and John was selling coffee to commercial accounts, but neither were making much money. John laughs as he explains the motivation for starting China Mist. "We were both going broke in our coffee businesses. I start businesses mostly out of fear. I've gotten fired from everything else I've ever done, mostly because I like to be my own boss and I don't like people to tell me what to do. Dan is a lawyer and he didn't want to go back to law. We really had no choice but to start a business again. We knew some things about the coffee and tea business and were anxious to learn more, and in talking we found that where Dan was weak, I was strong. So we sold our coffee businesses and went into the iced tea business to try again."

When Dan and John started there were no quality iced teas available for restaurants. There were only the bitter blends from Brazil and Argentina, made from ordinary tea bags or the oversweetened, artificially colored, instant teas distributed by giant food conglomerates. They saw the empty niche in the market and went after it. With a triple-beam scale from Dan's coffee store, some baggies for packaging the tea, some boxes purchased from U-Haul, and a lot of loose tea, the company was born on John's dining room table. They set out to make the ultimate iced tea. The tea was mixed by hand in big plastic trash cans. They weighed each portion on the scale and filled the baggies with the tea. John describes the development process like this: "We went through thousands of combinations before we got what we wanted. The proper way to taste tea, like wine or coffee, is to swirl it around in your mouth and then spit it out. You just can't do that all the time, so you end up drinking it and drinking it. There were a lot of sleepless nights from the caffeine while we were coming up with the recipe. We got a rubber stamp and some white labels and filled up the labeled baggies with tea. We called the blend the Restaurant Tea Special Blend, which it was called for about two years."

John still had some active coffee accounts and they sold the gourmet iced tea to those accounts initially. The first customer for the tea is still a customer, The Plaza Club in Phoenix. The Arizona Biltmore, another of the first customers, required twelve sales calls for John to convince them to take the tea—but ten years later, they are still a satisfied company.

Now the company's customers also include selected Hyatt Regency hotels, Jerry's Restaurants, Bombay Bicycle Clubs across the country, Westin Hotels, and almost all the Sheratons west of the Mississippi. And surprisingly, they do a lot of Burger Kings. "Burger King will spend a bit more for a better product because of the competitive nature of the business—but accounts like that are not the mainstay of our business. Most of our customers are small local chains and single-owner restaurants."

Most companies go into the retail business first and then go commercial with their food products. But John and Dan knew the commercial marketplace best. "We recently designed a retail package of the tea locally just for convenience, just because so many people started asking for the tea. I get two or three letters a week from people asking where they can buy the tea because they tried it in a restaurant." After phenomenal commercial success, retail distribution is in the plans, and, by the time you see this in print, you should be able to get China Mist teas in the market with pretty packages and some really unique things that John and Dan didn't want to talk about until the program was finalized.

John and Dan love what they do. Dan beams, "There are so many things that are wonderful about the businesses. It's an exciting business. I can come to work in shorts and a T-shirt. One of the most exciting things is putting other people in business, seeing the distributors be successful and putting their kids through school. The paycheck is nice and everything, but it is really exciting to see the other people succeed.

"We try to be the kind of suppliers we would like to have supplying to us. We teach local distributors how to sell to hotels and restaurants and then they distribute our tea. The tea-making machines are an important part of the product. We work with a local company, another home-based entrepreneur who at that time ran Coffee-Ins of America (now run by his son-in-law), and they make coffee and iced tea brewing machines in Phoenix. I used to buy coffee machines from them. We went to some big companies and asked them to modify some things about their machines for iced tea, but the companies said no. So we went to Coffee-Ins, and they said sure. We are now their largest customer. So, we've increased their business and they have supported ours and it's great."

As word got around about the superior flavor of the tea, the accounts grew. John took the tea around to restaurants, delis, and hotels. They were so successful in Arizona, they thought about expanding to other locations. A partner from one of John's other business ventures was his first distributor in California—A.J. Neiman—who helped them develop the marketing and sales training end of the business. "It was then that we developed the name China Mist, and developed a logo, and then we had a more appealing image than that conveyed by a product called RTS Special Blend. We never went into the business with the idea that we would go into national distribution. It never occurred to us when we started."

There is no question that Celestial Seasons has had some influence on the team—though John claims to be more inspired by Steve Jobs and Steve Wozniak because they did something that no one else had ever done—built a home computer. According to John, "They went head on with IBM and the big guys in the computer world. And we felt the same way about our tea. We went right into competition with Nestea and Lipton." John is the creative one and Dan is the more businesslike personality. John muses, "It's like Dan is the Jobs and I am the Wozniak in the partnership."

It quickly got cumbersome weighing out four ounces of tea into baggies and packing it into cases. So they got a packaging machine and set it up in the garage. They had to meet health regulations by sealing the floor of the garage and air conditioning it. As John remembers, "We were operating against the city codes, because you're not supposed to run a business out of your garage. After a while, we had eighteen-wheelers backing into the driveway every once in a while to pick up the shipments of tea, and we got a call from the zoning commission one day. They asked, 'What is it you're doing in your garage?' And my comment was, 'Oh, nothing.' We were out of the garage the next week and we sublet some space in a facility where the guy was making enclosures for outdoor pools. We took a corner of a warehouse and a desk. That lasted a couple of months because we didn't have a key and the only time we could get in was when the other guy with the pool business was there. We were constantly calling him to be there and when he wanted to leave we had to leave. Then, we got our first warehouse space."

The growth of China Mist was slow at first—but it's overwhelming now. "Our first year of business we did $3,000, but we were still encouraged. We knew we had something, we just had to let everyone else know we had something. We were closing 80 to 90 percent of the sales calls. Sales this year will be about $2.4 million. When we started we really did everything ourselves—the installations and the sales. I would hate to be doing it all now. Our first employee was a friend's daughter who helped us package the tea. The majority of our distributors are people who are like we were when we got started—they do everything and work out of their homes. In five years, we are going to be way up in sales. It took us seven years to get to a million in sales. It took us two years to go from 1 to 2 million. We are going to be a major force in the iced tea business nationally. We will be in all fifty states, and branch out into some close international business. For example, we do the Hyatt Regency in Aruba and have accounts in Bermuda, but we don't have distributors in those places." Based on this story, it's not surprising to hear John's advice for other entrepreneurs, "Don't quit, and don't let anybody tell you you can't do it."

As the business has grown, the roles of the partners have changed significantly. John explains, "Now we spend our time managing. That was the hardest and most important thing we had to learn—how to stop doing and start managing. You always feel like you are cheating when you aren't doing. You start to pay other people to do that thing that you used to do. For some reason when you initially make that first step to management, you feel like everybody else is doing the work, until you learn that management is work and is more difficult than you thought it would be. When we realized that we did not have the knowledge to bring the company up the stairs to growth, we hired a consultant to help us out. That is something I would recommend to any company owner, to push your ego aside, decide what is most important for the company, and then hire someone who knows what you don't. The consultant, who we gave some stock in the company, still works with us and his wife, who runs a home-based business, is our controller."

Dealing with success personally has been a personal challenge for Dan and John, mostly because they want to live a "regular" lifestyle and remain just like everybody else. John comments, "It's important for me from a lifestyle standpoint, to close the book on Friday evening and not even think about work again until Monday morning. There is more to life than just business. I went through a workaholic stage for a while, burned out, and then it was hard to get back into it. Learning to have balance in life is important. Finding balance in my life has been the biggest challenge."

Managing cash flow and using the money wisely to grow the business in uncertain economic times has been another major challenge for John in running the business. He glibly declares, "We forgot about the recession when we did all our business plans, and we still beat our projections. I don't know if that's luck or what, but it worked. Maybe we make good tea."

Both partners are very active in the community, sit on boards, and do fund-raising. Warm and generous, their employees regard them as family. John is like a proud father, too, when he talks about his employees: "We have given everyone a lot of opportunity. Our vice president and general manager, Rommie Dresher, now just twenty-three, started with us when she turned sixteen, while still in high school. Now she pretty much runs the company. She's in charge of all hiring, firing, and day-to-day management of the company. She's very savvy. She has no problem telling us when she thinks we're wrong. She is the third part of a triumvirate that runs the company. Everybody who meets her and knows her position in the company says, 'Every company needs a Rommie.' She's very loyal and hardworking, what more could you want."

China Mist still accounts for 90 percent of the business. The other 10 percent of the business is in flavored teas, including fiesta blend, mango, passion fruit, black current, peach, berry blend, prickly pear, Hawaiian spice, and strawberry. Several new flavors are in the works, including raspberry, mint, and possibly orange.

John believes that all people can succeed, if they put their minds to it. He offers this advice: "If you have some old family recipe or homemade mustard, or whatever it might be, you can create that product in your kitchen; you don't need a factory. Most kitchens more than meet health code standards. Canning and bottling are not that difficult. Then sell the product to your local stores, see how your friends and contacts like the product, and then go on from there. Do a business like that without jumping into it. Build it from the ground up—then jump into it with both feet. Pick one thing and do it absolutely the best you can. We were the only just iced tea company in the country. Other people have hot and cold teas—but we only do iced tea. We always try to be the best we can be and we are best at iced tea. You can't run a part-time business to be really successful, but it's important to lay some groundwork to get started. It doesn't take a lot of money to get started, but it takes a lot of commitment to get rich." If there's one thing John and Dan have demonstrated, it is a lot of commitment.

If you want to find a distributor for the ultimate iced teas in your area, write to China Mist Tea Company at:

14626 A North 78th Way
Scottsdale, AZ 85260

Saving Lives Leads to Savings in the Bank

Profile: Kay and Jim Zahn

Company Name: Arizona Security Control, a division of Alarm Screens, Inc.

Year Founded: 1982

Homemade
Success Secret: In bad economic times, look for business ideas in products and services that protect people's assets.

Business Profile: Provide twenty-four-hour monitoring of household and business alarm systems.

Start-up Capital: Nearly none

The Office: Starting out in a bedroom, they used the garage and the backyard for manufacturing. Kay and Jim no longer manufacture but with growth, they now work out of an office.

Working Hours: They are on call twenty-four hours a day.

Home Office
Technology: Alarm control panels send signals over telephone lines to the monitoring computers. The computers analyze the signals that come in or bring them to an operator's attention if the police, fire station, or paramedics have to be called.

Family Profile: Kay has a fifteen-year-old son from a previous marriage. Kay and Jim have a fifteen-month-old son.

Education: Jim and Kay went to college for a couple of years, but they don't have degrees.

Favorite Pastimes: They used to have more time for technical climbing (they honeymooned by rock climbing in Yosemite); now it's a twenty-four-hour business. They collect baseball cards as a family.

Only in their mid-thirties, Kay and Jim Zahn have secured their future by making other people's lives more secure. In 1992, they will have made about $620,000 in security system monitoring fees. According to Kay, "Since we got into the monitoring business, the business has been doubling or tripling every year."

Their story is straightforward—based on hard work and a business they knew. Here's how Kay puts it: "My husband's family has been in the alarm business for generations, starting with his grandfather. His father owned an alarm business. A cousin had a screen alarm business in Florida. On a vacation when we stayed with them, we started talking about starting our own screen business in Arizona and they showed us what they were doing and we took it with us. They became our supplier of materials and we went home and figured out how to build and market the product from home. We made up some business cards and some fact sheets about the product. Then we went door-to-door to all the alarm companies and just started doing it.

"We always wanted to work for ourselves. As a child, I don't remember playing house—I remember playing business. I had little notebooks and tried to get people to work for my little play store. I wasn't happy working as an employee, I wanted control of what I did. We realized as good as we could do was as good as our employer wanted us to do—the paychecks were ultimately limited.

"We made those screen alarms in our back porch and made a shop in the backyard. For about five years we built alarm screens. I worked for Coldwell Banker, in real estate, and my husband worked for alarm companies at the same time. After that first five years, we decided to take the plunge and I quit and Jim kept his job, and then we did that for about a year. Shortly after that, we went full-time into making alarm screens and got a small industrial space for manufacturing."

Then something happened to change the growth and the potential of the company. The company that Kay and Jim were contracting with to do the security monitoring went up for sale. The company was having some financial problems, and since their customers depended on this facility, they didn't want to see them go out of business. So, they simply bought the alarm monitoring business to service their customers.

Over the last two and a half years, the monitoring business has been so successful, they have stopped selling installations. They sold off the alarm screen part of the business and now they only provide monitoring services for other companies that sell and install the alarms. Here's Kay's explanation; "When we got a hold of the monitoring center, we loved it. It was so much more fun than the sales and installation side of the business. It's more exciting. It is a communications technology business, which is really growing. So we stopped doing installations, because we could afford to, and now all we do is alarm monitoring. "

Every day Jim and Kay save lives, homes, and property. Kay describes the satisfaction that goes beyond money: "We get calls all the time thanking us for saving a loved one who would have died if we hadn't been there. Every day we are doing something to help someone, so it's always rewarding. When we do our job and do it right, someone is very grateful for us being there."

The most exciting thing to Kay is just watching the business grow.

She explains, "In this business you make one sale and the revenue is recurring. The money multiplies as new accounts are added. I don't have to resell things—it's ongoing revenue. After you cover the overhead, everything is just pure profit."

As a businessperson, Kay is a "real person" with a lot of intuitive skills. In her own words: "I have learned to be a good businessperson. Because I don't take advantage of people, they don't take advantage of me. I'm not a suit. We are just ordinary people who have done well for ourselves. I am always comfortable—I work over the telephone, so I don't have to worry much about an image."

Kay expects the business to double or triple in size again in only a couple of years. Kay is modest about their role in the success of the business, however. "We didn't do this ourselves, the real growth has been because we have good employees who help us do a good job."

Kay understands the relationship of her business growth to the economy, as well. "We are in a good position right now—when the economy is bad, the alarm business does better, because people become concerned about protecting what they already have. Our industry is getting stronger right now. We were lucky to start in an industry that is going strong. We also have the guts to take risks. Quitting our jobs was a risk; buying the company was a big risk; we just bought a building, and that is a risk. We say, 'Let's do it now and then we'll work extra hard to make sure it works.' A positive attitude makes things happen. I never let myself feel scared, and it has always worked out."

To answer our question of advice for other business owners, Kay relates her favorite saying: "It doesn't matter whether you believe you can or you can't—you'll be right."

Kay and Jim and their staff provide monitoring services nationwide. If you are interested in obtaining information on monitoring services for your alarm system, you can contact them by calling Arizona Security Control

Phone Number: (800) 525-4829.

CHAPTER 7

Get Credible Information and Advice Before You Start

This book is not a how-to book, it is a book of inspiration and a book of possibilities. It does not present the best home-based businesses for you to try—instead it presents businesses that other people have tried and have been successful in implementing. In other words, if you try to copy someone else's success, step-by-step, you may not have the same results revealed in these pages. That's not to say you wouldn't succeed if you tried to write books, open a consulting agency, start a unique skin care line, or initiated other enterprises similar to the businesses in these pages—but you still need to adapt the idea and the execution to your situation and skills. You need to formulate your own idea and your own management style for your own business to succeed.

But how do you know if your own ideas are good ones? Well, when you do have a specific idea that excites you and you want to research the competition and the market potential before you get started, then there are places you can go to get information on the potential and the requirements for the business, as well as on the competition.

Check Out the Trade Magazines First

First, there are a number of books on home-based business opportunities. Some of these are good, but beware—if everyone interested in starting a home-based business reads the same books and chooses from the same lists, there will soon be a glut of similar businesses in the marketplace—and this may diminish the unique attributes that are so often necessary for home-based enterprises to prosper. That doesn't mean that there can't be other success stories in the same industry—but you have to be aware of the number of similar enterprises in the same area and you must have a clear idea about what will make your business different and better than the ones that already exist.

A frequent comment from the successful people profiled in this book is that you can never know too much about your profession, the competition, or the market before you get started. Many of the profiled entrepreneurs recommend that before you start your company, you should track down all of the magazines and newspapers relevant to your would-be profession and read them religiously. While you may think that no magazines cater to your kind of enterprise, with the enormous number of trade and specialty magazines, chances are that there are several publications that directly relate to your business and reading them will help you succeed. For example, if you were thinking of opening up a llama ranch on your home's unused acreage, you shouldn't be surprised to find *Llamas Magazine—The International Camelid Journal!*

There are several ways to track down publications that cater to your trade. You can visit a competitor and see what magazines are laid out on the table in the reception area and note the phone numbers for each one. (Look on the masthead located within the first couple of pages for subscription and circulation particulars.) A trip to a library or bookstore that offers a large number of magazines is another route, but to really get a handle on all the magazines and periodicals, look up a phone book-sized publication found in the reference section of most libraries called the *SRDS Guide to Magazines* from Standard Rate and Data Service. This volume lists just about every periodical for every industry.

In addition to industry-specific publications, more general interest magazines may be of use to you in your competitive and market analysis. Typically, several publications are available that cater to a broader readership such as small manufacturing companies, craft makers, and office technology. It helps to keep tabs on general business magazines as well. You may spot a trend that could be an opportunity for expansion and reading about others in business struggling with the same problems you're skirting can be a source of reassurance in times of rough seas. In addition to the obvious *Wall Street Journal, Business Week*, and *FORTUNE*, look up *Success, Entrepreneur, The Economist, Women Entrepreneur*, and *Home Office Computing*, which we'll talk about next.

Read these at the library if you can't afford to subscribe and keep in mind that many business or industry publications are available free to qualified readers by filling out a form that comes with the magazine. To "qualify" you need only be someone who buys products from the kind of advertisers that appear in the magazine. For example, in industry publications on computers like *InfoWorld* or *MacWeek*, you probably qualify if your company purchases computers or computer-related supplies occasionally.

Read *Home Office Computing*

While a growing number of computer magazines are beginning to run columns aimed at home-based businesses, one very useful publication for those starting (and running) companies at home is *Home Office Computing*. This is a magazine full of tips and how-to information written by home-based entrepreneurs for home-based entrepreneurs. In this magazine, you'll meet people like yourself, hear how they got started, and receive credible advice for making your business more successful. The magazine also features regular reviews and write-ups of home-office technology including fax machines, copiers, telephones, computers, software, and more. Since only products of use to home-based businesses are profiled, the magazine's reviews tend to cover only the kinds of products a home-based business is likely to buy. Best of all, the reviews of technical products such as computers are written for busy business people who need to get work done, not just the computer whizzes catered to in the computer trade.

Read Business Books and Listen to How-to and Motivational Tapes

One entrepreneur profiled in this book has a great plan for dealing with down days both in life and in her company—on a rainy day she heads to the library and curls up with a book on marketing, sales, promotion, or other business topics. On real bad days, she picks up a book on motivation or how to build and maintain a positive attitude. The payoff? The down days have become fewer and farther apart because the knowledge she has acquired at the library and the bookstore has been instrumental in helping her company reach homemade millionaire status. The motivational books have helped her to maintain a positive attitude even through trying times.

One related suggestion we heard from several people profiled was surprising, at least to us who have never tried this approach. These homemade millionaires buy a lot of motivational tapes on cassette and listen to them in their cars while running business errands or on the way to meet clients. They insist that these tapes keep them going and help revive their spirits if a deal falls through or when they seem to lack enthusiasm for their company. Maybe we should try a couple just to see what happens.

Join Clubs, Be Active in the Community, and Network as Much as Possible

Another piece of advice we heard frequently from the people in this book was that you should join a special interest society or club related to your business, even if it takes a chunk of change to do it. As Donna Hart (founder of *Parent & Child Magazine*) advises, "Join professional societies so you can take advantage of the knowledge of others in your field. These professionals are a source of ideas as well as business." Donna had to fork over $500 to join a society of publishers who specialize in how-to-raise-children publications, but she says it was worth it because other members have been there to provide her advice for growing her magazine when she's needed it and have been very supportive of her efforts.

In addition to advice, many societies and clubs provide events in which you can meet others that work in your kind of business. These contacts may be useful for locating new business and the idea sharing that frequently goes on at get togethers may provide you with information that can be used to improve business, find new customers, or work more efficiently. And having the phone numbers of a few people that operate similar ventures gives you someone to call when faced with a problem or a shoulder to cry on when required—we discovered that building a strong support system is an important component for most of the business owners we've interviewed.

Most cities have business clubs and entrepreneurial groups that get together for regular meetings or bring in speakers to discuss some aspect of business over lunch or dinner. Joining one or more of these organizations may provide you advantages similar to joining a professional organization. You may also pick up new business along the way, because many members of these clubs give their business to other members as a way of showing support for entrepreneurial values. There is usually an events calendar in your local newspaper that will list the meeting times and locations for business groups. The annual membership fees for belonging to these groups can add up—so consider only groups that allow you to "sample" a meeting or two without charge. Join only those groups where the business-building experience of the members is a step or two ahead of your own.

Another place you can find help, meet others like yourself, and chitchat about home-based business is through on-line services such as CompuServe, America Online, and Genie. This requires a computer and modem, but most home-based businesses will already own a computer and modem prices for a basic unit with basic software are now under $100. Logging onto CompuServe, you can meet working-at-home gurus Paul and Sarah Edwards (who are homemade million-aires who support other home-based businesses) and attend forums on working at home where the Edwards answer your questions and give advice to those getting started or running into barriers with their home-based companies. The cost of using these forums varies, but it is generally not very expensive.

Networking is vital for many of the entrepreneurs profiled and since networking is mentioned so frequently, we've emphasized it here. Some millionaires stake their entire businesses on their ongoing contacts, their work with community organizations, and other activities that get them in front of other people. If you work at home, it's very important that you are able to get the word out about your business—and networking seems to be one of the consistently cited ways of doing this, and it doesn't usually cost anything, except your time.

Don't Be Afraid to Get Professional Help When You Need It

As you read through the profiles in this chapter (and throughout the book), you'll notice that quite a few of the millionaires cite outside people who are brought in to bring the company to its next stage of growth or the use of government agencies to help formulate a plan or solve a financial crisis. These people were not afraid to admit their own limitations and searched out people who could help.

One source of widely available advice and even financial assistance is the Small Business Administration, a unit of the federal government (Canada has a smaller but similar organization). The SBA provides a wide range of services, from booklets to consulting to loans. They also have a library of literature available on request that explains the mechanics of starting and managing a small business. In addition, the business departments in major universities and colleges often provide business planning services. The SBA also supports the Small Business Development Centers on college compuses around the country. The SBDCs, which typically offer seminars and consulting services, vary in quality. The SBDC Connection is a clearinghouse for the centers and can provide you a list of centers in your area by calling (800) 633-6450. There are also privately funded, not-for-profit industrial development corporations that offer consulting services and seminars. These are hard to find in a phone book, but ask your local or state chamber of commerce about them. In fact, many chamber of commerce groups offer a small business division. Ask them about this when you call.

In many cities there is an unexpected source of extremely knowledgeable people—organizations of retired executives and senior military personnel. SCORE (Service Corps of Retired Executives) is one of these low-cost, high-value consulting groups. These groups will assign one or more of their members to you to advise you on running and building your company. Since these volunteers have spent a lifetime operating businesses of all kinds, their seasoned advice can show you new ways to solve vexing problems and assist you in maintaining control of your company through periods of rapid growth or when sales take a turn for the worst. Best of all, their advice is usually free or available at a very reasonable charge—the volunteers just like using their skills and keeping active. Otherwise this knowledge is available only through $150+ per hour business consultants who probably know less than these people do.

In the profiles in this chapter you will discover people who have been willing to ask for help when they needed it. There are many times in your own home-based endeavor when you will need to ask yourself, should I do it myself or let someone help? There is no pat answer. It depends on you, your willingness to look for answers and network with others, and the severity of the problems you are experiencing. The key thing is to realize that asking for help is not a sign of weakness—it is a sign of determination to succeed.

★　★　★

They're the Carpet Store at Your Door

Profile: Sandy & Joe Anderson

Company Name: Floor Coverings International

Year Founded: Sandy and Joe purchased their franchise in 1990.

Homemade Success Secret: Though the right franchise can provide the products and promotional materials to get you off to a quick start, it is still your own creativity, dedication, and basic business sense that are key to the profitability of the business.

Business Profile: Floor Coverings International franchisees such as Sandy travel to customer sites to demonstrate carpet, vinyl, hardwood, and other floor coverings right in the customer's home or place of business.

Start-up Capital: Less than twenty grand for the franchise and the purchase of a van.

The Office: A new room in their house with built-in U-shaped workstations for both Sandy and Joe.

Working Hours: Sandy runs the business full-time and Joe works part-time while he continues to run another home-based business that he plans to put up for sale. Sandy's day is typically 7:00 a.m. to early evening, depending on the number of scheduled appointments and the distance to be covered.

Home Office Technology: The usual—computer, fax, phones, etc.

Family Profile: Sandy and Joe are married and the Andersons have two children.

Education: Sandy completed one year of college and sang professionally with her identical twin sister. She credits her persuasive sales technique in part to her years on the stage.

Favorite Pastimes: Tennis and fixing up the house.

Can you be a *very* successful home-based business owner without investing a lot of money in a franchise, earning an advanced degree, or stumbling on a fluke like the Pet Rock? Yes, if Sandy and Joe Anderson's story is any indication of the possibilities. As one of the most straightforward success stories in this book, Sandy and Joe took the obvious path from Point A to Point B and not only made it work, they achieved financial independence with only a few years work! Sandy, a forty-three-year-old reformed Tupperware party hostess, and her husband wanted to open a home-based business that not only showed profit potential but would be fun to operate and give Sandy an outlet for her interior decorating skills.

To minimize risk they decided to look into franchises. Most franchise opportunities require substantial investments or store-front locations—but there are some legitimate franchise opportunities out there for people who want to remain home-based. Sandy and Joe both felt that with a good franchise, where much of the marketing homework is already done and clear methods are already in place, they would have a better chance of success than starting a business from scratch. Statistics bear them out, too—according to reports compiled by the federal government, franchise businesses have a much lower mortality than other kinds of start-up businesses, home-based and otherwise.

Their choice was a floor coverings business franchise called Floor

Coverings International. Most floor coverings in this area are sold through carpet specialty stores which consist of dusty showrooms with large rolls of carpets gracelessly arranged on a large floor. Oddly, the very stores that sell carpeting, ceramic tile, vinyl floor covering, and parquet flooring usually display them on bare concrete in unattractive warehouses. Floor Coverings International is different—its franchisees replace the dusty showroom with a well-equipped van that takes the samples directly to customer sites. Floor Coverings International is different in another sense as well. Where most franchise sellers insist that franchisees run a business from a storefront, Floor Coverings prefers that its franchisees run the business from their homes, in order to keep overhead to a minimum.

As the first step in purchasing the franchise, Sandy and Joe visited the company's headquarters and were impressed with what they saw—an organized and helpful staff, a well-integrated franchise program, complete with training, and a relatively low price for the franchise package. They quickly went ahead with the purchase and entered the training program soon thereafter. Sandy admits they had a bit of a head start with the business—a list of about twenty-five people who were already interested in floor coverings. Sandy's first customer was a friend and the sale went smoothly. She was very nervous about her second customer—someone she did not know. But after the "stranger" placed the order, Sandy breathed a sigh of relief. Then a problem came up that put Sandy in a panic—her first "real" customer and his choice of carpet was backordered. Fortunately, the customer was understanding and the sale went ahead as planned. After this experience, Sandy was ready to handle anything—and off she went to sell carpets around the city.

Sandy says that the idea of purchasing floor coverings where the store comes to the home or office is a new one to most people, but the reception to the idea has been quite positive. "We had one seventy-year-old lady who we went to see because she had no way of visiting a store. After she picked out some carpet, I let her know when the installers were coming around by sending her a thank-you card and then calling her the day before they arrived, so she was quite comfortable with the whole idea." A mobile carpet showroom is a great way for shut-ins, busy businesspeople, and people with allergies who can't handle the dust in a floor coverings store to make their choices. Sandy says that when she pulls up at a customer's site, she takes a hard look at the place to second guess what the person is looking for in color and pattern and then carefully chooses her samples from the van. "Sometimes I guess just right. Other times, I head back to the van several times to grab other samples." This is a highly personal level of service and Sandy explains that, "I have a lot of sleepless nights worrying whether what we choose for them was right or not, or if they're happy with it."

For Sandy, the business has been a dream—she gets to work with her husband instead of seeing him off in the morning, briefcase or lunch box in hand. And, in a local economy saddled with unemployment and doubt, their home-based franchise has been a success story from Day One. We asked Sandy about her advice for someone looking to start a home-based franchise. "First, read a couple of books on running your own business and read up on franchise operations as well. I think that a lot of people are fooled with the idea that when you run your own business you'll have a lot of free time on your hands with no boss over your head. But—if you're working out of home it's even harder. It's so easy to walk out of your office, sit down, and watch a soap opera."

What do Sandy and Joe think of the people at the mother company that sold them their franchise? "Sometimes I call them seven or eight times a day, especially when I work with commercial accounts. They're always great to work with and very supportive. That's why we liked the idea of a franchise — but remember, you only get out of it what you put into it."

If you are interested in covering your floors and live within the Anderson's large sales territory in Pennsylvania, you can contact Sandy and Joe at:

Phone Number: (814) 238-5552 or (814) 765-5268

★　　★　　★

A Second Mortgage Fosters a Magazine for Parents

Profile: Donna Hart

Company Name: Parent Communications, Inc.

Year Founded: 1988

Homemade
Success Secret: People want credible, quality information on things that are important in their lives. If you provide it on a consistent basis, the potential for reward is great.

Business Profile: Parent Communications, Inc. publishes the award-winning *Parent & Child* magazine. It is a free, regional publication distributed widely in Maryland and the Washington, D.C. area. Sustained by advertising revenue, *Parent & Child* is an expanding concern with increasing readership and growing national advertising. The free magazine, with a circulation of more than 50,000 readers, is experiencing an average growth rate of 32 percent per year.

Start-up Capital: A small second mortgage on the Hart's primary residence in Bethesda was used to start the business.

The Office: The office is in the basement of Donna's house which also doubles as a playroom, research center, and newsroom. Donna describes it as very cluttered and suggests, "Anyone who interviews to work with us should look around and decide if he or she can handle it or not."

Working Hours: Donna gets a 6:00 A.M. start when the publication is on a deadline. By 8:15 A.M. you can find her simultaneously packing her kid's lunches while talking on the phone with the magazine's production manager.

Home Office Technology: Several IBM-PC compatibles including one of the first Compaq "sewing machine" models. The PC files are sent to an independent designer's shop that produces the magazine using Macintosh computers.

Family Profile: Donna is married to Tom Hart, an attorney, and has two children, thirteen-year-old Joshua and six-year-old Julia.

Education: Among other degrees, Donna earned a Ph.D. in child development from George Washington University.

Favorite Pastimes: Donna likes gardening in her park-like yard. Donna and Tom enjoy attending concerts of acoustic folk music.

One of the toughest businesses to successfully launch in North America is a new magazine—even if you have tons of money to do it.

During the 1970s and 1980s, a plethora of new specialty magazines entered and ultimately overwhelmed the marketplace. By the end of the decade and into the 1990s, a number of magazines (and newspapers) had closed their doors for the last time or were sold off to competing publications only to be taken out of print a few months later. Donna Hart began *Parent & Child* magazine during one of the worst periods in publishing history with a fraction of the capital of most magazine start-ups and very little knowledge of the mechanics of magazine operation. Though Donna doesn't qualify as a millionaire yet, her publication is one of the few publishing success stories from this period—and with a growing readership, increasing ad revenues from more national advertisers, and the respect of many pediatricians and parenting experts, some of whom now contribute articles to *Parent & Child*, we expect her to hit tycoon status in no time.

Parent & Child was Donna's brainchild. At forty-six, she wanted to put her education and as Donna puts it, "a lot of creative energy," to work in a position of some sort, but found that traditional nine-to-five jobs prevented her from spending the kind of time she wanted to spend with her own children. Because of her background and interest in parenting, she envisioned a magazine full of useful, information-packed editorial describing how to raise, educate, and manage children, written in an journalistic style by influential parenting experts. She found other magazines on parenting to be only a vehicle for national advertisers as opposed to a source of authoritative information on the challenges, issues, and complexities of raising children. She wanted her magazine to be both—a source for quality products and a vehicle for distributed quality information on parenting. "I'm a teacher by trade; I'm a collector of information—I like reading the professional literature and then being able to pass that knowledge on to interested lay people in words they can understand." Donna was unwilling to settle for second-best or second-rate editorial pulled from press releases. Instead, she wanted a magazine that contained unique stories written by her, her staff, and experts in the field. As an example of the high-level editorial Donna prints, we caught her for the interview for this book just after she finished interviewing the outspoken former United States Surgeon General, General C. Everett Koop, for an upcoming issue of the magazine.

Donna started promoting the magazine by contacting a wide range of potential advertisers who sell quality child-care products. It was her persistence, the quality concept, and her boundless enthusiasm that convinced advertisers to place ads in the experimental venture. When she got enough advertisers interested and the money arrived for the ads, Donna was able to produce the first issue. She filled the issue with collected articles from her files—and brought the first magazines to supermarkets and stores all over Maryland and Washington, D.C. The first issue was well received. The parents called and wrote in, asking for more issues. So, Donna started the process all over again—selling ads, printing the magazine, and distributing it around the state. Initially, Donna chose to produce quarterly magazines to keep the work level manageable for one person. As the revenue expanded, she increased the number of issues to six per year.

For months, Donna did everything herself from her home base—and we mean everything. She wrote the articles (or got permission from others to use theirs), sold the ads, managed the production, and drove around from store to store to distribute the magazines. Because the magazine was well received and because the advertising revenue grew significantly, Donna now has helpers to distribute the publication, assist in article development, and help with the logistics—though she still does most of the selling and editorial work on her own.

Donna says that the highlight in the magazine's brief history was when it won the General Excellence Award from Medill University School of Journalism for editorial quality in early 1991. Other proud moments were when the magazine's printing run had to be increased several times to keep pace with the growth in readership which today is at 50,000 and growing. As Donna says, "A recent survey disclosed that more than 50 percent of our readers are well educated and make more than $100,000 per year." That's a very upscale readership—which is one of the things that attracts a growing number of national advertisers to the magazine. The advertisers pitch their products to the people with the income to buy them.

In addition to distributing the magazines in the stores, a growing number of people are requesting that the magazine be mailed to them. Still, Donna doesn't charge the subscribers for the magazine—she just sells advertising space. During the next five years, Donna plans to change the magazine over to a monthly format and expects circulation to more than double during the same period. She isn't sure about charging for subscriptions yet—she likes the fact that she can distribute quality information to parents for free. She figures parents have enough expenses already.

What advice does Donna have for home-based start-up companies? "I think that many people who go into business are like me—they don't have a good sense of how to run a business. Instead, they're doing it because they love what they're doing. It's very easy to get caught up in it. You probably should consult with a bookkeeper or accountant, especially in the early years. You need to have someone who asks the right questions so that you do better predictions. You need someone who will tear apart your expenses. You should also tell the person, 'I'm not coming here checkbook in hand. Instead, I want to buy a few hours of your services and then maybe in six months, I'll buy a few more.' "

As for her style of entrepreneurship, Donna explains that running her own magazine means juggling tasks and talents and being able to mentally switch gears whenever needed. "It helps to be very compulsive and obsessive and frequently very creative, especially if you're small and don't have a lot of money. You have to play a little of every role. I have to play editor, sell advertising—I even empty the trash."

If you are interested in a subscription to *Parent & Child* magazine, you can contact the publication at:

7048 Wilson Lane
Bethesda, MD 20817
Phone Number: (301) 229-2216

★ ★ ★

Next Time Someone Mentions Amway, Maybe You Should Listen

Profile: Tim & MaryAnne Mejdrich

Company Name: Mejdrich & Associates

Year Founded: 1988

Homemade Success Secret: Sales is sales, whether you work for a major corporation or get involved in a multilevel marketing program. You have to get out there to sell—there's no other way.

Business Profile: Tim and MaryAnne are Amway distributors. They already distribute products in almost every state and internationally in Korea, Mexico, Germany, Indonesia, and Taiwan. The next target for the business: the former Eastern block countries.

Start-up Capital: A couple of thousand dollars mostly spent for computers and bookkeeping software. The portion used to start the Amway franchise was approximately $100.

The Office: A bedroom that was turned into an office which was a big improvement over the original office that was installed in a modified closet. Amway no longer requires an inventory—products are shipped directly from the manufacturers. The Mejdrichs plan to turn their carport into a larger office when time permits.

Working Hours: Into the office at 8:00 A.M. to handle paperwork. Some lunches and evenings are spent with prospective Amway distributors.

Home Office Technology: A computer for bookkeeping requirements and letter writing.

Family Profile: The Mejdrichs have a black lab and a golden retriever. They are planning on starting a family someday.

Education: Tim has a bachelor's degree from Arizona State University and MaryAnne attended college for four years without finishing her degree.

Favorite Pastimes: Traveling, tennis, and skiing. Tim gave up his favorite sport, golf, to spend more time building the business.

Amway is one of the best known of the multilevel marketing ventures. Multilevel marketing operations like Amway rely on distributors who both sell products directly and find new distributors who will also sell the products. Of course individual distributors also consume the products themselves and they can buy them as a great discount from the retail price. We have always been skeptical about the income claims of multilevel marketing companies, and we were surprised when we found many people in network-selling businesses who actually qualified for the book. We included a couple because it's important for people considering a network marketing relationship to know what it takes to succeed.

Tim and MaryAnne Mejdrich, who easily meet our millionaire criteria, are very successful Amway distributors with only a few short years of service with the company. They had considered opening a traditional storefront franchise after a large corporation took them for a ride with big promises but no commitments—a distressing tale we heard over and over from people profiled in this book.

Salespeople are especially vulnerable to the corporate rip-offs. The story usually starts with an employer dangling the elusive carrot on a stick, only to yank it away every time it seems in reach. In a typical example, the employee delivers a stellar performance in sales and the employer writes out the large commission checks with resentment, trying to figure an angle for keeping more of the profit for the company instead of justly rewarding the hard work, diligence, and loyalty of the person responsible for the sales. Various ways of "lightening" the load include promotion to a management job with little incentive pay but just as much work, "redistricting" sales territories for "fairness," and outright unfulfilled promises, such as, "You make your numbers this year my boy and we will promote you to vice president of sales."

Tim's story follows the pattern. The minicomputer company he worked for promised him special incentives and promotions if he would just make the numbers. Well, he not only made his numbers but came in at a whopping 160 percent of quota with MaryAnne working at his side for free, coordinating activities and helping out on proposal writing. As to the promised promotion, while on a trip to Hawaii (a reward for meeting sales quotas), his boss came back and said he couldn't do it now, but reiterated the same promise if he would do it for a second year. Well, that was enough for Tim to get the message— he wasn't going to get rich working for someone else.

After being cheated by the computer company, Tim and Mary-Anne decided to look into franchising operations. They considered a submarine sandwich store priced at $75,000, an auto parts franchise costing more than $200,000, and a big-name fast food restaurant priced at more than $1 million—a proverbial mountain of cash for a young couple to raise. As Tim put it, "We were quietly, desperately seeking something that we could afford with the few thousand we had saved. When a friend showed us the Amway marketing plan I instantly knew it was a concept that would work. But when I said, 'Well wait a minute, what's the cost?' He told us we could get in for under a hundred dollars. We figured that the worst that would happen is that we would save 30 percent on the product." MaryAnne chimes in, "We thought that if it was only half as good as what we were told, it would be worth a try. We checked it out and found out that it was a company with great integrity and decided to give it a go."

Today, after just a few short years, Tim and MaryAnne have successfully leveraged themselves into financial independence selling Amway products—something that Tim claims is surprisingly common. But being skeptical, mostly because of our lack of knowledge of the company and its products, we sat down with the Mejdrichs over lunch. When we asked them the mission for their business, their response was not only positive but surprising as well. Tim is clear and precise. "Our mission is to essentially share a dream, to let someone know that he or she doesn't have to be in bondage to a corporation, a job, or bills. Our mission, the way we see it, is just to share the dream of freedom with people. They can create whatever kind of freedom they want. Financial freedom to start with and that goes from there to whatever is important in their life." MaryAnne intercedes, "The one thing with this business, unlike other home-based businesses, is that we are not only helping ourselves fill our plate—once that is full we can turn around and help others. Before, when Tim and I were working for corporations, all we could do was to help ourselves become wealthy but we couldn't turn around and help others. With this business we can teach and train others to do the same thing."

The message of doing it for yourself as well as others is the message of Amway today. Is this the same company that used to sell miracle cleaning products via networks of home-based distributors? Well, as it turned out, not only has the world turned, but Amway has become a world-class corporation with an amazingly broad range of products and services. As Tim explains, "The product lines they're dealing includes everything—phone service through MCI, VISA cards, Coca-Cola products, General Motors cars, and even cellular phones. The fact of the matter is today we're dealing with hundreds of companies representing thousands of product lines and services. You can even buy a house, a new Mercedes Benz automobile, or be worked on by a chiropractor! Amway customers and clients don't buy retail, we buy from our own business and pay wholesale. Amway-developed products now make up only about four percent of the product line."

Tim and MaryAnne make every contact count and work whatever hours it takes to make things happen. We learned from Tim and MaryAnne that there is no magic to success at Amway—it just takes work and persistence. The Mejdrichs have this advice to give before others decide to go it on their own, "I went to a really fine business school but I wasn't taught to be a businessperson in school, instead I was taught how to be an employee. So, as a result you need to learn the discipline of working for yourself and also need to know why you're doing it. You need to decide what you really want out of it. What's your dream? What's your goal?"

Tim and MaryAnne are certainly on the road to meeting their goals. Their success has been phenomenal. In addition to the money, they are quick to emphasize the other benefits they've realized since joining Amway. "We could be building our dreams instead of someone else's. It's something we can do together. When we got married we got married to be together. When we were always apart we couldn't be in control. Now we are." Always in synch and always supportive, Tim adds, "One pair of associates were growing apart from the stress of nine-to-five jobs. When they came into our business they were already separated and they were on the verge of divorce. Within the first few weeks of running the business the wife saw such a change in her husband, they got back together. It rekindled the dream between them. It was a nice feeling for us." When we asked them what they saw for the growth of their business over the next handful of years, MaryAnne's proclamation was simply, "Phenomenal!"

If you are interested in finding out about distributing Amway products or buying them, you can contact Tim and MaryAnne at:
6048 East Calle Del Paisano
Scottsdale, AZ 85251
Phone Number: (602) 420-1413

★　　★　　★

Selling Humanistic Programs to Corporations with Dollars and Sense

Profile:	Jane Porter
Company Name:	The Porter Group
Year Founded:	1990
Homemade Success Secret:	Make your network work for you—and never burn your bridges. You never know when an old boss or colleague may be the key to new business in the future.
Business Profile:	"We are a management consulting firm that specializes in working families." The firm finds ways businesses can reconcile work and family issues,

including child care, elder care, and working hours.

Start-up Capital: Had tucked away some money from her Wall Street tenure and sold her prestigious Tiberon house on the San Francisco Bay to reduce her debt load. In total, she put about $80,000 into the business.

The Office: The kitchen was the original office; now she has an office in downtown San Francisco and a small office in Manhattan.

Working Hours: Works as much as necessary, but still makes time for her life.

Home Office Technology: Computers, faxes, and other office equipment are central components of the office. "We couldn't do our business without technology. Seventy-five percent of our business is computer-based."

Family Profile: Divorced; has two sons—nine and sixteen. "I'm glad I'm a single parent." Her oldest son, now in high school, recently started his own home-based business called "One Man Fits All," which provides handy-man services around the neighborhood. He earned enough money to buy and maintain his own car.

Education: BA in biology from Skidmore College. "I was going to be a doctor, but I got married when I was twenty and that derailed that."

Favorite Pastimes: Very fitness oriented. She used to go to the gym but now she has brought the gym to her house. She reads a great deal and enjoys the movies. She also loves to travel, but not on business.

Pushing thirty-nine, Jane Porter decided that she better get going on her own or she would miss the goal of being independent by the age of forty. She had spent more than twenty years in corporations, including a decade at Saloman Brothers as a vice president in human resources and a two-year stint at The Gap. But in spite of high salary and prestige, this dynamic, energetic lady increasingly felt her hands were tied. "I would look at employees across the desk from me who were literally burned out from trying to work twenty hours a day and raise a family, and pretend they didn't have other things going on. The people would come to me and say, 'I can't do this anymore. I have kids. I need help. I don't know where to find help and I don't feel I can talk to my boss about it.' I could talk to them and do certain things, but mostly I couldn't fix it—and it drove me crazy. I said, 'When I start a business, I will concentrate on those issues. After all, my background was human resources, and I don't know anything else. It wouldn't make any sense for me to open a restaurant or something. The thing that saved me was that I earned enough money to always have live-in help. If I hadn't been in that position, I would have been royally screwed up, and 99 percent of the world isn't in that position, and I used to hear those stories, so I wanted to help. That's what gave me the idea."

"I just quit my job and started the business. Being in human resources there was no way to start part-time, the community was just too small—and I was one of the few females in a position of that seniority, so I would have been caught trying to sneak around. I had to quit and jump in with both feet. If I hadn't done it that way, it would have been a mediocre effort. "

"The first thing I did was go to Europe for a month and I sat on a beach and thought about things. I hadn't had a vacation longer than a week, ever. I said, 'I am going to go, I am going by myself, and I will try to formulate what I am going to do'—and that's what I did."

Her New York accent is only occasionally apparent through the street sounds of San Francisco in the background. She continues the story of her business: "I came up with the framework of the idea. I used to work with women after hours and on weekends, while I was at Saloman Brothers, and would try to find them suitable child care facilities. So, I have to get that into this somewhere. I didn't want to work one-on-one with employees, but wanted to work with corporations. I know how to work with corporations. I drafted an idea when I got back; I was relatively new to San Francisco and really didn't know anybody. So, I just picked up my phone and called the Big Six firms in San Francisco. I called the partners in charge and invited them to lunch to talk about my idea. They actually came.

"It turned out that they didn't poke too many holes in the idea, and Ernst and Young liked the idea very much. They were the ones who suggested very strongly that I leave my home office and get a real office. They even gave me a piece of space within their building—in a very prestigious address, and in return in the future, when we are rich and famous, I promised we would let them do the audit. So that's how I got out of my kitchen office."

"I thought the address was important and necessary for the types of clients I wanted to work with. Now, I could go back to my kitchen and do it without the office. Our name is out and recognized. In fact, I could operate from a beach now, as long as there is a fax machine and a phone."

In spite of the downtown facility, the work continues to come home with Jane. "My office opens at home at 6 A.M.—because so many of my clients are in New York. And at night, I pick up calls when I get home from downtown. It's like having two offices at this point."

Jane Porter offers a very unique service for corporations—a way to save money by providing better benefits to their employees. Her very first client was Smith and Hawkin, a gardening products company. She makes contact with her clients through her extensive network. "I do not do cold calling and I never will. Between the three partners, we have such an extensive network of clients we will never run out of leads for the business. My New York partner knows everybody. She had been in banking for twenty years, and she owned a bank for high-wealth individuals—she ended up marrying one of her partners in that endeavor, and decided it would be a good family decision to go off on her own. She is the most networked executive woman in the United States. So, we can just go straight to the CEO of a company and it cuts out so much of the other stuff. An assignment that would take two years from the cold-call level to get to the decision maker—it doesn't happen with us. We know where the right people are and how to get to them."

Jane's other partner was originally a free lance employee. Jane describes how the relationship developed. "I decided I would write a business plan because I was going to raise capital. As a former corporate person, I also knew I needed a mission statement and organizational plan. I bring it out every two or three weeks to make sure we are still going in the same direction we thought we were. When I started to actually do it, I realized I needed to hire someone to help me with the plan, so I hired Pamela Fyffe. She comes with a background from McKinsey and Company and Arthur Andersen Consulting, and we were quite compatible in working styles.

"After she wrote the plan, I asked her if she would be interested in getting involved in the business, and she said no. After all, she did have another job as a consultant. Then, after a few weeks, she came back to me and said that she had rethought it, and of course she had done all the research to see that the market was really ripe for the idea, so she joined me then."

"My New York partner, Susan Greenwood, joined six months later. She came in because I had sent her the business plan because she owned a bank and I thought she might want to invest. She called one day and said, 'The bad news is I am leaving the bank now. The good news is that I am now in the market for a job, and I would very much like to get into this thing with you.' She worked out of her home for six months—everyone has to work out of their home to get started—and then we opened our office in New York on Broadway six months later. We sublet a space that costs an arm and a leg, of course everything costs an arm and a leg there."

The partnership is an important part of Jane's success formula. She describes the advantages of the triumvirate: "What we bring as skill-sets to the business is important. Each of us could do 75 percent of everything, but for the other twenty-five percent, each of us brings a different skillset and level of expertise. My buddy in New York spends her life on the phone networking. I couldn't do that for all the tea in China. She only sleeps three hours a night, and always has, so she is like having two people. She sends over two thousand birthday cards a year—she has a computer full of names and addresses of people she knows. Pamela's strengths are in support documentation and research. She can do all the beautiful word crafting to come up with great proposals, and she is also very financially minded, so she likes to develop the cost models. I am somewhere in between the two things. I enjoy the marketing part and enjoy helping with the proposals, but the thing I bring most is that I can speak the language of the corporate people. I can figure out where their hot buttons are. They feel comfortable dealing with me because they know I have spent many years doing jobs like theirs. They know I am out to make them heroes and I make sure they know that. I was bound and determined to have partners who can do things I can't do and vice versa. You end up with one super human being if you put the three of us together."

The biggest challenge for Jane now is to stay focused. "We get asked to do things that if we were bigger or had more hours in the day, we would be able to take on, but it starts to go outside what the company is all about, and I have to reign it in periodically. Having to say no is a challenge, because every time you say no you are turning down money. But, I don't want to dilute the nature of the business by getting into all sorts of ancillary stuff that we shouldn't be in at this point in time. I refuse to increase my payroll; I use free-lancers all the time for large assignments. It's going to be that way for a long time."

Aggressive, intelligent, creative, and fun, Jane loves what she does. "If it's not fun, I don't want to do it." But she is also savvy about what it takes to succeed in the corporate world. "In most board rooms it's still men who are over fifty and have had wives who stayed at home to take care of the home and children—so the issues of home and family are so remote to them that they just don't get it. I had to ask, 'How am I going to appeal to this group?' The way to appeal to them is to show them what the company is losing by not doing it, and prove it. Then we go one step further, we become financial partners with the client by taking some of the financial risk in implementing the programs. By osmosis, the employees get what I want them to get—but I have to sell it the way it is going to sell. I am trying to capitalize on the mind-set of the people who sign the checks.

"We work with corporations to teach them ways to help their employees balance careers and family lives. We take the approach of the return of investment to the company, rather than trying to sell programs. We do a lot of financial justifications and cost modeling of the programs. We measure the cost of not doing the program and then prove the benefit to the companies of implementing certain policies."

"For example, we may do a needs assessment on elder care and child care. We put the tools into the employees hands so they can control their own destinies. We offer a 1-800 network of answers to questions on day care, health care, and elder care. Questions range from Where can I find a day care center? to My father has been diagnosed with Alzheimer's disease, what do I do? We then do some research and provide employees with referrals to services, education, and other support facilities. This is something that any employee can use—not just employees with children or employees without children.

"We find that people who can shape some of their own destiny with regard to their lives are happier on their jobs and more loyal to their employers. If you make someone's life easier for him or her, that person won't go down the street for a $5,000 raise. On the other hand, if you don't, that person may go down the street for $5,000 less, just to be with the employer who recognizes that there are things going on in the employee's life other than work."

The business is growing by 200-300 percent a year. One of the most exciting things for Jane, other than getting new clients, is that the competitors in the business now know that The Porter Group is a threat. Jane relays, "They have sent their spies in to see how we do business. We have arrived. We have also gotten a lot of good press, which is exciting, and gets people to notice that we're here."

Jane Porter and her partners, Pamela Fyffe and Susan Greenwood, have one neat business—their company helps improve the lives of employees while saving money for the client company. Jane is quick to share the secrets of her prosperity: "You should sit down and really examine whether you have the guts and the fortitude to walk into a situation where there's no guarantee of a pay check. You've got to be a risk-taker to do this. If you are going to be up every night worrying about it, you are just going to make yourself miserable. The next thing to do is make a list of everybody you know. Everybody. Everywhere. What I do, and what I tell other people to do, is to sit down and make your list and divide them into an A, B, and C list. Then, go to the C list people first, because you don't have that much to lose with them. Try your ideas out and your techniques. By the time you get to the A list, you've perfected your presentation. It's like a funnel, you start with the people who can do the least amount of damage, but can provide some degree of input. You end up buying a lot of cups of coffee—don't do too many lunches, it will bankrupt you. It works well to get people excited about your idea. Then you can ask them for people they know—it works like a charm. The follow-up is also extremely important. We always send thank-you notes. We are very courteous. We always do what we say we'll do.

"Quality service is what makes a business successful—it's important to remember that even if people can't help you now, they remember you if you are nice and polite. Every person we deal with is a business opportunity at some time in the future. Great word of mouth comes out of the pro bono work we do as well. You want to have a good reputation in the marketplace. Those are the most important things when you start. You have to go into it optimistically and you have to really want to do it. If there is any degree of hesitancy about being your own boss, you shouldn't do it. You'll drive yourself and your family members crazy.

"I am always more impressed with people who take the risk and fail than those who take no risk at all. I've found that 95 percent of the risks prove to be successful—if you could go to Las Vegas and have those same odds, you'd be a rich person. I like to see women helping other women overcome some of the stereotypes that happen in big organizations, too—they can't be like the guys. I don't think they should be like the guys. I think they should be like themselves and have the guts just to take that extra step. Nice things happen when you do. Don't listen to negative adjectives."

So what does this articulate entrepreneur envision for the future? "In five years, I would like to take a less active role in this business and I would like to start another one." We should have expected that.

If you are interested in obtaining information on innovative employee benefit programs contact The Porter Group at their headquarters: Phone Number: (415) 955-4154

★   ★   ★

Direct Mail Is a Twice-Traveled Route to Success

Profile: Carlyn R. Horowietz-Millea

Company Name: Sentron West, Inc.

Year Founded: 1989 (The original business in Albany, New York was started in 1982.)

Homemade
Success Secret: If you can do it once, you can do it twice.

Business Profile: Sentron West provides complete direct mail mailing services. The business has more than doubled its revenue each year.

Start-up Capital: $10,000 in savings—pretty much all of the money the Carlyn family had in the bank.

The Office: Started from home, the business was forced into a conventional office facility because of overwhelming success.

Working Hours: Carlyn says she works as long as it takes. When the shop is overflowing with business, her entire family pitches in and works all weekend if necessary to get the mail out.

Home Office
Technology: Computers for handling mailings lists and tracking jobs. Mass mailing equipment for folding, stuffing, labeling, and adding postage to direct mail pieces.

Family Profile: Carlyn is married to Brian, who now works in the business. They have two kids.

Education: Carlyn has a bachelor's degree in marketing communications from Temple University.

Favorite Pastimes: Carlyn likes her time with the family, when she gets any.

Almost everyone has seen the ads in the back of magazines claiming that you can make "$100 a day or more" stuffing envelopes. If you send in the fee for the "free" information, according to the Postmaster General of the United States, if you are "lucky" you will receive information that instructs you to place ads similar to the one you responded to and then sell the same information you purchased to customers responding to the ad. This is, to put it mildly, a con game, and it is illegal in this country. But the basic premise of these ads—that there is money to be made in direct mailing—is true, and Carlyn R. Horowietz-Millea has proved that it is possible to build a thriving mailing business with almost no money—just hard work, a commitment to quality, and an aim to please customers.

Carlyn started a business from her kitchen table in Albany, New York stuffing envelopes, sending out mailers, and coordinating direct mail programs. The business is a quick success story—Carlyn got so much work so fast that she had to open a shop to handle the volume of mail customers were bringing in. But Carlyn fell in love with the Arizona deserts after a visit to see her parents who moved to Scottsdale, Arizona. When she got back, she asked her husband if they could move there if she sold the business. He tentatively agreed, assuming that the business wouldn't sell—since they really had no tangible assets in the business, other than Carlyn's skill and hard work. Three days later, at a friend's cocktail party, she mentioned the company to a man they didn't know very well, who bought it on the spot for $100,000 cash—and they made "a very nice profit from the deal." So, they moved to Arizona.

Once in her new home, Carlyn found herself without a business or a job. But, based on her last success, she decided to rebuild the mailing business from scratch, this time with her husband participating. Four months after arriving in The Grand Canyon state, Carlyn was in business again and Sentron, Inc. was handling mailings for all kinds of customers. Carlyn describes the reasons for her company's success: "We come through and we're dependable. If we tell someone we're going to meet a deadline, we meet it. I treat every job as if it were my own. Quality control is very important to us. I can count on my right hand all the mistakes made in the past seven years of business that were of any consequence. We're successful because we don't mess up on a regular basis like many of our competitors do."

Carlyn has built her business on being a different type of mailing service: "We really are full-service—we do all the letter shop services, such as folding, inserting, labeling, metering—but beyond that we will help people target their pieces. We will help them maintain lists and develop lists if they don't have them. We do personalized laser printed letters when people are catering to more elite clientele. We offer the service of a complete direct mail specialist. I approach this business much differently than what I call a letter shop. A letter shop is primarily a company that will affix labels to bulk mail—they handle large volumes for businesses. That *is* my business too, but I specialize in dealing with people who are looking for more personalized attention."

The mailing business is really more complicated than it sounds. There's a lot more to it than simply stuffing envelopes and putting on labels. There are regulations to master, equipment to maintain, and deadlines to meet. How did Carlyn learn the business so quickly? Carlyn responds, "My Mom had known someone doing this out of her home in Philadelphia who is now in a 22,000-square-foot-warehouse. She started in her garage and I thought, if she can do it, I can do it. I had been a traveling rep for a major lingerie concern for five years and I had a lot of sales experience. I had my first child and I didn't want to leave her, but I got tired of coffee klatches and lunch with the girls. So my Mom said why don't you investigate this—I don't know much about it. So I did some research and learned what bulk mail is and what is involved and it didn't seem that complicated, although there's a lot of hard work involved. I set myself up, made myself up a name, filed a DBA (doing business as), opened a business checking account, and began making cold calls. And I grabbed my first client after just two days of cold calls! He handed me a mailing list and I called the post office and said, now what do I do? They sent over a representative and she helped me through the whole mailing and taught me what is necessary to expedite a bulk mailing. Now I advise clients how to do the same thing . . . We're doing invoices for clients; we handle all the mailing for one of the major hospitals and a large cable TV company. We're doing one of the major political parties this fall which will probably amount to 1.2 million pieces!"

Carlyn has this advice for up-and-coming homemade millionaires. "We did it with a lot of determination and a little bit of luck. Anyone can be successful if he or she wants it badly enough. It does take tons of hard work, and there have been many nights I've gone home stressed out to the max and in tears—and I won't say there isn't that side of it. But it's a real adrenaline rush every time we get a new client and we can show them how good we are."

If you are interested in someone to help you direct your direct mail, you can contact Carlyn and company at:

7848 East Redfield Rd.
Scottsdale, AZ 85260
Phone Number: (602) 443-0334

Professional Dancer Falls into
Successful Public Relations Act

Profile: Connie Connors

Company Name: Connors Communications

Year Founded: 1985

*Homemade
Success Secret:* Getting into financial trouble is no reason to quit the business. This only means it's time to reassess your situation and ask others for help.

Business Profile: Connors Communications handles strategic communications planning, public relations, and publicity for some of the largest book publishers in the country, including Random House's new line of computer and small business books. They also handle PR for education and technology companies.

Start-up Capital: An IBM PC purchased from the advance on a writing job.

The Office: The business started in Connie's seventeen hundred-square-foot converted butter factory loft in New York where she still lives today. By 1989 rapid growth pushed the business into an office because Connie could no longer fit the growing business and staff in her house.

Working Hours: The day begins at around 9:00 A.M. Connie often works on her laptop until late at night while lounging in her pajamas.

*Home Office
Technology:* Computers, fax machines, copiers, and a very good phone system.

Family Profile: Connie is single. "Someday I'd like to have time to get married."

Education: Connie has a bachelor's degree in theater from the University of Santa Clara.

Favorite Pastimes: "I love to travel in the third world." On one of her adventures, she traveled through South America with a medicine man.

While not everyone knows it, many of the stories carried in newspapers, magazines, and on TV news, entertainment, and documentary programs are really promotions placed by publicity and public relations firms. Companies, corporations, and not-for-profit organizations submit news on their new products, inventions, discoveries, and activities to publications and broadcast media and the stories are aired or run at no charge, thus providing almost free advertising for the company. Since "paid for" advertising is very expensive, you can imagine this form of free advertising, called publicity, is highly sought after. As a result, there are far more submissions than radio and TV stations, papers, and magazines have room to accommodate. To guarantee companies a better chance of getting their "news" placed, public relations firms help companies produce professional quality new releases, call editors to explain newsworthy events, and build awareness of the client organization's products or services. Good public relations agencies develop publicity programs that catch the attention of broadcast and print media outlets—so the releases get coverage in the media instead of thrown in the waste basket.

One of these firms was started by Connie Connors right in her home. She eventually became so successful that it almost went out of control—but that's another story . . . Let's go back to the beginning. Connie started a career as an actress and professional dancer and "accidentally" ended up as the proprietress of a very successful public relations company. Connie began her love affair with computers and technology, when, as a struggling actress, she taught computer classes to make some extra money. She wasn't a technical whiz, so she simply memorized the lines of the training, without really knowing much about the subject. As she puts it, "I wanted to continue dancing, so I taught the classes as an actress would—I read the dialogs. When there was a question I would say, 'That's a good question—we'll get to it later,' because I didn't know the answers." Teaching these classes ultimately got Connie interested in computers, so she taught herself computer technology and began writing manuals and catalogs for computer companies.

Then a tragic accident—especially for a dancer. Connie found herself bedridden after being hit by an errant New York taxicab. Unable to teach computer workshops or dance, a friend gave her a project writing a catalog for Scholastic. This led to other projects for other divisions of Scholastic. The company eventually asked her to handle their public relations needs. Connie replied, "What's PR?" But, in the same way she taught herself technology and computers, she quickly learned the mechanics of public relations. And with her charming demeanor, bright smile, and bountiful persistence, Connie began to master public relations and build a network of editorial contacts within the echelons of print and broadcast media. As a testament to her ability, Scholastic remains a client of Connors Communications to this day.

Connie's home office was located in her New York loft. The office area was a ten-by-ten-foot room crowded with computers and people. Connie reminisces, "By 1988 there were three people working at the house and we still worked in that ten-by-ten space. We all gathered together and we had one stapler, one note pad, three computers, and two phone lines. We'd laugh because one phone would ring and you'd have to crawl over somebody to get to it. Then at night we'd do mailings on the coffee table and on the living room carpet—if I needed privacy, I'd go sit in the bedroom on the floor." Connie's desks were made from old doors picked up off the street. Computer cables were conveniently run through the hole in each door where the doorknobs had been.

Connie finally gave up working from home by the time eight people were working in her crowded space, but she still regrets making the move. She misses working from home, because as she puts it, "To work at home is great. You're out in the open, people are more open with each other. There aren't all those machinations about what a business should be. We liked our home office so much it took us nine months to find the storefront we are in now. I still have my old IBM at home and I use it at night to send electronic mail, and I have a laptop I use at home to keep up with my work."

Success almost turned into failure for Connie, however. After her expansion into the storefront, things began to spiral out of control because of growth. (Yes, while some people would love to have this kind of problem, uncontrolled growth can kill a business just as fast as no growth.) Then a burglar broke in and stole all of her equipment. But after dealing with the burglary, Connie, fortunately, recognized the problems she was having. With the help of a management consultant and her staff, she wrestled the business back on track, regained control of expenses, and redefined her company. Within a year, the business was back on its feet—and doing better than ever.

Connie's advice for people thinking of starting a home-based business is stated with authority, "Pick out something you love to do, that you're passionate about—don't do it for the money!"

Afternote: We first saw Connie's story in one of our back issues of *Home Office Magazine.* It wasn't until we set up an interview with her that she realized that one of her employees was talking to us on the other line about promoting one of our books. "Oh you're that Connie Connors!" we said to save face. Somehow, we hadn't made the connection.

If you are interested in having Connors Communications help you get the word out about your product or service, you can contact the agency at:

873 Broadway, Suite 201
New York, NY 10003
Phone Number: (212) 995-2200

CHAPTER 8

The Truths About
Home-Based Entrepreneurs

While it is probably pure coincidence that the two youngest entrepreneurs in this book are respectively named Daryl and Daryn, some of the other facts hidden in the book are not only amusing but also informative. While the selection of the people profiled in this book was for the most part random, and no effort was made to ensure that people from every state were included, some statistics that can be derived from the book bear elaboration and point to important social trends regarding home-based enterprises.

There Are a Disproportionately Large Number of Home-Based Businesses Started by Women

When we began working on this book, we expected to find an even balance of homemade millionaires among couples, men, and women, but as we worked on the project, one fact came to light in spite of our unscientific selection methods—there are a lot of women entrepreneurs who have come through a divorce with dependent children and almost no money and then put themselves on track by building successful home-based businesses.

Considering the small percentage of women in senior executive positions in major corporations, our millionaire search uncovered a disproportionate number of women who started businesses at home with stratospheric success. At first it appeared that maybe it was simply an accident, since we were looking for success stories that were interesting and diverse. Then an article in the *Wall Street Journal* titled "Pay-as-You-Go Approach Is Giving Women an Edge" caught our eye and further substantiated our suspicions. The article explains that unlike their male counterparts, women start home-based businesses because they have difficulty obtaining bank loans to establish conventional office-based businesses. It's an accidental strategy that actually pays off because the tightening of lending practices had no impact because these female-owned companies had no bank loans to worry about anyway. As Sharon Hadary, of National Association of Women Business Owners, explains in the article, "The bad news was we couldn't get credit, but the good news was when banks were calling in loans, they weren't calling in ours because we didn't have them."

Another reason that so many women run home-based businesses is apparent from the profiles in this book. In addition to expressing a wish to work where their children were, several of the most successful women profiled didn't have a dime to start their companies, let alone enough money to rent an office. But, with the inner strength of Hercules (or maybe *The Bionic Woman*), these upstart entrepreneurs seized an opportunity and grasped their way to success rung by rung. So, can a woman alone, or with a partner or spouse get rich running a home-based business? Is the sky blue? Is the Pope Polish? Does a bear . . . Anyway, corporations that fail to move women up the ranks of management are driving women into the marketplace to compete on their own. This is a great story about the ability of women to overcome obstacles and prosper in the face of adversity—but a sorry comment about the equality of the sexes in business in general.

It Looks Like 1985 through 1989 Were Watershed Years for Homemade Millionaires

No effort was made on our part to select companies based on their years in business, but the majority of enterprises profiled in these pages opened their doors within the eye blink of economic time toward the end of the Reagan boom years or during George Bush's first year in office during 1989. According to John J. DeMarco, senior vice president of PSI, a Tampa, Florida, financial research firm, the number of millionaire households has shot up by more than 66 percent since 1985, from 1.3 million to 2.1 million in 1991—so it isn't surprising that many of our millionaires are part of this phenomenon, even though our selection criteria were somewhat random based on personal contacts and press coverage. As a result, we likely missed many established companies that started from home years ago. And, it's likely that companies that started later than this have not had time to make their millions yet—though there are a couple of exceptional businesses in these pages that made a million within the first year or two of business.

The Recession has Had Some Affect, but Not as Much as You'd Expect

It was late 1992 when the majority of the research for this book was completed, with the nation stuck in a shallow but persistent recession that spawned a record number of layoffs in the ranks of the formerly sacrosanct white collar workers and managers—not to mention the loss in high-paying blue-collar jobs, which were hit even harder. To characterize the times, the usually upbeat *Wall Street Journal* quoted a laid-off hotel catering manager who described her inability to land a job and her evaporating saving account as putting her "two steps away from a sewer grate or a homeless shelter." Another equally gloomy 1992 article in *FORTUNE* was titled "The Job Drought" and its title says enough that we needn't go into more detail about the employment prospects in the U.S. at this writing.

But, in spite of the recession, the home-based millionaires we talked with are mostly forecasting growth and prosperity. The expansion plans of some of these companies has slowed a bit over the recession, but most of them prospered even in the worst of times. The people profiled in this book see the best years still ahead for their businesses, at a time when the air has chilled in corporate America. In fact, with the exception of two companies planning to deliberately *limit* their growth because they did not want to become any larger (wouldn't most businesses *love* a problem like that?), the entrepreneurs we profiled all see a bright future and many claim the recession has actually helped their companies. To the skeptical, this may appear as Pollyanna sentiment when the sorry state of the economy is examined, but when you consider that many of the companies profiled specialize in superior service over their office-, store-, or factory-based competitors and they often charge less because of lower overhead, the advantage of working from home in recessionary times is clear.

Homemade Millionaires Are Ageless!

In this chapter you will find that people from young to old can start successful home-based enterprises. The youngest person profiled in this book, Daryl Bernstein, is profiled in this chapter. Daryl, at the ripe old age of sixteen, is not quite yet a homemade millionaire but he's been running several businesses since he was eight years old and with his first book already published and his second in progress, we don't think it's going to take him too long to fully qualify as a teenage tycoon. Daryn Ross's mail-order business qualified him for the book while he was still in college—now at the ripe old age of twenty-five, he only sees more millions in his future. You don't have to be young to be successful however, as Mona Tolin, also profiled in this chapter, has proved—she only operated her business for three years. She asked us to leave her exact age out of this book, because as she puts it, "I look like I'm in my fifties so there's no point in telling anyone my real age."

The majority of people profiled range in age from their early thirties to mid-forties. This may be a fluke because of our totally random selection criteria or it may reflect deeper trends. Since most of the homemade millionaire set worked in nine-to-five jobs of one sort or another before getting fed up and staring their own companies, many younger people have not yet decided to go it on their own. Older people may not appear for two reasons, one of which we stumbled on in our search for likely candidates for this book. First (a guess), many older people have made enough money off their enterprises, sold them, and quietly retired to the good life in an exclusive section of the city or are sailing around the world enjoying their oversized nest egg. Second (and we heard this from several successful entrepreneurs in their late sixties or older who don't make enough to qualify for this volume, but are certainly successful), older entrepreneurs intentionally make a choice to limit their companies' growth to a comfortable size. One of these silver entrepreneurs, a gentleman who'd been forced to retire at age sixty-two, commented, "I've grown the company to nearly $75,000 a year and that's all I can handle. It's a comfortable arrangement and I don't want to get any bigger because I'd have to hire a staff and I don't want that—I want to enjoy my business."

In this chapter, you'll also see that physical handicaps, like Jerry Seagrave's blindness, are no obstacle to home-based success. In fact, for many people with physical limitations, a home-based business provides resources and accommodations that are more difficult to implement in traditional office settings, thereby enabling physically limited workers to be more productive. You will also find profiles in this chapter that show how part-time businesses can become just as successful as full-time endeavors and that you can start a business with no capital at all. The profiles in this chapter combine to illustrate the one universal truth we uncovered about home-based businesses and that is that almost anyone can start a profitable business from home.

Of course, our findings may not be scientifically valid, but they are something to ponder. If the statistics and success criteria in this book hold up for a larger portion of the population, almost anyone can open a business at home in America regardless of age, sex, financial condition, time available, or background. And these businesses, at least on the surface, appear to be less susceptible to recessionary fluctuations than do conventional companies with their higher operational costs. If what we've found here is true, then there's no reason not to consider a home-based business, as long as you have the other common attributes of our successful home-based moguls which we discussed earlier, including ideas, creativity, persistence, the willingness to take a risk, the ability to focus your time on work, and the overriding will to succeed.

★ ★ ★

Don't Underestimate the Power of a Gas Can or the Impact of this Entrepreneur

Profile: Jerry Seagraves

Company Name: Jetson Industries (The name is a reference to the 1960s cartoon show. Jerry changes the name of the company every few years as he sees fit or when it amuses him to do so.)

Year Founded: Sometime in the 1970s.

Homemade Business Secret: There are no challenges in business that intelligence cannot conquer.

Business Profile: Jerry's company builds mainstream software that he feels will be needed three years down the road for major software publishers. His company completes the product before offering it for sale.

Start-up Capital: $100 earned from fixing a student's computer software problems.

The Office: Jerry's control center was created out of two bedrooms that were made into one office in his home in a top-secret residential location somewhere in the sprawling San Francisco Bay Area. The windows are blacked out to highlight the computer displays and his big screen TV projection system. To his left is a Merlin telephone. To his right is the "bobsled," a table that he had a carpenter friend build. It has controls on one side of it and coffee on the other side while he's working. A projection TV serves as his monitor. "It's like a theater. I can hit a switch right now and switch over to CNN or whatever and see a screen of TV or a video disk."

Working Hours: Jerry lives his work.

Home Office
Technology: Jerry uses computers in his home office to create his product—software. "I have a virtual world. I'm completely connected." He calls this arrangement the "brain bank."

Family Profile: Jerry is married to Suzie. They have two Siberian huskies, Dometri and Domenic. Jerry trained them both to respond to a second name, Gentlemen. Now when his friends come over, Jerry commands, "Gentlemen come," and both dogs come over! But, since they also have individual names, he can have one sit while the other remains standing. He says "Dometri, roll over," and only one dog responds. "Everyone thinks the dogs are really smart."

Education: A bachelor's degree in marketing and part of an MBA in marketing from Arizona State University.

Favorite Pastimes: He designs educational toys that he patents and plays chess via electronic mail.

This book is full of amazing people, but Jerry Seagraves is one of the most amazing, brilliant, and at the same time most singular people in this book. We could probably write a book on him alone—he certainly is one guy who has let nothing stop him in life. More than legally blind with 20/400 vision (and that's *with* glasses), he designs computer software that he later sells to major software companies who market it under their own logo and then pretend to be the geniuses who came up with the uncommon functionality and brilliant ideas.

How does someone who can't see his own face in the mirror write software? No problem for Jerry—he developed a special, home-based working environment to be able to see what he is doing while assembling computer programs. Jerry replaced a conventional computer monitor with a ten-foot projection TV system that blows the image up to a massive size to make the text readable.

We'll let effervescent Jerry explain what it is he does instead of trying to interpret it in our own words. "I identify what I think would be really cool in terms of a software product two or three years from now, because that's how long it usually takes to build it, and then I design it and build it. Then two or three years later, I take it to various top publishers. I usually find one very quickly. It's really a challenge trying to figure out what will be good two or three years from now because there are so many factors you have to watch—hardware development and software marketers—all sorts of stuff. You have to predict where everything's going to be then and also try to think of a really cool new idea that maybe no one else is going to do. I've done a lot of software products for the top publishers."

Deliberately remaining vague on the identity of the product names because of contract limitations, Jerry mentions the kind of products his company has delivered. "We've done over twenty products, many of which have been very good sellers you've seen in software stores. We've done spreadsheets, word processing, database, graphics, telecommunications—all mass-market oriented." Jerry receives clandestine royalties on the sales of his programs with the purchasing company pretending it developed the software on its own. You may be using one of Jerry's products on your own computer even though you thought it was developed by a big company with a reputation for innovation.

Coming from a broken home and suffering the ridicule of other children, Jerry talks frankly about how he got started in science and technology. "In early grades I used to read the big print books of which my school library only had about fifteen. After reading all of them about five times, I started roaming through the science section, which happened to be next to the big print books. Usually people wouldn't go to that section until about fifth or sixth grade. I started reading all the science books but I had to read them slower because I had to get about one inch away to see regular sized print. I started dreaming about science and I read about Thomas Edison. Like him, I started making experiments and building little circuits—by seventh grade I had written this electron theory for my science fair project. In eighth grade I built a little digital computer using relays. I used a hamster cage for my chassis and I went to a friend's dad who ran a gas station and he took me to a junk yard for electronic stuff. I saved up my money and bought some relays and stuff." If you think this is amazing, it gets better.

A turning point in Jerry's life came when he decided that "the system" as he calls it was not going to work for him. The same day he realized this, he decided to stand up for himself and make his life work. In the doldrums at age sixteen and realizing that he had little to look forward to in a society that was going to do little to help him, Jerry decided to go outside the system and make his own decisions in life.

Passing on the offer of a seeing eye dog and a free bus pass on the municipal bus system, he figured out an alternative method of transportation that would get him around town and to the distant university where he wanted access to their computers.

"I got a five-gallon gas can—a plastic one—five gallons for better visibility and larger capacity and plastic because it was light. I cut a trap door in the back and I'd put my books in there and then I'd hitchhike. If people think you're out of gas, they pull right over. They'd always say, oh, I never pick up hitchhikers, but I could see you needed a lift. And that's how I got around. Senator Barry Goldwater picked me up once. It gave me an opportunity to talk to people in an interesting way."

Now with transportation freely available, Jerry, still in high school, would travel via gas can to the university, which gave him access to mainframe computers. Upon arriving at the computer room, he'd hunt through the trash can to find the computer punch cards with people's account numbers on them. These he would use to get access to the computer. "I'd go through the trash to get the punch cards. Then I'd get them all ready and I'd throw out the ones that were punched most of the way across, but a lot of cards people would just punch about halfway or less. Then I'd take them and flip them upside down and backwards and use the other half. Then I'd punch them in a special way that would tell the computer to disregard the rest of the card. I'd go up to the guy at the cardreader and tell him to put them in upside down and backward and he'd say, 'Oh, I'm not going to get fired for that,' but eventually he would comply. There was a sign that said turnaround time is two hours, but my first few cards would take full control of the computer and my job would come out immediately. The people in the computer room already thought I was really crazy. There's this guy in the computer room that's got a gas can! What is he a saboteur or something?"

Jerry explains that at one point he wanted to write jokes for a living, sending his material unsolicited to Johnny Carson, who at first promptly returned them. "While I was in high school I sent some stuff in and they sent it back saying, 'Sorry, no way pal,' and then I'd send it in again. Finally they broke down and put some stuff of mine on the air. I sent in this whole thing on nictophobia—the fear of backing into doorknobs. I sent this plaque in with a doorknob mounted on it that said it was the American Nictophobic Associated League of Scholars which is spelled ANALS. Carson held up the plaque on the show. I wrote to them again and told them I was only eighteen and really wanted to be a joke writer. Instead of a canned letter they wrote me a real letter saying you've got to be in the Writer's Guild or they couldn't put anything else on the air. But they also said, if you're thinking of moving out to this area, you should definitely come see us. But I was eighteen and I wasn't ready to make the big move. I just kind of went off to college and did computers and I never got back to the jokes."

By the time Jerry started at Arizona State University, he was already very proficient with computers. After realizing that the computer science department wouldn't let him test out of the computer program even though he was more proficient than many of the professors, Jerry gave up the idea of a computer science degree because he was concerned that he would be bored attending the classes.

Instead, he started on a degree in marketing. This didn't stop him from profiting from the other students who needed his computer help, however. "I used to put these signs up that said, 'I can do anything on a computer—$30 an hour. This was in 1974 dollars.' I knew that $30 an hour in college was a lot of money and nobody would call until two or three weeks before the end of the semester. I'd always get one or two calls. It would be Ph.D. candidates who were right down to the wire."

So Jerry worked his way through college, and after starting an MBA program, Jerry pondered what to do next in life. He considered interviewing with some companies or printing up some business cards and going into business—but what company to work for or what kind of business to start? With a 4.0 average in his postgraduate work, he decided to start a business because he only had $100 left in his account. Dropping out of the MBA program, Jerry didn't know how to advertise or exactly what to do to generate new business. Then he talked to a friend of his in the computer business: "Somebody told me, 'Hey Jerry, you don't have to do that—people advertise when they need business.' And I go, 'You're kidding!'"

"I couldn't believe it. There are things called RFPs, requests for proposals. Big companies put these RFPs out and they ask computer companies to tell them how much they would charge. I mean I couldn't even believe it—they do it for you; they even write out roughly what they want! I started looking in the paper and calling around and Greyhound Lines had an RFP out for a twenty- or thirty-multiterminal on-line reservation system for the charter buses. People would call in and say our church needs two charter busses and we want to go to Wyoming and Greyhound would have to figure out how much it's going to cost and what cities they need to stop in and if they need to make a driver change. Then they give them a price and they make sure they send the bus to the right place and so on. That's what they wanted the system to do."

"So I wrote this proposal and of course it was my first one and so I went way overboard. It was 180 pages. Later I found out that most companies would send in a ten- or twenty-page proposal that was pretty detailed and here I am with this huge book. The system was fully designed with all the frills and incorporated things they hadn't even dreamed of! Luckily the fellow who was the head of the computer department at Greyhound happened to be an academic. This thing came in and dripped both of academia and excitement and I was immediately selected. But since they didn't know me they said, 'We want this system but we've got to have some company financials. We want to make sure you've been in business for a while, you look kind of young.'

"So I thought, I don't have any financials, but I told them that I had some partners and I thought to myself, I'd better get some partners fast! I designed the system so it would run on almost anybody's computer system, so I started calling all these minicomputer companies and I said, 'I've got this huge deal. Do you just want to sell them the hardware? You can just go in, sell the hardware, and have all the commission you want! I want to do the software.' Of course this sounded really flaky to most of them and they didn't want to talk to me. But one of the guys I got through to was the head guy at Quantel and he met me for lunch the next day at the campus. I told him what I needed and apparently it was the biggest sale he'd ever made—the guy couldn't even believe it. I'd just walked in and thrown this huge deal in his lap. Quantel's headquarters in Fremont couldn't believe it either. It was the biggest deal they had ever sold! And so they flew in their vice president to meet with Greyhound and assure them that everything would be all right. And the whole deal was signed. I heard from a friend about two years ago that Greyhound is still using the system."

After Greyhound, Jerry worked on more projects. He would have two or three projects going at a time and a "handful" of free-lance employees assembling programs. We asked if Jerry had ever run his company from a conventional office? He has. For a year the company set up shop high atop the famous Transamerica office tower in San Francisco where Jerry always dreamed of having a swank office. As Jerry describes it: "We did it for a year and everybody said, 'Gee, Jerry it is kind of cool but maybe we ought to work at home again.' They were starting to get older, too, and having kids and getting married. So I said, 'Okay let's go back and work at home and if it keeps working then there is no real sense in having an office.' "

While almost all of his software designs have been huge successes, he's had a couple of flops where his vision for a product was simply too far ahead of its time. "I have had two duds that I spent three years building. One of them was a product that I tried to write very early on the mainframe in 1973, my first year of college. I called it Project DI-VORG—my name for digital virtual organism. Now that sounds catchy, like the Terminator or something. I was trying to model a biological organism for the purposes of training medical people to understand genetics or for testing drugs without having to use animals or people. I had to modify the FORTRAN source code for the simulation software because it wasn't powerful enough. I worked on this for years and years and I finally gave up. I put the tapes in my sock drawer where they remain to this day. I'm going to fire up the DI-VORG project again soon, maybe in 1993. I can't afford a Cray super-computer but I can afford a lot of power, that's what I didn't have back in 1973."

Jerry is currently working on several products that integrate a variety of devices into a single cohesive package. Always the visionary, he sees that in two or three years this is the next obvious direction in automation and communication. His systems will tie together telephone communications, video, and computers into a single system. Maybe after these projects are completed it will be back to DIVORG for a few years.

You don't run into a genius very often and not everyone in this book is one. Most of the people profiled are certainly bright, dedicated, and in love with their work, but Jerry is one step beyond with his wild obsession with his work, insights, and absolutely wild sense of humor. Talking to him is like plugging into a light socket—you walk away feeling invigorated and ready to take on the world. Jerry took a limitation with his eyes and built his own world, writing the scripts to his own life instead of following. We look to him as a source of inspiration and we hope that after reading about him, you will feel inspired to take on the world as he has.

This Lady Knows How Much Your Business Is Really Worth

Profile: O. Mona Tolin

Company Name: Tolin Business Appraisers

Year Founded: 1989

Homemade Success Secret: Many of the most prosperous people find a niche and then make themselves an expert in that area. If you do this, people will come to you for your advice. If you charge for the advice, you have started a business.

Business Profile: Tolin Business Appraisers specializes in appraising small- to medium-sized businesses in the Southern California area. Her clients include service, retail, distribution, manufacturing, and wholesale businesses.

Start-up Capital: The will to succeed.

The Office: The twelve-by-twelve foot front bedroom was turned into an office complete with a big desk and bookcases in a sixty-seven-year-old house. Mona had to make some changes to make it work. "I had to have an electrician come in and put in a half box in the electrical panel so that we could put in extra plugs for the computer and the printer." She equipped the rest of the office with furniture from the Salvation Army.

Working Hours: Mona works as much as she needs to. As she puts it, "Here, I can work early in the morning. I can work late at night. Sometimes I've been down here in the office at two o'clock in the morning—something gets on your mind and you can't sleep, so you might as well get up and do it."

Home Office Technology: A fax machine, computer, and a printer. The computer helps her assemble all the data for the finished appraisals.

Family Profile: Mona has a grown son from her first marriage. Her husband, who is around home most of the time, is her chief "go-for" and is retired.

Education: She is certified by the American Business Consultants as a business appraiser and has a degree in teaching from UCLA.

Favorite Pastimes: Mona likes to travel and is planning a trip to Australia and New Zealand.

Mona Tolin has a long career of running companies of her own. Recently profiled in the book, *The Women Entrepreneurs*, Mona started her first business, a beauty supply store, before she was twenty. She is a rare woman who ran her own show long before most women did. She learned how to value businesses after seeing one of her own destroyed through arson. Mona's breadth of experience equips her to be able to look at someone else's company and establish a hard dollar price for it.

Computing the value of a company is extremely difficult because a business is *not* a tangible item like a car, house, or bar of gold, and its value is highly subjective. Most companies have few corporeal assets outside of business equipment and inventory (if any). And, every aspect of a company must be evaluated to establish market value. As Mona explains, the process begins with documentation. "I have a checklist that I give to the owner that lists the documents and papers that I will need to do the appraisal: financial statements, copies of licenses, leases, corporate papers, and an inventory if it's the kind of business that has inventory. They also have to give me a list of all the things the business owns such as real estate, furniture, fixtures, equipment, and if it has large equipment such as a machine shop, they need to take pictures of the equipment and identify it with serial numbers. There are about thirty different pieces of information I need from the owner. The file's pretty thick by the time I get all the stuff!"

We asked what got her interested in the business appraisal business. She explains: "I also hold a real estate license and I am a business opportunity specialist. I've owned four businesses, but when I got my real estate license I knew one thing I did not want to do was to sell houses. I knew I wanted to sell businesses. I had the expertise—I had gone through every emotion that a buyer goes through and every emotion that a seller goes through. In selling businesses, I had to know how much they were worth, and it was very difficult without some appraisal knowledge. So, at the time I found out that the only appraisal school in California is out of Sunnyvale and there is no mandatory certification in California. The department of real estate does not require it. They require it for appraisal of real estate but not for businesses. There are two kinds of property—real property and personal property—a business is personal property. So I decided I needed to get that education and get myself a certification and set up a business doing appraisals. And that's what I did."

Once certified, Mona hired a marketing firm and sent out about fifteen hundred letters to lawyers, financial planners, and insurance people telling them that she was a certified appraiser. "I got my first big appraisal from a lawyer. It was an income tax problem with a research and development company and she wanted me to appraise it and find out what it was worth so she could price the stock. Unfortunately, it had a great big negative because the firm had never produced a product—they were only doing research. They had a vast office, but everything was rented and they didn't own a thing. When I was done, she was very pleased with the appraisal."

Mona's services are typically called upon when a change is anticipated. She explains, "The reason I do the appraisal is usually to find out how much the business is worth for a sale, a dissolution of partnerships, dissolution of marriage, insurance, or IRS reasons. Most of my appraisals come through referrals and my referrals come through lawyers, financial planners, and other business owners. Once they give me all the documentation, I estimate how many days it will take to do the appraisal and I have a daily fee. I can figure whether it will be a one-, two-, three-, or four-day appraisal. I don't appraise real estate, so I have an outside company come in to appraise the real estate owned by the company."

She's had some interesting clients as you can imagine. One of the more amusing was, in her words, "a company with two partners and one wanted to retire out of the business and the other was going to buy him out. I went over for the interview and about a week later I got all the documentation and information that I needed. I did the appraisal and delivered it within a week after receiving the information. When I talked to one of the partners on the phone, he gave me no indication that there was any urgency. When I delivered it to him, he said, 'Oh! Well my partner wanted to leave early so I just went ahead and bought him out, but I paid a lot more for it than the dollar figure in Mona's appraisal.' We all think of our businesses as our babies and they're worth a million dollars, when they may really be worth only $50,000."

What does Mona think about working from home? "Oh, I love it! I wouldn't work in an office for anything! I can schedule my appointments so I can have time off if I need it. I don't like to commute to an office—I did that for five years. You get to the office and you're three hours between appointments and you don't have anything else to do—I think it's time wasted." We asked about how she deals with clients, many of whom obviously want the appraisal done for reasons that might upset day-to-day operations. Mona explains that she keeps her activities as low key as possible. "I usually see clients at their businesses, homes, or at coffee shops. Clients become very paranoid about me walking into their businesses because they don't want employees to know what's going on. It's a very confidential kind of business." This also made opening a conventional office unnecessary. "I usually see clients in the field so there's no reason to rent an office space."

Mona says she keeps herself going with a "goal card" (we thought she said *Gold Card* at first). "I write my financial goal down on a three-by-five card and I put it on the bathroom mirror and I say, I will earn X number of dollars or more by December 31." Her advice to wanna-be home entrepreneurs is good. "They must know their subject and educate themselves completely and do research—find out what other people are doing, talk to other people, network. You don't open a business in your home and expect people to beat a path to your door!" Of this book, Mona commented, "I think it's very intimidating for someone who wants to start his or her home-based business to see all these highly successful people who have been in it for years and think, Oh I'll never be able to do that." But readers, Mona did it and so did a hundred other people in this book. You can, too!

If you need your company appraised, you can contact Mona at:
Phone Number: (714) 832-1630

★   ★   ★

The Weekend Entrepreneur

Profile:	Susan Ratliff
Company Name:	About Me! of Arizona
Year Founded:	1985
Homemade Success Secret:	Starting out part-time or on weekends is a low-risk way to learn about your own business skills and abilities. If the part-time business is a success, it can be easily grown into a full-time endeavor.
Business Profile:	About Me! produces a line of personalized chil-

dren's books. Susan also wrote a book called *How to Be a Weekend Entrepreneur* and does seminars on this topic when she has time for her second business called *The Weekend Entrepreneur*.

Start-up Capital: $5,000 in savings.

The Office: The den of Susan's upscale townhouse is set up as an office for her and her husband.

Working Hours: Seven days a week. Susan often attends trade shows and special events on Friday, Saturday, and Sunday, where she produces her children's books on site. Her day starts at 7:00 A.M. and she describes her schedule as "unrigid and totally flexible."

Home Office Technology: Computer and laser printer to produce her personalized kid's books.

Family Profile: Married with a son.

Education: Two years of college in Baltimore.

Favorite Pastimes: Reading and spending time with her family.

One of the best adventures any child can have is to actively participate in an exciting story. About Me! produces personalized books for children. Parents can have a book produced which makes their child the lead character in a delightful story. Thus, the child "participates" directly in the adventure.

Susan didn't come up with the idea for personal books on her own—she saw an ad for a similar product in a magazine. Susan decided this was something that would be both fun and potentially profitable. Like many of the people profiled in this book, Susan chose to work at home to be able to spend more time with her family. Susan started out in the spa business, later got into real estate, and eventually became pregnant with her first child. Upon becoming a parent, she realized that she wanted to spend more time with her child than a conventional job would allow. She decided that the only way she could make this work was to start a business of her own from home, because few jobs or employers would allow her the time she wanted for her family. To choose a business, she spent time reading the entrepreneur magazines. Doing as she puts it, "unscientific research," she settled on the idea of selling personalized books because of her interest in reading and children.

Susan started out part-time. She began selling and assembling the personalized books at sidewalk crafts shows. To create the books, Susan sets up a table with a computer and laser printer. The story and illustrations are already in the computer. Susan then adds the child's name to the book on the computer and generates pages with the story tailored for the child using the merge-function of the computer which puts the child's name in all the correct places in the story. She can produce a completely customized book while the people wait! She also had fliers printed up and distributed at the shows and soon people started calling in orders for the books. Her part-time endeavor was soon bringing in full-time profits. She now advertises nationally and sells the idea to other people as a franchise.

Her business won her the 1992 Small Business of the Year Award in her home city. Among her clients are celebrities like musician Graham Nash of Crosby, Stills, Nash & Young and his stage crew. Singer Debbie Boone of *You Light Up My Life* fame is also a children's book author and one of *About Me!* books, personalized for her, was presented to her as a gift on the "Home Show."

Susan describes the keys to her prosperity as "tuning out the negative influences—the people and things that were trying to tell me what to do. A supportive husband and my background in sales and marketing has been extremely helpful. I've been successful right from the very beginning—it's scary!"

Susan also has a new second business that she started based on the success of her book, *How to Be a Weekend Entrepreneur*. She describes selling her book to her publisher as one of the most exciting events of her life. Her book describes ways for people to start businesses that they run only on the weekends to raise additional income. Once established, these companies can then be grown into full-time enterprises.

Susan says the future looks bright for her two companies. "I see continued expansion even though there are now a lot of competitors. We are number three in the nation distributing these books and with the success of my business book, I see only growth. What's really exciting is my speaking career and the fact that I'm in demand to teach the subject of weekend entrepreneurship."

We asked Susan what makes her tick as an entrepreneur running two companies, raising a family, and pursuing a writing career. "Drive. I'm a very driven person. I work very well under pressure. I'm the type of person who's not happy unless I've got about six things going at once. I have difficulty relaxing and I feel unproductive laying around enjoying my leisure time." Susan advises fledgling entrepreneurs to "get involved in a business that you really love. The enthusiasm you have for the products goes a long way to make up for your lack of sales and other skills."

Susan's weekend entrepreneur approach to starting a home-based business while maintaining a nine-to-five job sounds like a workable get-rich-quick scheme: "Readers thinking of starting a business need to be aware of the $5 billion exhibit marketing industry. You don't have to go into business seven days a week. There is an incredible opportunity out there for weekend vending. It's really exciting—there's absolutely nobody tapping into this niche. I have not come across any product or service that can't be sold at a convention, trade show, craft fair, swap meet, or through some sort of exhibit marking avenue. The average vendor makes $3,000 per weekend. The superior ones do $5,000 a weekend and this lady I met who sells sweaters from Peru did $34,000 in four days! Another lady who sells hand-painted T-shirts got $28,000 worth of orders at her first wholesale trade show. The buyer for Harrods of London was there and she is now supplying Harrods of London with her T-Shirts. Best of all, you can start one of these companies with no money down!" Maybe a trip to the swap meet for "market research" would be a good idea this weekend.

If you are interested in *About Me!* books or weekend entrepreneuring, you can contact Susan at:

8100 E. Camelback #79
Scottsdale, AZ 85251
Phone Number: (602) 946-9202

To order a copy of *How to Be a Weekend Entrepreneur* direct, call (800) 745-5047.

★　★　★

The Exceptional Entertainment Company Delights Corporations

Profile: Donna Friedman

Company Name: The Exceptional Entertainment Company, Inc. and Ultimate Team Concept, Inc.

Year Founded: 1986

Homemade Success Secret: Read the best-selling business books. There are ideas in these that can be used to develop products and services for business. And don't be afraid to clown around in the process. Also, realize that personal growth and business growth go hand-in-hand.

Business Profile: The Exceptional Entertainment Company produces special events for corporations. Ultimate Team Concept helps companies with team building.

Start-up Capital: "Nothing—Zilch, Zero, Zip!"

The Office: A two-room apartment where the bedroom became the office and the living room became a bedroom. Donna had to roll up the bed to entertain. Donna eventually moved the business to a loft as it quickly got too large for her abode.

Working Hours: Typically nine-to-five or six although with the start of Ultimate Team Concept, Donna finds herself working longer hours.

Home Office Technology: Three personal computers, a fax, postage meter, and "lots of phones and lots of phone lines."

Family Profile: Donna is single.

Education: She completed part of an MBA. She quit the program when she chose to build the Exceptional Entertainment Company.

Favorite Pastimes: Sunbathing and racquetball. Donna loves talking to people of all kinds. "I just love people!"

Donna Friedman's Exceptional Entertainment Company brightens up corporate events to make them more memorable. Launched from a two-room apartment in 1986, her organization is used by companies to make their events, such as product launches, more special. Donna also promotes the Ultimate Team Concept, a program used by corporations to help make employees into productive teams. With just a hint of a New York accent, Donna explains, "My company produces events that are designed to heighten respect for the individuality of each colleague while we sharpen their individual competitive spirit and the group is driven to a higher performance standard." Donna describes her special events. "They are physical activities and they are mind activities. They are dramatic and they are musical depending on the client's needs."

Donna explains how she got started while she was still working for Merrill Lynch. "I used to be a professional clown in a white face and colorful suit. I was an executive secretary on Wall Street full-time and I was a clown on weekends. One day my friends at Merrill Lynch wanted me to find a clown. I told them I wasn't going to clown any more after this summer, as I had been accepted into an MBA program and I thought that getting my MBA would be important if I was going to start my own business. Two weeks later they called back and said they wanted me to put a show together for the grand opening of their new corporate headquarters, and that was when I recognized the opportunity to book talent for corporate events. That was in 1986."

Donna grew The Exceptional Entertainment Company quickly— and she never finished her MBA. As more opportunities became available, she changed the focus of the company. Instead of offering her services writing and rehearsing talent for shows that had other vendors involved, she began packaging the complete event so she would have control over the entire process. The change in orientation was instigated after a disastrous event where Donna's people performed flawlessly, but because of problems caused by others, she couldn't hold the event together. Donna explains, "The company went from just a talent booking agency type of thing to an event management company two years later. We did an event for a bank and produced a family Christmas show. It was a nice event. It looked like an off-Broadway show—that was the quality of the event. And, when we got there the only thing that went right was ourselves. So what I proposed the following year was that the company hire us to review their logistics and revamp the entire event. Through this we began to meet other kinds of people and became an event management company—we now handle soup to nuts for our clients."

Donna decided to run her business from home because, like many of the other success stories in the book, she didn't have any money to rent an office. "I had no capital, but this is a business you can do from home. Initially there was no inventory although eventually there were costumes. At one point I was supplying Santa Clauses to the department stores, so I made a phone call to my dad. 'Listen, I need some space in your attic for about eleven months a year.' I did this just to save on expenses, but eventually we ended up getting warehouse space."

We asked Donna what the biggest challenge was to running her business from a two-room apartment and "privacy!" was her reply. Now that her business has been forced into an office due to success, her biggest challenge is "dragging myself away and leaving to go home." This is one entrepreneur who loves her work! Ever confident Donna describes the keys to her success as multifaceted "First, I'm always open to personal growth. Second, the way I work with people is special. The third key is I play up the strengths of the people I work with, by letting them know how wonderful they are. One of the things I do is to build teamwork. I do that by getting people to recognize the strengths of the individuals in a group and get them feeling good about who they are."

In an enterprise rich with amusing stories and mishaps, one of Donna's favorites goes like this: "We were doing an event for an insurance firm. It was their annual employee appreciation day and there were about seven hundred people there. It was an outdoor event and when the CEO got up to speak it started to rain. He looked at me in dismay. I said to him, 'Don't worry, we'll stop the rain.' Of course, I was kidding. He took the microphone and said, Donna Friedman will stop the rain! I walked over to the DJ and the MC and told them that we needed to do something. So, we instructed all the people at the event to do sort of a rain dance. To our surprise, the rain simply stopped!" It seems that Donna is still discovering the true extent of her powers.

Donna finds her work rewarding because she draws people together as friends, people who would otherwise be in competition or simply the people at work. Donna beams as she relates her feelings about the business. "It's wonderful to get a thousand stockbrokers together in a room and have them all clapping hands and singing holiday songs. It's exciting to get 250 salespeople together from different areas of the company and have them intermingling together as a whole team—that's what I get off on!"

If you are interested in exceptional entertainment or team building, you can contact Donna and her crew at:
57 East 11th Street, Ninth Floor
New York, NY 10003
Phone Number: (212) 254-1190

Partners in Venture Become Partners in Life

Profile: Brian Lillie & Nadia Semczuk
Company Name: The Party Staff

Year Founded: 1988

Homemade
Success Secret: Service, service, service—there can never be enough of it.

Business Profile: The Party Staff provides temporary professional staffing for special events. An offshoot of the company provides training and consulting services to restaurants with service problems.

Start-up Capital: Nadia's modest savings of $1,000 from other jobs and the rest was charged on credit cards.

The Office: The company was started in the bedroom of Nadia's apartment and the living room was used as the conference room for meeting with clients. Today, with 150 employees, the company has moved to an office.

Working Hours: 10:00 A.M. to as late as 9:00 or 10:00 P.M., seven days a week.

Home Office
Technology: A Macintosh computer.

Family Profile: Brian and Nadia started as business partners, now they are married to each other.

Education: Nadia studied at UC Berkeley and UCLA. Brian graduated from UCLA with a bachelor's degree in political science.

Favorite Pastimes: Dining out, what else? If she had time, Nadia would enjoy traveling and spending time in the outdoors.

We did a stint as professional restaurant critics back in mid-1980s while we were living in the suburbs of Seattle. In fact, our first book was a Seattle-area restaurant review guide, that still sells after all these years in spite of the fact that it is now hopelessly out of date. Being a restaurant reviewer is everybody's idea of the ultimate cushy job—but eating out twice a day, seven days a week wears thin real fast as you gain weight and tire of tracking a hundred different details to monitor a restaurant's operation while trying to quietly enjoy your lunch. What really makes the job loathsome is that you have to eat in at least as many bad restaurants as good ones.

After a year of "research," in more than one hundred restaurants, a never-ending problem we observed was that consistently professional and courteous servers are surprisingly hard to find outside of a handful of premium restaurants. Servers exhibit attitude problems, show up for work drunk or drugged (a more common problem than many people realize), are hopelessly inexperienced, or lack even a speck of the charm prerequisite to effectively working with guests. Oddly, restaurant staff that are gracious on one visit too often pull a Jeckyll-and-Hyde turnaround on subsequent visits and appear preoccupied or unfriendly. The worst service is usually found when restaurants handle special events or catering and hire temporary employees who have not previously worked together.

The partners in The Party Staff know all the horror stories about restaurant help. They used to work in hospitality and food service at the best restaurants and resorts in Los Angeles. Now their company helps the situation, by providing all kinds of serving and food preparation personnel and, unlike some of the cretins who have waited on us, they know how to do it right. Proprietors Brian Lillie and Nadia Semczuk take on only experienced servers with the right kind of professional attitude. Then they train them for several months in all phases of food service before allowing them to work with guests.

They charge for their services and the servers by the hour. Brian and Nadia can provide event coordinators, servers, bartenders, hostesses, chefs, and set-up and clean-up crews for restaurants that need extra staff for outside catering. They have coordinated people for events such as the 1991 Academy Awards and the Five Living Presidents luncheon which brought together President Bush and former Presidents Carter, Ford, Nixon, and Reagan.

Live wire Nadia sold lemonade and cookies as a child and after she was on her own as a young adult, she sold free-lance photographic services and helped a former boyfriend run a disk jockey business. "I have always been the type of person who believed that I was going to have a business—I wasn't sure what—I knew I was going to be a businesswomen. I tried different things. Through college I worked in restaurants and in the hospitality industry." Brian picked up the skills to run the financial end of the business working in corporate America after completing an associate degree in business at a local community college.

The two decided to form their own company after Brian recognized a growth trend in upscale food service and special event coordination in the Los Angeles area. Working together for a couple of years, Brian and Nadia got hitched. Today they are partners in both life and business. But at first, running the budding enterprise was a challenge that didn't leave time for romance. Nadia explains, "It's hard when you start a business. Everybody thinks of how great it will be! And it sounds great because you want to be your own boss, you want to do your own things. You have to have a lot of willpower, because you can't go out and buy this or that or go out of town and have a good time, because you've got to watch every penny. Everything you make goes toward the business. The more you make, the more you put back into the pot."

Twenty-nine-year-old Nadia and twenty-six-year-old Brian are modest about their success, in spite of a client list that includes celebrities like Peter Bogdonovich and Dustin Hoffman and elite Los Angeles restaurants such as Chasens and Spago. According to Nadia, "I know that in a certain number of years, all this is going to pay off and that's what keeps me going. I'll be more independent and be able to take some time off to do the kind of things I want to do." She explains that getting the first clients is the toughest problem that most businesses experience: "When you first start a business there's a certain point that is really hard to deal with. You're afraid, you're scared—you wonder if you're really going to be successful. You have to go through this time period before people really start hearing about you. Then, you start getting popular and word of mouth starts working and your reputation results in new business. It's like climbing a ladder."

We asked what advice she has for those who are considering a home-based business. After a thoughtful pause, she recommends, "Really think about what you want to do. Because it takes so much time and money and energy, you really want to plan it out and really think about your goals and what you want the business to become. You've really got to look into the future to anticipate what could and should happen. It's important to do a business plan beforehand. Write it all down. All the facts. Everything you need to do—where you plan on going, the kind of clients you want to get. Then describe your market and determine the amount of money you're going to need to start up. Listen to motivational tapes. They've been very helpful for us."

Nadia is looking forward to a large expansion of the company. "In the next five years I'd like to have five other offices in major cities and I'm starting to develop videos on service that I'm distributing nationwide." It's the feedback they get that Nadia likes best. Comments like, "You guys are the greatest" and "If it wasn't for you guys, it wouldn't have been such a success" are very rewarding. How good are they? As the catering director of Spago says, "They're absolutely the best in the business."

If you are interested in improving your restaurant's service through hiring and training top-notch personnel, you can contact The Party Staff at:

9328 Civic Center Drive, Suite A
Beverly Hills, CA 90210
Phone Number: (310) 859-6500

A True Believer in the American Dream

Profile: Kenneth V. Bates

Company Name: The Buyer's Source, Inc.

Year Founded: 1987

Homemade Success Secret: Learn from the mistakes that others have made and then start a business that avoids them.

Business Profile: Buyers Source brokers real estate and a division of the company builds custom houses and handles the financing for individual buyers.

Start-up Capital: $1,300 paid as an insurance settlement after a burglar broke into a previous residence.

The Office: Living on an acre, Kenneth uses his entire home as a model for his clients. His home office is located upstairs in what would be a spare room if Kenneth ever sells his house. He uses it as a showroom and two agents work with him there to help sell houses.

Working Hours: Kenneth works typically eighty hours a week to keep up with all his building projects.

Home Office Technology: A computer and fax machine.

Family Profile: Kenneth is married to Jennifer and is planning on having a family soon, now that the business is on its feet.

Education: A degree in finance.

Favorite Pastimes: Trips with his wife to Central America. The Bate's also enjoy a tight knit group of friends with whom they go on outdoor trips.

Born in England, thirty-three-year-old Kenneth Bates is one of the homemade millionaires who pulled himself up with his own boot-straps. Coming to the United States in 1979 after graduating from high school, he looked around and quickly realized that, compared to his homeland, this was the land of opportunity. With his family paying the first year of his tuition, he was accepted into college. He eventually found a job to put himself through school.

After graduating with a degree in finance, Kenneth chose to stay in the United States and build a career for himself. He felt that returning to England would limit his future because of the social class structure still alive there. With only a trace of a melodious English accent, Kenneth comments, "America is probably the only place in the world where somebody can start a business up and make a good living. I came from a working class background in England. I didn't have wealthy parents to set me up and get me going, and England today is still very class striated. I don't have the right school tie to start a business there."

Kenneth took a traditional corporate job with a home builder who trained and groomed him for a long career with the company. "When I got out of college I went to work for General Homes. They had a management training package that trains you how to build and sell homes." Kenneth feels bad about the demise of his former employer. "I learned a whole lot from that company and it could still be around today employing a whole lot of people."

His stint working for the company changed him much in the way various companies influenced many people profiled in this book. He watched in frustration as the company strangled itself by not listening to its own people and later as it sank without a trace after the market for new homes went sour in the mid-1980s, "I don't think I could work for corporate America again. For five years I sold my soul to a corporation and I've actually turned down work from people that work in that atmosphere and have that frame of mind. It's the dog-eat-dog atmosphere, middle management being stupid and not listening to the people who are selling or building the product. This is why I left General Homes. I can't work under the 'you and us' atmosphere. There are six or seven of us from General Homes who are very successful now, who pretty much weren't listened to for years and years, and that's why General Homes is no longer in business."

Today, Kenneth handles the entire home-building process from working with buyers to producing plans and finding lots, from getting the projects financed to managing the construction—all from his home office which doubles as a model home. Kenneth talks about his unique home-office/office-home. "For me in particular, people can see my product. They can come here and they can see exactly what I do for a living. My home is always in tip-top condition. It's really easy to demonstrate my product without having to have the additional overhead of a model home. I get up in the morning and I'm at the office right away—no commute!"

Kenneth made the transition from corporate worker to home-based enterprise in economically shaky times. "It's everybody's dream to run his or her own business. When General Homes went out of business, I had the knowledge I earned at General Homes. At the time, we were running into a recession and there were few jobs out there." So Kenneth decided that since no other opportunities were available with the squeeze in home building bankrupting the well-established builders, he'd take a chance and set up his own outfit where he could call the shots and build on the lessons he learned at General Homes. Starting out with just $1300, he assembled a small business and built it up brick by brick into the success it is today. But success hasn't spoiled Kenneth Bates. He modestly reports, "I'm just an honest guy trying to make an honest living. I'm a pretty average guy I think. If I won $10 million tomorrow, I'd probably still be doing the same thing."

How is this man so successful when other builders are throwing in the towel? According to Kenneth the secret is, "Luck, luck, luck and eighty hours a week—I spend Monday and Tuesday checking out my job sites to determine that the work I've been billed for by subcontractors is completed on time. I'm still active in the real estate market searching out lots and homes to remodel. Friday is pretty much spent in the office returning phone calls and billing banks and owners."

Kenneth's goal for his company is further financial stability so he can raise a family. Over the long term, he plans to add several houses to his large property so his in-laws and other family members can share in his success. His large property is located in an area where residents traditionally ride horses for pleasure, but it's close enough to the city that urban conveniences and entertainment are close by. He envisions his property becoming a family compound, rather than just a house on horse property. He describes where he lives and works, "It's an equestrian or country-type atmosphere in the city." As for his company, Kenneth sees growth all the way, but as he explains, "I have no intention of going public or becoming a big company."

Relying on his finance background, Kenneth has this advice for entrepreneurs just getting started, "Before going into business absolutely count every single bill you have. Pay them off. Don't have a car payment, don't have a furniture payment, don't have outstanding payments on your credit cards, because if you are paying 21 percent interest on a credit card, you don't have the sense to run a business." Guess we all better, er, um, pay off a few bills.

If you need a custom house designed, financed, and constructed, you can contact Kenneth at:
7490 East Cactus Road
Scottsdale, AZ 85260
Phone Number: (602) 451-0040

★　　★　　★

An-Up and-Coming Millionaire—Sixteen-Year-Old Started on Road to Success at Age Eight!

Profile:	Daryl Bernstein
Company Name:	Daryl Designs
Year Founded:	1989
Homemade Success Secret:	All the success factors that apply to adults can be used by kids to start profitable businesses at home. As with any endeavor, encouragement and support from the family is important for kids to realize their potential as entrepreneurs.
Business Profile:	Daryl uses computer graphic tools to create logos and flyers for small businesses. He also wrote a book for child entrepreneurs titled *Better than a Lemonade Stand.* He is already working on his second book.
Start-up Capital:	"Basically nothing. I used some money I had made from earlier businesses to buy a computer."
The Office:	His bedroom at home, which Daryl describes as leaving little room for sleeping with all of his office equipment.
Working Hours:	"I go to school during the day. My hours tend to be long if a project comes in from five to ten at

night. A lot of times I'll also work 3:30 to 6:30 in the morning.

Home Office
Technology: A personal computer, laser printer, and a fax machine. Daryl says that his pieces of equipment are stacked on top of each other to save space in his bedroom.

Family Profile: Daryl is the son of David and Bianca Bernstein.

Education: Daryl is a junior in high school. He plans to attend an Ivy League college upon graduating. His ten-year-old sister Sara contributed some of the ideas for Daryl's book.

Favorite Pastimes: Baseball and tennis are Daryl's favorite activities outside of business.

> *"A fifteen year old who has published a book? Daryl Bernstein will have no problem being successful in business."*
> — James Stewart, Pulitzer prize-winning journalist
> and author of *Den of Thieves*

Well, he's not quite a homemade millionaire—but he's not very old either. We'd call him a business prodigy. A prodigy is someone who displays an atypical talent for one of the arts or mathematics at an age much earlier than other kids. A search of our CD-ROM database found plenty of well-known prodigies: including Mozart for music, Blaise Pascal for mathematics, and Bobby Fischer for chess, but no listing could be found for prodigies in business. But someone who started in business at age eight must be somewhat akin to one. At an age when most of us were still fiddling with Erector sets and Barbie dolls, Daryl was out earning a legitimate buck as a businessperson! Today, his company designs flyers and logos for small companies which he creates on his computer using desktop publishing software.

Probably one of a few high school students who regularly reads *The Wall Street Journal*, Daryl has just completed his first book, written for Beyond Words Publishing, Inc., a small Oregon-based publisher of books of "integrity" (their word, not ours). Daryl's first book is great, titled, *Better than a Lemonade Stand: Small Business Ideas for Kids*. It's a guidebook to fifty-one businesses that kids can start and run on their own. Each suggested enterprise provides information on what, if any equipment is required, how to price the goods or services, and how to promote the business. Daryl has tried most of the businesses himself. (As you read this profile, remember, at this writing, this guy is just sixteen years old! When we interviewed him and in subsequent phone conversations, he sounds more like a twenty-five-year-old white collar professional than a teenage boy.) Daryl recently completed a national book-signing trip promoting his book with a stop at NBC's "The Today Show" as part of the tour. Daryl also invests in the stock, bond, and options markets.

Daryl explains how he became interested in business so early in life. "I always wanted money to buy things that I liked and wanted and I never got a big allowance. I decided to just go forward and try to make my own money. I learned about the American free enterprise system very early in life. I started knocking on doors and picking up the phone—it started early for me."

Sounding like many of the adult entrepreneurs we've talked to, Daryl describes the biggest challenge in running his business as, "Picking up customers. People are always reluctant to spend money. In the business I'm in, a lot of people feel that their hand-drawn logos and typed letterhead is enough for them and they really don't need anything else. My hardest job is convincing these people how much a nice logo, letterhead, or flyer can help them improve their business and get new customers.

"I always laugh when people call and say, 'Can I talk to the accounting department?' I tell them, 'Well you're talking to him,' or once in a while I say, 'Well let me call downstairs,' or 'They're on the thirty-third floor, let me get them for you.' People over the phone don't really know you—as far as they're concerned I'm a huge corporation."

We asked Daryl what the keys to his success are, and he replies in worldly fashion, "Determination—I call over and over. A lot of people ask me how you get a first book published because a lot of people take two or three years to pull that off. My answer: It happened in three days. I sent in the idea, they called me and loved it. But if it hadn't been accepted, I would have been on every publisher's doorstep in the United States until it got published. I'm very determined. When I set myself on a goal, I end up achieving it eventually." Like most of the people in this book, Daryl says that "I'm not thrilled with the idea of working for someone else."

What does Daryl see for himself five years in the future? "Well I'll be finishing college. Hopefully at that point I'll be ready to start up a business from a storefront, maybe go to law school, or go for an MBA. Eventually I'd like to start up a big business and I don't exactly know what yet. I'd like to have lots of different businesses and industries and merge them into some sort of a conglomerate. I really enjoy the challenge of business—convincing customers, selling products, and pleasing people. I can't say that money is my first motivation. It is the challenge of free enterprise."

Daryl has this advice for home-based entrepreneurs: "Go for it. When you have a dream, just follow it no matter how high or lofty or unique or possibly impossible it is. Follow your dreams, know your goals, and make all the follow-up necessary." We expect to hear more from Daryl over the years as he achieves his own goals—most likely on the front pages of the *Wall Street Journal* or *FORTUNE*.

If you are interested in obtaining *Better than a Lemonade Stand* and your local bookstore is sold out, you can contact Daryl's publisher, Beyond Words Publishing at:

Phone Number: (800) 284-9673

Avoid the Losers and
the Dabblers at All Cost

You have now read about a wide range of homemade millionaires and home-based businesses. But, before you put the book down, we'd like to offer some final advice to ponder before you get started in your own endeavor. Home-based entrepreneurs agree that as soon as you open a home-based business, you'll run into the losers and the dabblers. Almost every person we profiled told us so. Loosely described, the losers are a mix of people who like to sit around and complain rather than do any work. Their idea of running a company is waiting around for the phone to ring with orders even though they never do any selling or promotion. Of course, when the customers don't materialize it's time to blame the world for the failure—never themselves.

Fortunately this group is easy to recognize. At any given time members of the losers club will be making comments such as, "It's the miserable economy—there's no business out there, so why bother looking." As you become more successful, you may find that these people try to stick to you and your company like glue.

You'll meet some of these people in business clubs and organizations. They will try to get you to join their factions by involving you in their conversations and luring you into the groups with offers of free rides to meetings and "how about a beer after the meeting to talk business." The real pervasive ones may even show up at your door and waste your afternoon complaining about the world and telling you why your company isn't going to succeed. After they leave, you'll feel low enough to start updating your resume to find a regular job.

A subset of this group is "the dabblers." These are people who go through the motion of running home-based businesses by buying equipment, printing business cards and letterhead, and setting up a desk in the study, but never get any clients or seem to do any real work. While they play at running an enterprise, they'll pester you for advice and waste your time over long lunches. Discussion topics will include long explanations of the companies they have started and agonizing explanations of why clients have failed to place the big orders they were counting on. They may secretly hope that you will feel sorry for them and send them some of your customers. And by buying you an expensive lunch they hope you will feel guilty and soon reciprocate the warm gesture. Of course, when these people should be digging up sales leads and prospective work, they are off casing Office Max or other large office supply stores for "just the right" answering machine to handle the customer calls that will never materialize.

One person we spoke with explained how a loose mixture of dabblers and a loser almost made her go back to work at a regular job. Fortunately a friend who was a successful home-based entrepreneur helped her realize where her time was going and how she was being emotionally manipulated into developing a negative outlook. She dropped the so-called friends and instead started a regular Monday lunch meeting with a handful of successful home-based businesswomen. With their positive feedback and proven advice she built a company that makes enough profit to qualify her for a place in the book!

The thing to remember if you want to succeed in your own endeavor is to stay away from the dabblers and losers at all costs. If they start latching on to you, discourage them by becoming a perpetual optimist in their presence or leaving them accidentally on hold when they phone. Pass on their invitations to lunches, parties, and dinners with the flimsiest excuses. Don't be home if they show up unannounced. Through these tactics it will eventually sink in that you want nothing to do with the losers club because you have no intention of becoming a member yourself.

Index

About Me! of Arizona, 232-235
Academy Awards, 240
Adams, Mason, 137
Aerial Advantage Photography, 56-59
Aetna Life & Casualty, 147
Alarm systems, business and household, 184-185
Alcoa Corporation, 147
America Online, 191
American Business Consultants, 230
American Civil Liberties Union, 133
Amway, 35, 200-204
Anderson, Joe, 193-196
Anderson, Sandy, 193-196
Animal containment and exercise facilities, 174-178
Apple Computer Corporation, 23, 24-25, 53, 54
Appraisals (of business worth), 229-232
Arizona Security Control, 184-187
Arizona Sun, 152-156
Around the World in Eighty Days, 126
Artificial fur business, 98-101
Arthur Andersen Consulting, 207
ASK Computer Systems, Inc., 27-28
Attic Babies, 85-89
Avoiding losers & dabblers, 249-250

Banking, 32
The Bare Facts, 49-52
Barry, Dave, 29
Bates, Kenneth, 35, 242-245
Beaver Valley, 171-174
Bedke, Janelle, 26
Ben & Jerry's Ice Cream, 150
Bernstein, Daryl, 220, 245-248
Best, Janis, 156-160
Best & Kintzer, 156-160

Better than a Lemonade Stand, 245, 246, 248
Beyond Words Publishing, Inc., 246
Big Ass Comics, 132
Blake, Dianne, 56-59
Bloom County, 29
Blooming Cookies, Flowers, and Baskets, 160-165
Bloomingdale's, 90
Bogdonovich, Peter, 241
Book distribution, 131-134
Boom, Michael, 130, 137-140
Boondoggle technologies, 129
Boone, Debbie, 234
Borland International, 28-29
Bowerman, Bill, 30
Breathed, Berke, 29
Briggs, Bob, 51
Brokerage, real estate, 242-245
The Brothers K, 77
Bryant, Lena, 31
Bundgaard, Joyce, 124-127
Bundgaard, Mike, 124-127
Bush, George, 29, 110, 156, 240
Bushnell, Nolan, 23
Business appraisals, 229-232
Business books, as information, 190
Business Week, 189
Butterick, 100
The Buyer's Source, Inc., 242-245

Carter, Jimmy, 240
Catalog production for fashion industry, 156-160
Celestial Seasons, 182
Chapman, Tom, 34, 43-52
Chapman Design Concepts, Inc., 43-52
Chappell, Kate, 102-105

251

Chappell, Tom, 102-105
Charity events, 35-39
Charlie Horse, 29
Chasens, 241
Cheeseborough Ponds, 154
Children's books, personalized, 232-235
China Mist Tea Company, *see* Restaurant Tea Service, Inc.
Close, Glenn, 107
Club Med, 69
Clue, 32
CNN, 222-228
Coca Cola, 53, 69, 203
Codner, Robert, 140-144
Comics manufacturing, 131-134
Communications & public relations, 214-217
Complete Guide to Growing Marijuana, 132
CompuServe, 191
Computer book and manual writing, 137-139
Computer Currents, 140
Computer graphic design, 245-248
Computer Magazine, 139
Computer millionaires, 22
Connors Communications, 214-217
Connors, Connie, 214-217
Cotton, Sandra, 59-63
Cotton-Naaken, Caroline, 59-63
Craig, Jennie, 173
Cruise, Tom, 51
Crumb, R., 132
Curriculum material for teachers, 140-144
Custom Towels, Inc., 52-55

DaRin, Ray, 93-96
DaRin, William, 94
Daryl Designs, 245-248
Davidson, Art, 31
Davidson, Walter, 31
Davidson, William, 31
Decorative lights, 39-42
Den of Thieves, 246
Direct mailing services, 211-214
Disney, Walt, 23, 42
Dresher, Rommie, 183
Duncan, David James, 77
Dunlap, John, 32

Eastside Eats, 133, 134
The Economist, 189
Edwards, Paul & Sara, 192
The 8-Week Cholesterol Cure, 114
Elsel, Ingrid, 34, 46-49
Ingrid Elsel Associates, 46-49

Emerson, Ralph Waldo, 123-124
Employee development & sales promotional programs, 144-149
Engel, Catherine, 105-109
Entrepreneur, 57, 189
Entrepreneurial ideas, sources of, 34-35
Entrepreneurial Megabucks, 27
Environmental consulting, 46-49
Ernst & Young, 206
Estevez, Emilio, 161
The Exceptional Entertainment Company, 235-238

FTD (florists), 53
The Fabulous Furry Freak Brothers, 132
Fagan, Carol, 105-109
Fake fur business, 98-101
The Far Side, 29
Fischer, Bobby, 246
Five Living Presidents' luncheon, 240
Flakey Foont, 132
Floor Coverings International, 193-196
Forbes magazine, 31
Forbes, Malcolm, 31
Ford, Gerald, 240
The Ford Foundation, 112
FORTUNE, 135, 189, 220, 248
FORTUNE 500, 22,
Friedman, Donna, 235-238
From Teacher to Tycoon, 142
Frommer, Arthur, 137, 142, 143, 144
Fucini, Joseph and Suzy, 32
Fyffe, Pamela, 207

The Gap, 205
Gates, Bill, 26
General Electric, 27, 69
General Homes, 243
General Hospital, 60
General Motors, 70, 203
Genie, 191
Georgio cosmetics, 55
Getz, George, 34, 35
Ghegan, Ashley, 160-165
Gibbons, Fred, 26-27
Gift baskets of cookies and flowers, 160-165
Goldberg, Whoopi, 173
Gone with the Wind, 164
Grant, Carolyn W., 110-114
Great American Duck Races, 35-39
Greenwood, Susan, 208
Greyhound Lines, 226
Griffith, Bill, 132
Gumbel, Bryant, 173
Guthrie, Janice R., 118-122, 130

HK Consulting, 82-85
Hallmark, 55
The Hard Rock Cafe, 42
Harley, Bill, 31
Harley Davidson, 31
Harris, Paul, 69
Harrods of London, 235
Hart, Donna, 191, 196-200
Hart, Tom, 197
Harvard Graphics, 26
Harvey, Paul, 100
Hatfield, Jim, 134
Jim Hatfield Productions, 134
Hawn, Goldie, 170
Health Plus, 114-118
The Health Resource, Inc., 118-122
Herz, Bill, 34, 68-71
Hewlett, William R., 23
Hewlett-Packard, 23-24, 25,27
High Times, 133
Hillar, Ron, 79-82
Hoffman, Dustin, 241
Home building, 242-245
Home Office Computing, 189, 190
Home Office Magazine, 51, 217
Home repairs and improvements, 43-46
Homestead Book Company, 131-134
Horowietz-Millea, Carlyn R., 211-214
Hosada, Craig, 49-52
Hot air balloons, sales, rides & lessons, 125-127
How to Be a Weekend Entrepreneur, 233
Howard the Duck, 50
Hughes, Gene, 122-124
Hughes, Kristine, 122-124
Hush Puppy, 29

IBM, 25, 69, 73, 118, 182
Ideal Toy Company, 172
Imprinted towels, 52-55
Imprinted paraphernalia, 63-65
Information gathering, 188-192
InfoWorld, 190
Innovative Concepts, 63-65
Interior landscapes, 110-114
Introduction to Windows 3.1, 140
Jetson Industries, 222-228
Jim Beam, 55
The Joan Rivers Show, 51
Jobs, Steve, 23, 24, 182
Johnson, Jeff, 30
Johnson, Michele, 174-178
Johnson, Ron, 174-178
Kahn, Phillipe, 28-29
King, Ann, 160-165
Kintzer, Ruth, 156

Klopp, Hap, 82-85
Knight, Philip, 30
Koop, C. Everett, US Surgeon General, 198
Kowalski, Robert E., 114
Kurta, Bill, 137
Kurtzig, Sandra, 27-28

Lamb Chop, 29
Lane Bryant, 31
LaPaz Cocktail Mix, 62
Larsen, Gary, 29
Law office automation, 71-75
Learn Microsoft Word for the Macintosh Now, 140
Levy, Marian, 168-171
Levy, Richard, 168-171
Lewis, Shari, 29-30
Lifecycle Balloon School, Ltd., 124-127
Lillie, Brian, 238-242
Lipton tea, 179, 182
Literary agencies, 76-79
Llamas Magazine—The International Camelid Journal, 189
Lloyd, Christopher, 107
Lloyd's of London, 170
Lou Grant show, 137
Lubecke Enterprises, 114
Lubecke, Don, 114-118
Lubecke, Kay, 114-118
Lunchbag Lizards, 81
Lunchbox Lizards, 81

MacWeek, 190
Macy's, 42, 90
Madonna, 161
Magic tricks for corporations, 68-71
Magicorp Productions, 68-71
Mailboxes, Etc., 170
Malsin, Albert, 31
Management consulting firm, 204-211
Marketing, in-store, 59-63
Martin, Tom and Deborah, 52-55
Martinson, John S., 178-184
Maschino, Marty, 85-89
MCC Publications, 140-144
MCI, 203
McKinsey and Company, 207
Medical information services, 118-122
Mejdrich family, 35
Mejdrich, MaryAnn, 200-204
Mejdrich, Tom, 200-204
Mejdrich & Associates, 200-204
Melchor, Jack, 27
Memorex, 25

The Men and Women behind Famous Brand Names and How They Made It, 32
Merrill Lynch, 237
Michener, James, 29
Microcomputer Systems Corporation, 25
Microsoft Corporation, 26
Millar, Judy, 79-82
Monopoly, 32
Morton, Lynn, 138
Mother Theresa, 170
Motivational tapes, 190
Motorola, 169
The Movie Collectors' World, 51
Moyers, Bill, 161
Mozart, 246
Mulholland, Nora, 165-168
Museum of Modern Art, 42
Music through MIDI, 140

Nabisco, 59
Nader, Ralph, 104
The NANCI Corporation
Nash, Graham, 234
Mr. Natural, 132
The Nature Company, 42
Nature's Sunshine Products, 122-124
NCR Corporation, 57
Neiman, A. J., 181
Neiman Marcus, 42, 107, 161, 163
Nestle, 182
Network, 168
Networking, gathering information, 191
New York Times, 79
News & Advance, 104
Nike, 30
Nilan, Kaylee, 171-174
Nixon, Richard, 240
Nordstrom's, 42
The Northface, 82-84
Nutritional/weight management products, 114-118, 122-124

The Office Furniture Broker, 150, 165-168
On the Waterway, 136
Osborne, Adam, 23
PPG, 147
Pac Expediters, 168-171
Packaging and shipping services, 93-96, 168-171
Packard, David, 23
Page, John, 27
Parent & Child Magazine, 191, 197-200
Parent Communications, Inc., 196-200
Parker Brothers, 32

The Party Staff, 238-242
Pascal, 28,
Pascal, Blaise, 247
Peanuts cartoon, 29
Peck, Gregory, 170
J.C. Penney's, 107
Pet Rock, 33, 194
Peter Principle, 73
Photography, aerial, 56-59
Pitney Bowes, 129
Plants by Grant, 110-115
Playboy, 50, 51
Pope John Paul II, 170
Porter, Jane, 204-211
The Porter Group, 204-211
Power of Attorney, 71-75
Price-Waterhouse, 30
Primal Lite/Primal Design, 39-43
Professional staffing, temporary, 238-242
Public Broadcasting System, 29, 134
Publishing, 49-52, 196-200, 232-235
Publishing: curriculum material for teachers, 140-144

Quantel, 227
QuattroPro, 29

Ragu Foods, 94
Random House Electronic Publishing, 140, 214
Ratliff, Susan, 232-235
Reagan, Ronald, 240
Real estate brokerage, 242-245
Red Horse Clay Company, 90-93
Red Rose tea, 179
Redford, Robert, 170
Restaurant Tea Service, Inc., 178-184
Revlon, 154
Risk, 32
The River Why, 77
R Johnson MD Barns, Trailers and Equipment, Inc., 174-178
Robards, Jason, 137
RONNO Productions, 79-82
Roosevelt, Teddy, 172
Ross, Daryn, 55, 63-65, 220
Roth, Kyle, 66, 71-75
Russell Stover Candies, Inc., 33

Saloman Brothers, 205, 206
Salyers, Donna, 98-101
Donna Salyer's Fabulous-Furs, 98-101
San Diego Zoo, 108
San Francisco Art Institute, 40
San Francisco Opera, 53
Schechter, Eric, 34, 35-39

Scholastic, 216
Schroeder, Pat, 126
Schulz, Charles, 29
SCORE, 193
Scott, Sue, 34, 39-43
Script writing, 134-137
Seagraves, Jerry, 23, 222-228
Secrets of the Astonishing Executive, 69
Semczuk, Nadia, 238-242
Sentron West, Inc., 211-214
Sew News, 100
Sheen, Charlie, 44
Sheldon, Gilbert, 132
Sherwood, Carol, 90-93
Siemasko, Dan, 35, 130, 144-149
Siemasko Program Development,
    144-149
Silicon Valley, 22
Silver, A. David, 27
Simon, Neil, 161
Small Business Administration, 192
Small Business Development Centers,
    192
Smith, Amanda W., 21
Smith, Julia, 120
Smith, Robert, 21
Smith & Hawkin, 207
Mrs. Smith's Delicious Homemade Pies,
    Inc., 21
Smithsonian Museum, 170
Snell, Mike, 66, 76-79
The Michael Snell Literary Agency,
    76-79
Software manufacturing, 222-228
Software millionaires, 26, 222-228
Software Publishing Corporation, 26
Song Support, 79
Spago, 241
Special events production, 236
SPI, see Sunshine Promotions, Inc.
SRDS Guide to Magazines, 189
Sunshine Promotions, Inc., 59-63
Suntan products manufacturing, 152
"Star Trek," 30
Steele, Danielle, 29
Steif of Germany, 172
Stewart, James, 246
Stover, Clara, 32, 33
Stover, Russell, 32-33
Streisand, Barbara, 161
Stuffed animal manufacturing, 171
Swinnerton Parker, George, 32
Switt, Loretta, 100

Tan, Amy, 29
Tarcher, Jeremy, 30

Tate, George, 26
Tatelman, David, 131-134
Tea manufacturing, packaging and sales,
    178-184
Team building, 235-238
Technology as an investment, 128-129
"The Today Show," 247
Tolin, Mona O., 221
Tolin Business Appraisers, 229-232
Tom's of Maine, 102-105
Top Gun, 51
Toreson, James, 25-26
Towels, imprinted, 52-55
Toxic Screen Dump, Inc., 137-140
Trade publications, 188-192
Tramiel, Jack, 23
Tri-City Packaging Industries, Inc., 93-96
"Two on Two," 135

USA Today, 173
Ultimate Team Concept, Inc., 235-238
University of Oregon, 30

V-8 vegetable juice, 53
Video Review Magazine, 51
VISA, 203
Vogue, 100

The Wall Street Journal, 30, 135, 189,
    218, 220, 246, 248
Wallace, Bob, 150, 152-156
Wallace, Ellen, 152-156
The Weekend Entrepreneur, 233
Westinghouse, 147
Weight management and nutrition
    products, 114-118, 122-124
What Color Is Your Parachute?, 120
Williams, Robin, 170
Wilson, S. Clay, 132
Wind art, 105-109
Wind Related, Inc., 105-109
Wolverton, Van, 140
Women Entrepreneurs, 100, 189
The Women Entrepreneurs, 230
Wozniak, Steve, 23, 24, 182

Xebec Corporation, 25-26
Xerox Corporation, 94

Zahn, Jim, 184-187
Zahn, Kay, 184-187
Zippy the Pinhead, 132

About the Authors

SUNNY BAKER has more than fifteen years of teaching, counseling, and curriculum development experience in colleges and universities. KIM BAKER is a teacher, artist, and marketing communications professional. Together, they are the authors of *On Time/On Budget: A Step-by-Step Guide for Managing Any Project*. The Bakers live in Mesa, Arizona.